AF650290

A TEXTBOOK OF

PHYSICAL ACTIVITY TRAINER

Subject Code 845 | Skill Education
Including Part A and Part B
(As per Latest NEP Guidelines)

12
CBSE

Name ....
Class .... Section .... Roll No. ....
School ....
Address ....
Phone ....

Dr. Rakesh Bharti
Dr. Mali Ram Yadav

A TEXTBOOK OF
PHYSICAL ACTIVITY TRAINER

Subject Code 845 | Skill Education
Including Part A and Part B
(As per Latest NEP Guidelines)

CLASS XII

By:

Dr. Rakesh Bharti
Dr. Mali Ram Yadav

S.K. KATARIA & SONS®
Educational Publishers
4885/109, Prakash Mahal, Dr. Subhash Bhargav Lane,
Opposite Delhi Medical Association, Daryaganj, New Delhi-110002 (INDIA)
Phone: +91-11-43551243; Mobile: +91-9871775858, 7678425209
e-mail: katariabook@gmail.com; katariabooks@yahoo.com
Website: www.skkatariaandsons.com
(e-books, subscriptions and bulk buying also available on our website)

Published by:
S.K. Kataria & Sons®
4885/109, Prakash Mahal, Dr. Subhash Bhargav Lane,
Opposite Delhi Medical Association, Daryaganj, New Delhi-110002 (INDIA)
Phone: +91-11-43551243; Mobile: +91-9871775858, 7678425209
e-mail: katariabook@gmail.com; katariabooks@yahoo.com
Website: www.skkatariaandsons.com

First Edition: 2025-2026 Reprint: 2026-2027

ISBN: 978-93-49499-15-7

Laser Typesetting by : S.K. Computers, Delhi

Printed at : Atharv Enterprises

PREFACE

Physical education plays a vital role in the holistic development of individuals, fostering physical fitness, mental well-being, and social skills. This work aims to highlight the importance of physical education in shaping a healthy and active lifestyle, emphasizing its impact on overall growth, discipline, teamwork, and resilience.

Through this study, I explore various aspects of physical education, including its significance in academic settings, the benefits of sports and fitness activities, and the challenges faced in its implementation. By shedding light on these areas, I hope to contribute to a greater appreciation of physical education and its essential role in personal and societal well-being.

Authors

ACKNOWLEDGEMENT

I extend my sincere gratitude to all those who have contributed to the completion of this work. My heartfelt thanks go to my mentors and teachers for their invaluable guidance, support, and encouragement throughout this journey. Their expertise and insights have been instrumental in shaping this study.

I am also deeply grateful to the physical education instructors, coaches, and students who shared their experiences and knowledge, enriching this research with real-world perspectives. Their dedication to promoting fitness and well-being has been truly inspiring.

Lastly, I express my appreciation to my family and friends for their constant encouragement and belief in my efforts. Their unwavering support has been a source of motivation throughout this endeavor.

Authors

CBSE | DEPARTMENT OF SKILL EDUCATION
CURRICULUM FOR CLASS-XII
PHYSICAL ACTIVITY TRAINER
(Subject Code 845)

COURSE OVERVIEW

Physical Education Assistant (Primary Years) works in a primary school, an apartment and clubs to teach basic sports to build sports skills and fitness for children up to the age of 12 years. He/she is involved in conducting play activities, coaching, mentoring and training children at primary level. Physical fitness is considered a measure of the body's ability to function efficiently, effectively and without injury in work and leisure activities. The responsibilities of the individual include the implementation and delivery of an appropriately broad, balanced, relevant and differentiated physical education curriculum for students and preparing and inducting students for competitive sports. S/he needs to ensure that students are physically active within the physical education class.

COURSE OUTCOMES

On completion of the course, students should be able to:

1. Apply effective oral and written communication skills to interact with people and customers
2. Identify the principal components of a computer system
3. Demonstrate the basic skills of using computer
4. Demonstrate self-management skills
5. Demonstrate the ability to provide a self-analysis in context of entrepreneurial skills and abilities
6. Demonstrate the knowledge of the importance of physical activity in child development
7. Demonstrate the knowledge of hygiene and safety
8. Demonstrate the application of Ms. Excel in maintenance of records
9. Describe the purpose of emergency management
10. Follow steps for maintaining health and hygiene in the play area
11. Demonstrate the knowledge of the importance of green skills in meeting the challenges of sustainable development and environment protection and perform assessment and evaluation of students.

SYLLABUS

CBSE | DEPARTMENT OF SKILL EDUCATION

PHYSICAL ACTIVITY TRAINER

CLASS XII (SESSION 2026-2027)

(Subject Code 845)

Total Marks: 100 **(Theory-50 + Practical-50)**

	Units	No. of Hours for Theory and Practical		Max. Marks for Theory and Practical
PART A	**Employability Skills**			
	Unit 1: Communication Skills-IV	15		2
	Unit 2: Self-Management Skills-IV	10		2
	Unit 3: Information Communication Technology Skills-IV	15		2
	Unit 4: Entrepreneurial Skills-IV	10		2
	Unit 5: Green Skills-IV	10		2
	TOTAL	**60**		**10**
PART B	**Subject Specific Skills**	**Theory**	**Practical**	**Total**
	Unit 1: Overview of Physical Educaion and Sports Sector	18	19	10
	Unit 2: Assessment of Students	18	19	10
	Unit 3: Emergency Management	18	23	10
	Unit 4: Health and Hygiene in Play Area	21	14	10
	Total	**75**	**75**	**40**
PART C	**Practical Work**			
	Practical Examination			15
	Written Test			10
	Viva Voce			10
	TOTAL			**35**
PART D	**Project Work/Field Visit**			
	Practical File/Student Portfolio			10
	Viva Voce			05
	TOTAL			**15**
	TOTAL	**210**		**100**

SYLLABUS

DETAILED CURRICULUM/TOPICS FOR CLASS XII

PHYSICAL ACTIVITY TRAINER

(Subject Code 845)

Part-A: EMPLOYABILITY SKILLS

S.No.	Units	Duration in Hours
1.	Unit 1: Communication Skills-IV	13
2.	Unit 2: Self-Management Skills-IV	7
3.	Unit 3: Information and Communication Technology Skills-IV	13
4.	Unit 4: Entrepreneurial Skills-IV	10
5.	Unit 5: Green Skills-IV	7
	TOTAL	**50**

NOTE: Detailed Curriculum/ Topics to be covered under Part A: Employability Skills can be downloaded from CBSE website.

Part-B – SUBJECT SPECIFIC SKILLS

- Unit 1: Overview of Physical Education and Sports Sector
- Unit 2: Assessment of Students
- Unit 3: Emergency Management
- Unit 4: Health and Hygiene in Play Area

UNIT-1: OVERVIEW OF PHYSICAL EDUCATION AND SPORTS SECTOR

Learning Outcomes	Theory	Practical
1. Describe the job profile and career opportunities of a Physical Education Assistant	1. Teaching Physical Education 2. Coaching 3. Sports Management 4. Fitness sector 5. Equipment managers 6. Sports journalism 7. Photography 8. Sports Medicine 9. Sports Psychologists 10. Sports Nutritionists	1. List the skills required for teaching physical education 2. Discussion on various occupations in physical education and sports
2. Differentiating between Physical Activity, Games, Sports and Recreation	1. Physical activity 2. Games 3. Sports 4. Recreation	1. Demonstrate the knowledge of difference between physical activities, games, sports and recreation for different age groups

3. Describe the importance of life skills in sports	1. Life skills 2. Learn on how to deal with failure 3. Importance of working hard 4. Sports will teach you how to be a team member 5. Learning how to make sacrifices 6. Learning discipline 7. Time management	1. Divide teams in your class to conduct a competition for the following sports and observe (a) Foot Ball (b) Kho – Kho

UNIT-2: ASSESSMENT OF STUDENTS

Learning Outcomes	Theory	Practical
1. Compare the various types of assessment and purpose of evaluation	1. Meaning of assessment 2. Types of assessment: • Self-assessment • Peer assessment • Teacher Observation • Homework 3. Factors influencing assessment: • Physical factors • School factors • Teacher factors 4. Assessment tools: • Checklist • Rubrics • Benchmark 5. Types of evaluation: • Formative evaluation • Summative Evaluation • Diagnostic Evaluation	1. Discussion on the importance of assessment and evaluation 2. Group discussion on factors influencing assessment 3. Preparation of chart on types of assessment
2. Identify the steps of qualitative and quantitative assessment	1. Meaning and steps in qualitative assessment 2. Meaning and steps in quantitative assessment	1. Draw a chart showing the steps of qualitative assessment 2. Group discussion on qualitative and quantitative assessment
3. Organize assessment and evaluation of students	1. Elements of teaching process 2. Ongoing evaluation 3. Key success factors for imparting high quality Physical Education 4. Organizing an evaluation plan	1. Prepare a chart for the four elements that make up the whole process of teaching 2. List four key success factors which show that high quality physical education has been imparted to students

4. Demonstrate the knowledge of organizing interaction with parents	1. Parent-Teacher Meeting 2. Managing Parent-Teacher meeting 3. Interaction with parents post assessments 4. Explanation of performance evaluation 5. Steps to improve performance of slow learners	1. Identify methods of reaching out to the parents 2. Role play for explanation of student's report to parents

UNIT-3: EMERGENCY MANAGEMENT

Learning Outcomes	Theory	Practical
1. Identify the importance of emergency response	1. Meaning of emergency response 2. Need and importance of emergency response: • dealing with heat stroke • allergies • asthma attacks • sudden cardiac arrest 3. CPR	1. Group discussion on emergency response 2. Preparation of a plan for emergency response 3. Create a poster showing the steps of CPR
2. Identify and respond to emergencies in playfield	1. First Aid 2. DRABC of First Aid 3. First Aid –Purpose and Basic principles 4. Basic sports injuries: • Sprain • Strain 5. Instructions for R.I.C.E. 6. Concept of First Aid kit 7. Area inspection for safety 8. Roles and responsibilities of first responder 9. Equal opportunities 10. First Aid procedures	1. Group discussion on importance of first responder 2. Demonstration of first aid procedures 3. Preparation of an emergency plan

UNIT-4: HEALTH AND HYGIENE IN PLAY AREA

Learning Outcomes	Theory	Practical
1. Demonstrate knowledge about players' health and hygiene	1. Maintenance of player's health and hygiene 2. General Hygiene and Sanitation rules 3. Hygiene tips	1. Prepare chart on general hygiene and sanitation rules
2. Describe the hygiene and health in play area	1. Inspection and maintenance of sports facilities and kits • Low frequency inspections • High frequency inspections 2. Personal items and kits inspections 3. Maintenance of Hygiene in play area	1. Write a paragraph about importance of play area inspection

WORK DETAIL

S.No.	Chapter Name	Date	Teacher's Signature

MY PERFORMANCE

Date	Text/ Exam	Marks/Grades Obtained			Highest Marks/Grade in the class	Teacher's Remarks	Parents Signature
		Theory	Practical	Total			

CONTENT

PART A

EMPLOYABILITY SKILLS

- **UNIT-1:** Communication Skills – IV
- **UNIT-2:** Self-Management Skills – IV
- **UNIT-3:** Information and Communication Technology Skills – IV
- **UNIT-4:** Entrepreneurial Skills – IV
- **UNIT-5:** Green Skills – IV

UNIT 1

COMMUNICATION SKILLS – IV

- **Session 1:** Importance of Active Listening at Workplace
- **Session 2:** Steps to Active Listening
- **Session 3:** Writing Skills to the Following

Session–1: Importance of Active Listening at Workplace

1.1 Introduction

It is commonly said that we have one mouth and two ears for a reason: to listen more and speak less. This makes sense because listening is important. But what's the difference between listening and hearing?

To see **Difference Between Hearing and Listening** in Action

Scan QR Code

Listening is more than just hearing sounds. It is a mental activity. For instance, when you are listening to a lecture, you are trying to understand and gain knowledge. On the other hand, hearing is simply the physical act of detecting sound. Imagine sitting in a classroom with your friend, chatting away during lunch, but not paying attention to what's being said around you. You are hearing the noise, but you are not actively listening. You might have heard the saying, "There's a difference between listening and waiting for your turn to speak." This means that true listening involves fully concentrating on what's being said, rather than just waiting for your chance to talk. Active listening isn't always easy, but it's worth the effort because it can greatly improve relationships, followership, and overall results.

This way ...

Fig. 1.1 Listening: A Skill That's Harder Than It Seems

- Listening is the ability to accurately receive messages in the communication process.
- Listening is not the same as hearing.
- Listening is a cognitive act (for knowledge); hearing is a physical act (which can't be avoided).

- Good listening skills can lead to better customer satisfaction, greater productivity with fewer mistakes, and increased sharing of information that in turn can lead to more creative and innovative work.
- A good listener will listen not only to what is being said, but also to what is left unsaid or only partially said.
- Listening is not the same as hearing and in order to listen effectively you need to use more than just your ears.

1.2 Difference Between Hearing And Listening

Hearing	Listening
Hearing is an activity of receiving sound waves through the ear.	Listening is the activity of hearing sound waves and then analysing and understanding it.
It is an ability.	It is a skill.
It is a continuous activity.	It is temporary. We listen only when we care about sounds.
It happens at the subconscious level.	It happens at the conscious level.
It just happens all the time – whether someone likes it or not.	Listening requires concentration so that the brain can understand the meaning of sound and spoken words.
Hearing simply happens.	Listening leads to learning.
Hearing uses only ears.	Listening uses different senses, like the sense of hearing, seeing, or sense of touch.
Hearing is an involuntary act.	Listening is a voluntary skill where the brain tries to understand the meaning of sound.
Concentration is not required for hearing.	Concentration is required for listening.
It involves physiology (only the ear).	It involves psychology, also (active brain).

Traits of a Good Listener:

"Traits" refer to essential qualities. A proficient listener possesses specific traits enabling accurate comprehension of sounds and words. Proficient listening fosters constructive responses, and deeper comprehension, and fosters robust relationships.

A good listener must have the following qualities:

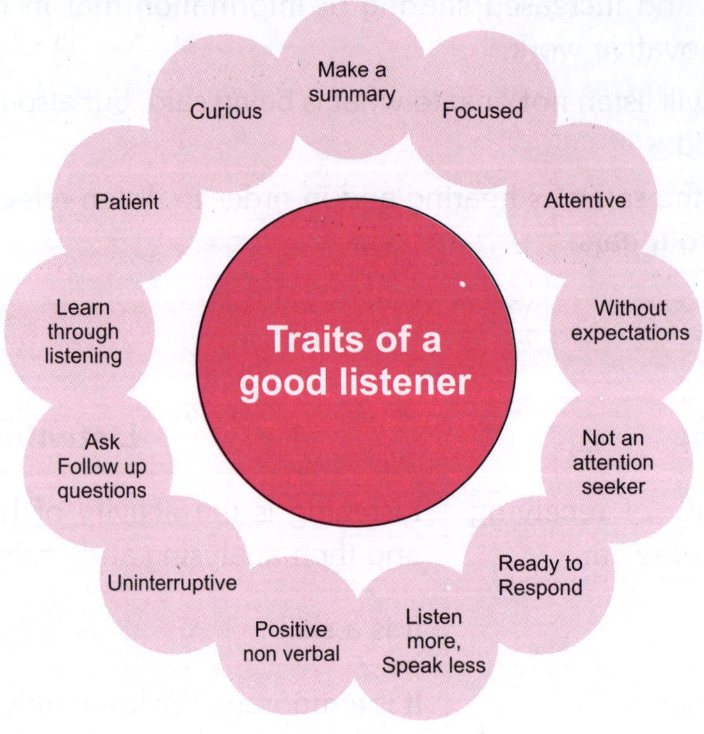

Fig. 1.2

1. Focused

Being focused means understanding the central point of something.

A listener is focused when listening to the speaker. He maintains good eye contact to show his focus. This helps him to understand speech better. He does not care much about 'how to react' rather he should listen, process, and understand. He listens to comprehend, not respond.

2. Attentive

Being attentive means 'listening or watching carefully'. A listener is engaged in the current moment instead of remembering the past or thinking about the next. The listener avoids all distractions, including phones and other people. He remains active in writing queries or taking notes.

3. Without expectation

A good listener listens without any expectations. He is not attached to any outcome. He allows the speaker to speak freely. Any expectation by the listener forces the conversation in the listener's desired direction. He accepts the conversation as it goes naturally.

4. Not an attention seeker

'Attention seeker means a person who tries to get attention, typically in an inappropriate (wrong) manner.'

A good listener helps the speaker whenever he get stuck somewhere. But he doesn't disturb the speaker unnecessarily. He does not take attention away from the speaker.

5. Ready to respond

A good listener is ready to respond to the speaker either through positive body language or through words. Both ways he boosts the energy of the speaker. Remember, the listener responds responsibly not with a critical (wrong or harsh) mind. A listener's positive response prepares a smooth environment for building good relations with the speaker.

6. Listens more and speak less

A good listener must not show his knowledge while listening. Instead, he focuses on speech and responds when necessary. He doesn't aim to dominate the conversation but rather tries to listen even more than he listens.

7. Uses positive body gestures

A listener must show a positive response even through his body language. This may include a smile, posture, facial expression, nodding, etc. It encourages the speaker to continue. One of the best ways to show attentiveness is to keep eye contact with the speaker. These non-verbal cues have an especially important place in listening.

8. Does not interrupt

It is frustrating for a speaker to speak and constantly get interrupted by listeners. A listener should not interrupt the speaker in the middle. Unnecessary interruption becomes the reason for losing the train of thought or even getting the whole point derailed and forgotten. A good listener understands this and simply listens until the speaker completes his point. If he is confused, he asks after the speaker has made his point.

9. Asks follow-up questions

An important part of listening is engagement with the speaker. A listener asks follow-up questions after the speech of the speaker. A good listener encourages the speaker by asking relevant questions. He tries to get more details. He clears his doubts by asking questions.

10. Listens to learn

A good listener believes in learning something new from each speech. He actively listens to understand new information and asks the speaker to elaborate. He remains interested and invests time in each meeting.

11. Exercises patience

A good listener does not make haste to judge the speaker and speech. He waits until the speaker has finished his point of view. Patience makes a person a good listener.

12. Curious to know

Curious means 'finding more about anything'. A good listener is genuinely curious and wants to find out more from the speech. He wants answers, and he is excited about how the speaker will handle his queries.

13. Summarizes after listening

A good listener prepares a summary of the speech. This helps to highlight important moments and any outstanding issues. It helps a listener for future references related to this topic.

In a Nutshell

A good listener demonstrates active engagement by focusing on you with their eyes, displaying empathy through their body language, and striving to comprehend your emotions. They refrain from interrupting you and maintain receptivity to your words. They adeptly interpret non-verbal signals and mirror your statements to indicate their attentiveness. Patient and inquisitive, they seek further understanding through questioning without passing judgement. They exhibit respect by retaining and recalling your disclosures, occasionally allowing silence for you to articulate yourself freely. Subsequently, they offer feedback as evidence of comprehension and encouragement.

Listening Modes:

To see
To see Listening Modes
in Action

Scan QR Code

Listening is the process of receiving and interpreting sound signals (messages) sent by the sender. Listening is one of the skills of communication. It can be developed by practising regularly. Various methods of listening are also called modes of listening.

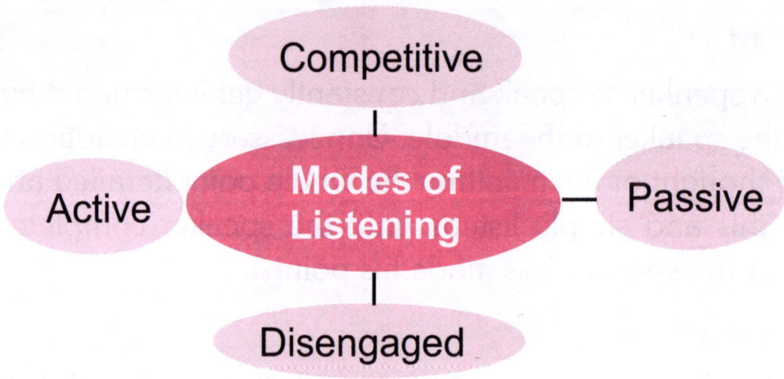

Fig. 1.3 Modes of Listening

Types of Listening:

1. Disengaged Listening:

- The listener's body is present, but the mind is elsewhere.
- **Example:** A student in class planning a friend's birthday instead of paying attention to the lesson.
- **Key feature:** Only physical presence.

2. Competitive Listening:

The listener tries to prove they know more than the speaker.

- **Example:** In a meeting, everyone tries to show they are the smartest.
- **Key feature:** Speaking more than listening and overpowering the speaker.

3. Active Listening:

- The listener pays full attention and engages with the speaker.
- **Example:** Nodding, making eye contact, and asking questions.
- **Key feature:** Proper feedback and learning.

4. Passive Listening:

- The listener pays attention but doesn't ask questions or show interest.
- **Example:** In a group discussion, some people just listen without participating.
- **Key feature:** Avoiding feedback.

Difference Between Active and Passive Modes of Listening:

Active Listening	Passive Listening
The listener is very active.	The listener is not active.
The listener gives proper feedback to the speaker	The listener doesn't give feedback.
Doubts and inquiries are asked.	No query from the listener.

Difference Between Passive and Disengaged Modes of Listening:

Passive Listening	Disengaged Listening
Passive listening involves merely hearing without active engagement or focused attention.	Disengaged listening entails deliberate withdrawing of attention or interest from the speaker or the subject matter.
The listener doesn't give feedback.	The listener doesn't listen.
No query from the listener.	The listener is busy with his thoughts.

Other than these, we also have additional types of listening:

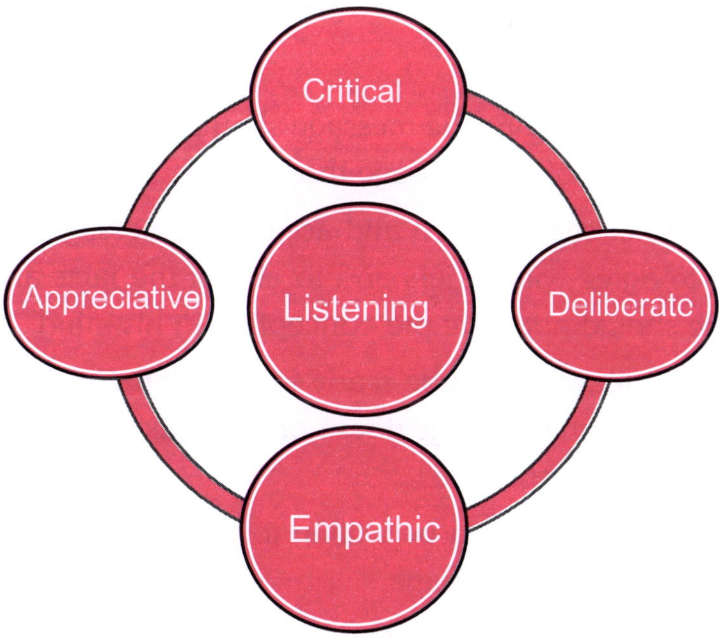

Fig. 1.4 Types of Listening

Types of Listening:

> To see
> **Types of Listening**
> in Action
>
> **Scan QR Code**

1. Appreciative:

- Listening for fun.
- Listening to enjoy or appreciate a speaker's message or performance.
- Used in social situations like concerts, plays or sporting events.

2. Critical:

- Listening to lectures in class.
- Listening to announcements or getting directions, (used when you need to remember something important).
- Listening to comprehend ideas and information in order to achieve a specific purpose or goal.

3. Empathetic:

- Listening to understand, participate, and enhance a relationship.
- Usually used in interactions between two people or a small group.
- The goal is to develop an understanding and appreciation of the meanings and feelings of the sender.
- Trying to put yourself in the other person's place, but not necessarily agree with them.

4. Deliberative:

- Listening to understand, analyse, and evaluate messages.
- Used when receiving and evaluating persuasive messages.
- Used when you must make decisions. It should make you think.

Important Elements of Effective Listening:

(a) **Intensity:** The person receiving the message should listen attentively. He should try to understand the emotions of the message thoroughly.

(b) **Empathy:** The listener should listen and accept the message with an open mind. He should be ready to agree with others and to accept the facts and realities. He should not be biased. He should not have pre-conception in his mind.

(c) **Acceptance:** The listener should be ready to accept the message. He should readily accept the truths, even if the message does not serve his purpose. He should try to think from the other person's perspective.

(d) **Willingness:** The listener should be willing to take responsibility. He should have a positive attitude to follow the message.

Importance of active listening at the workplace: Active listening is crucial in the workplace because it fosters clear communication, enhances teamwork, and builds trust among colleagues. By fully engaging in conversations, employees can understand instructions accurately, provide constructive feedback, and address concerns effectively. This attentive listening reduces misunderstandings, increases productivity, and creates a positive work environment where everyone feels heard and valued. Ultimately, active listening helps in making informed decisions and achieving organizational goals efficiently.

Key Takeaway:

Listening is the ability to accurately receive messages in the communication process. The major barriers to listening are forged attention, premature evaluation of the subject matter, hard listening, poor interpersonal relations, over-excitement, different language varieties and accents, distraction, etc. These barriers can be overcome by preparing oneself to listen rather than speak, putting the speaker at ease, removing distractions, empathizing, being patient, avoiding personal prejudice, listening for ideas – not just words and paying more attention to non-verbal communication.

1.3 Practical Exercise: Becoming an Active Listener

PS-1 Demonstration of the key aspects of becoming an active listener

Objective:

To help students develop and practise active listening skills by demonstrating key aspects such as full attention, proper feedback, and engagement.

Materials Needed:

- A list of discussion topics
- Notebooks and pens
- Timer

Duration:

45 minutes

Steps:

1. *Introduction (5 minutes):*
   - Briefly explain the importance of active listening.
   - Outline the key aspects giving full attention, providing proper feedback, and engaging with the speaker.
2. *Group Activity (10 minutes):*
   - Divide the class into pairs.
   - Give each pair a discussion topic (e.g., favourite book, recent movie watched, a hobby they enjoy).
   - Assign roles: one student as the speaker and the other as the listener.

3. *Listening Practice (10 minutes)*
   - The speaker talks about the given topic for 3 minutes while the listener practices active listening.
   - Encourage listeners to show they are paying full attention (e.g., making eye contact, nodding), provide feedback (e.g., "That's interesting," "I see"), and ask relevant questions (e.g., "What did you like most about it?").
4. *Role Reversal (10 minutes)*
   - Have students switch roles and repeat the exercise with a new topic.
5. *Reflection and Feedback (10 minutes):*
   - After both rounds, each pair discusses their experience. Listeners share what they found challenging and speakers provide feedback on the listener's engagement.
   - Open the floor for a class discussion where students can share insights and reflections on their active listening experience.
6. *Conclusion (5 minutes)*
   - Summarize the key takeaways from the exercise.
   - Emphasize the importance of practicing active listening in daily interactions.

Suggested Discussion Topics:

1. Your favourite subject and why you like it.
2. A memorable family vacation.
3. The most interesting project you have worked on in school.
4. Your plans for the future.

Assessment Criteria:

- Evaluate students based on their participation and demonstration of active listening skills during the exercise.
- Provide constructive feedback to help them improve further in body language, communication skills, and listening skills.

SESSION–2: STEPS TO ACTIVE LISTENING

Attentive Listening: The Key to Communication

Attentive listening is a critical component of effective communication. It involves full concentration on the speaker, understanding their message, and responding thoughtfully.

Here's why attentive listening is so important:

1. Builds Trust and Respect:

- When you listen attentively, you show respect for the speaker, which helps build trust and strengthen relationships.

2. Improves Understanding:

- By paying close attention, you can better understand the speaker's message, including their emotions and intentions.

3. Reduces Misunderstandings:

- Active listening helps clarify information and reduce the chances of miscommunication, ensuring that all parties are on the same page.

4. Enhances Problem-Solving:

- By fully understanding the issues at hand, you can contribute more effectively to find solutions.

5. Encourages Openness:

- When people feel heard, they are encouraged and more likely to share their thoughts and feelings openly, fostering a more collaborative and positive communication environment.

6. Promotes Empathy:

- Attentive listening helps you to put yourself in the speaker's shoes, enhancing empathy and emotional intelligence.

Incorporating attentive listening into your communication style can significantly improve both personal and professional interactions. It requires practice and mindfulness but is ultimately rewarding for all parties involved.

2.1 Steps to Active Listening

1. Pay attention:

The first step to listening actively is paying attention to the speaker. Peter Drucker said, "The most important thing in communication is hearing what isn't said."

To see **Attentive Listening** in Action

Scan QR Code

Here are some ways in which you can give your undivided attention to the speaker:

- Look at the speaker directly
- Stop other activities while you are listening
- Don't prepare a response or a rebuttal in your mind as you listen
- Avoid being distracted by external factors such as noise or side conversations
- Pay attention to the speaker's body language

2. Show that you are listening:

Sometimes even though you give your undivided attention to the person speaking, they look doubtful or ask if you've understood what they said. This is because they don't see any sign of attentive listening.

Your active listening skills must be visible to the speaker. How do you convey your interest? It's simple. You can use non-verbal signs such as nodding your head or smiling whenever appropriate. Even your posture says a lot about your interest and attentiveness.

So, the next time you are all ears to someone, try to let them know this through your gestures and body language:

- Maintain eye contact with the speaker
- Use body language to show interest—sit straight or lean in, and stop fidgeting
- Nod, smile, and use appropriate facial expressions
- Encourage the speaker to continue with comments such as 'yes' or 'hmm'

3. Ask questions and give feedback:

People sometimes listen without understanding what the speaker is saying. Always engage with the speaker by sharing your feedback or asking questions for effective communication.

- Ask thoughtful questions to clarify your doubts
- Try to summarize the speaker's points to confirm if you understood them clearly
- Reflect on what the speaker has said by paraphrasing

4. Respond appropriately:

The soul of active listening lies in respecting the speaker and understanding what is being said. Those who listen with genuine interest don't have reactions. They formulate appropriate responses that enrich the conversation. A well thought-out and respectful response shows that you have listened closely to the speaker. It encourages them to share more information.

So, how can you ensure that you respond and not react? Here are a few tips:

- Reflect on what you have heard instead of reacting immediately
- Be open, honest, and candid when you respond
- Do not attack the speaker or challenge them rudely
- Be respectful yet assertive with your opinions

Practical Session Exercise

PS-1 List out and describe the essential steps involved in active listening. How can each step improve communication in a classroom setting?

PS-2 Prepare a poster that includes all the steps of active listening. Make sure to highlight how each step can enhance communication in the classroom.

Note: Ensure that your poster is clear, colourful, and engaging to effectively convey the steps and their benefits.

Session 3: Writing Skills To The Following

3.1 Introduction

Effective writing is the cornerstone of clear communication. Mastering the fundamentals of writing, including sentences, phrases, and paragraphs, enhances clarity and coherence in your work. This session will explore key aspects of writing, including the construction of sentences and paragraphs, and the roles of various parts of speech.

To see **Sentences and Phrases** in Action

Scan QR Code

Sentences and Phrases:

Sentences: A sentence is a group of words that express a complete thought. It typically includes a subject and a predicate.

1. **Simple Sentence:** Contains one independent clause.

   Example: "The dog barks."

2. **Compound Sentence:** Contains two or more independent clauses joined by a conjunction or a semicolon.

   Example: "The dog barks, and the cat meows."

3. **Complex Sentence:** Contains one independent clause and at least one dependent clause.

   Example: "The dog barks because it sees a stranger."

4. **Compound-Complex Sentence:** Contains two or more independent clauses and at least one dependent clause.

   Example: "The dog barks when the mailman arrives, and the cat hides under the bed."

Phrases:

A phrase is a group of related words that do not contain both a subject and a predicate. Phrases add detail and clarity to sentences.

1. **Noun Phrase:** Includes a noun and its modifiers.

   Example: "The big, brown dog."

2. **Verb Phrase:** Includes a main verb and its auxiliaries.

   Example: "Has been barking loudly."

3. **Adjective Phrase:** Modifies a noun or pronoun.

   Example: "Full of excitement."

4. **Adverbial Phrase:** Modifies a verb, adjective, or adverb.

   Example: "With great enthusiasm."

Kinds of Sentences:

Understanding the different types of sentences helps convey the right tone and intention.

1. **Declarative Sentence:** Makes a statement.

   Example: "She enjoys reading."

2. **Interrogative Sentence:** Asks a question.

   Example: "Do you enjoy reading?"

3. **Imperative Sentence:** Gives a command or request.

   Example: "Please close the door."

4. **Exclamatory Sentence:** Expresses strong emotion.

   Example: "What a beautiful day!"

3.2 Parts of a Sentence

Every sentence has essential components:

1. **Subject:** The person or thing, that is acting.

   Example: "The teacher" in "The teacher explains the lesson."

2. **Predicate:** The part of the sentence that tells what the subject does or is.

   Example: "explains the lesson" in "The teacher explains the lesson."

3. **Object:** The recipient of the action.

   Example: "the lesson" in "The teacher explains the lesson."

4. **Complement:** Adds more information about the subject or object.

   Example: "The best student" in "She is the best student."

3.2.1 Parts of Speech

Parts of speech are categories of words based on their function in a sentence.

1. **Nouns:** Represent people, places, things, or ideas.

   Example: "dog," "city," "happiness."

2. **Pronouns:** Replace nouns to avoid repetition.

   Example: "he," "she," "it."

3. **Verbs:** Express actions or states of being.

   Example: "run," "is," "seem."

4. **Adjectives:** Modify nouns or pronouns.

   Example: "blue," "quick," "happy."

5. **Adverbs:** Modify verbs, adjectives, or other adverbs.

   Example: "quickly," "very," "well."

6. **Prepositions:** Show relationships between nouns (or pronouns) and other words in a sentence.

Example: "on," "at," "by."

7. **Conjunctions:** Connect words, phrases, or clauses.

   Example: "and," "but," "or."

8. **Interjections:** Express strong emotions or reactions.

   Example: "Wow!," "Oh!"

3.2.2 Articles

To see **Articles** in Action

Scan QR Code

Articles define the specificity of nouns.

1. **Definite Article:** "The" refers to a specific noun.

   Example: "The book on the table."

2. **Indefinite Articles:** "A" and "An" refer to non-specific nouns.

   Example: "A book," "An apple."

3.2.3 Construction of a Paragraph

A well-constructed paragraph presents a single idea and is structured as follows:

- **Topic Sentence:** Introduces the main idea.

  Example: "Effective communication is crucial in every aspect of life."

- **Supporting Sentences:** Provide details, examples, and explanations to support the topic sentence.

  Example: "It helps in personal relationships, professional settings, and academic environments."

- **Concluding Sentence:** Summarizes the paragraph or transitions to the next idea.

  Example: "Thus, mastering communication skills can significantly impact success."

Mastering writing skills involves understanding and effectively using sentences, phrases, parts of speech, and the structure of paragraphs. By applying these principles, you can improve the clarity and impact of your written communication.

Practical Session Exercise

Q.1. Write five sentences on the topic "Technology in Education." Ensure that you include a mix of simple, compound, complex, and compound-complex sentences. After writing the sentences, identify and label each type of sentence.

Q.2. Create a short paragraph (4-5 sentences) on a topic, the importance of reading books, Underline or highlight the different types of phrases (noun phrases, verb phrases, adjective phrases, adverbial phrases) within your paragraph and label them accordingly.

Q.3. Write a brief dialogue (5-6 exchanges) between two characters discussing a school project. Ensure that the dialogue includes examples of declarative, interrogative, imperative, and exclamatory sentences. After writing the dialogue, identify and label each type of sentence.

Q.4. Write three sentences about innovations in science. For each sentence, identify and label the subject, predicate, object, and complement. Provide a brief explanation of how each part contributes to the meaning of the sentence.

Q.5. Write a well-organized paragraph (5-6 sentences) on how technology affects daily life. Ensure that the paragraph includes a clear topic sentence, supporting details, and a concluding sentence. Submit a brief outline showing the structure of your paragraph.

UNIT 2

SELF-MANAGEMENT SKILLS–IV

- Session 1: Inspire and Aspire: Exploring the Foundations of Motivation
- Session 2: The Essence of Character: Understanding Personality and its Impact

SESSION-1: INSPIRE AND ASPIRE: EXPLORING THE FOUNDATIONS OF MOTIVATION

1.1 SELF-MANAGEMENT SKILLS

Self-management skills encompass a range of abilities that help individuals to control their thoughts, emotions, and actions to achieve personal and professional goals. Key aspects include goal setting, time management, self-motivation, self-discipline, stress management, emotional regulation, adaptability, problem-solving, accountability, and maintaining healthy habits. These skills are vital for enhancing productivity, improving well-being, fostering better relationships, building resilience, and achieving professional success. Developing self-management skills requires continuous learning and practice, leading to more organized, productive, and fulfilling lives.

To see *Self-Management Skills* in Action

Scan QR Code

Fig. 1.1 Power of Motivation

1.2 INTRODUCTION TO MOTIVATION

Motivation is the drive or desire to achieve your goals. It pushes you each day to improve the quality of your life. For instance, if you want to be fit, you'll be driven to watch fitness videos, follow a strict diet, and work toward a healthy lifestyle. Your desires to earn more, help others, or commit to change, all stem from different types of motivation that are influenced by internal and external factors.

To see *Introduction to Motivation* in Action

Scan QR Code

1.2.1 Categories of Motivation

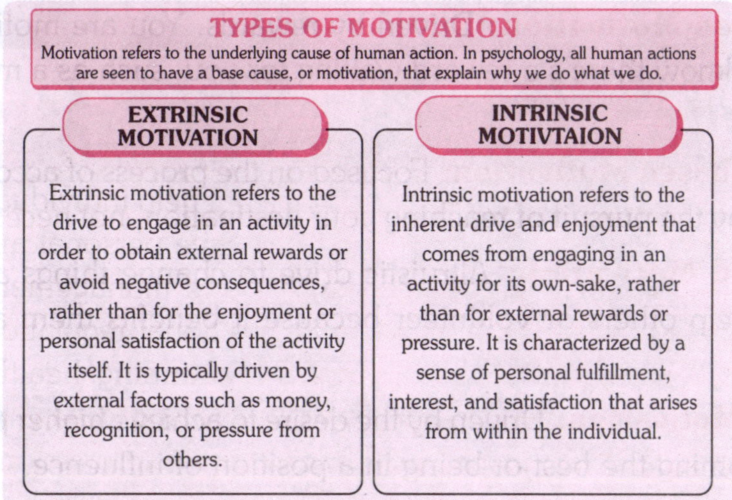

Fig. 1.2 Extrinsic & Intrinsic Motivation

In essence, there are two broad categories of motivation:

1. **Internal (Intrinsic) Motivation:** This type of motivation is driven by self-fulfillment. It is something you do for self-satisfaction, like finishing your summer reading list.
2. **External (Extrinsic) Motivation:** This type of motivation is driven by external rewards, like a promotion at work or receiving praise from others.

To see *Types of Motivation* in Action

Scan QR Code

Both positive and negative factors motivate you to improve the way you do things so you can achieve your desired outcomes.

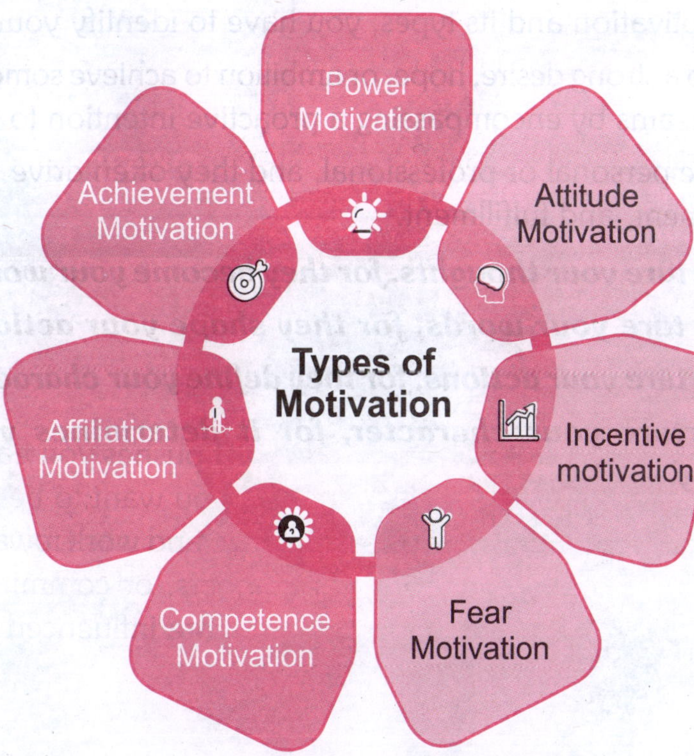

Fig. 1.3 Types of Motivation

1.2.2 Types of Motivation

1. **Incentive-based Motivation:** Driven by rewards. You are motivated to complete a task when you know there's a reward waiting for you, such as a monetary incentive or a raise.
2. **Achievement-based Motivation:** Focused on the process of accomplishing goals. You are motivated by the pursuit of reaching your destination, not necessarily by the reward.
3. **Attitude-based Motivation:** Altruistic drive to change things around you. You are motivated to help others or volunteer because it benefits them and aligns with your values.
4. **Power-based Motivation:** Driven by the desire to achieve higher positions or authority. It is about becoming the best or being in a position of influence.
5. **Affiliation-based Motivation:** Driven by social interactions and teamwork. You perform better with praise from managers and enjoy working in a team to accomplish larger goals.
6. **Competence-based Motivation:** Driven by the desire to improve and become the best version of yourself. You enjoy learning and tackling challenges to enhance your skills.
7. **Fear-based Motivation:** Motivated by the fear of negative consequences, such as bad grades or getting fired. This type of motivation can drive you to work productively to avoid undesirable outcomes.

1.3 Identifying Your Motivations

- To understand motivation and its types, you have to identify your aspirations.
- Aspirations refer to a strong desire, hope, or ambition to achieve something. It goes beyond mere wishes or dreams by encompassing a proactive intention to reach a specific goal.
- Aspirations can be personal or professional, and they often drive individuals to pursue growth, improvement, and fulfillment.

Nurture your thoughts, for they become your words.

Nurture your words, for they shape your actions.

Nurture your actions, for they define your character.

Nurture your character, for it determines your destiny.

1.3.1 Positive Thinking and its Impact

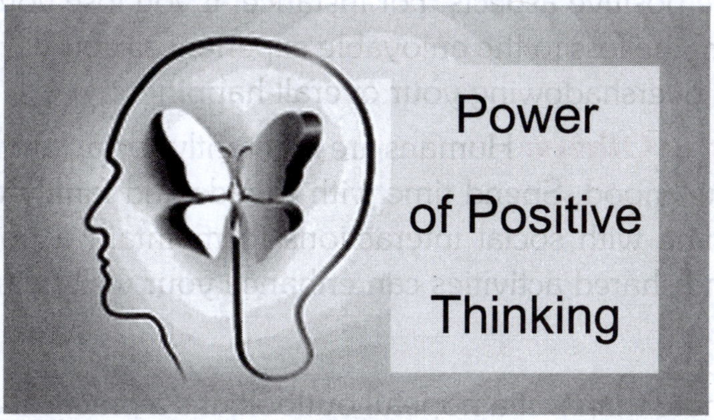

Fig. 1.4

Positive thinking involves maintaining an optimistic and realistic outlook on life. It is about focusing on the good in any situation and leveraging this mindset to drive personal and professional growth. Understanding how to harness the power of positive thinking can significantly impact your life, especially when faced with challenges.

To see **Power of Positive Thoughts** in Action

Scan QR Code

Impact of Negative Thinking

Negative thoughts can have profound effect on your outlook and self-esteem. For example, Radhika, a talented artist, won many competitions in her youth. However, a single criticism about her art made her question her abilities and led her to stop painting. This illustrates how negative feedback can erode confidence and hinder progress. Negative thoughts can cloud your judgment, making you doubt yourself and become pessimistic.

Benefits of Positive Thinking

Adopting a positive mindset can transform how you handle life's ups and downs.

Here are some key benefits:

1. **Lifts Your Spirits:** Positive thinking can elevate your mood, even during difficult times.
2. **Increases Motivation:** It drives you to perform well and persist through challenges.
3. **Encourages Skill Development:** You are more likely to seek opportunities and enhance your skills.
4. **Builds Resilience:** Positive thinking helps you bounce back from failures and setbacks.
5. **Overcomes Setbacks:** It empowers you to face obstacles with a constructive attitude.

How to Develop Positive Thinking

Cultivating a positive mindset involves intentional practices and habits. Here's how you can foster positivity:

Practices Gratitude: Regularly acknowledge and appreciate the good things in your life. Whether it's a supportive friend, personal achievements, or simple daily joys, expressing gratitude helps reinforce a positive outlook. Saying "thank you" and recognizing your powers can strengthen relationships and boost your mood.

Focus on the Positive: While it's natural to encounter both good and bad experiences, try to concentrate on the positive aspects. For instance, if you lose your phone during a great trip, shift your focus from the loss to the enjoyable experiences you've had. This helps prevent negative incidents from overshadowing your overall happiness.

Seek the Company of Others: Humans are inherently social, and connecting with others can greatly improve your mood. Spend time with friends and family who uplift and support you. Balance solitary time with social interactions to maintain a positive emotional state. Engaging in laughter and shared activities can enhance your well-being.

Key Takeaways

Positive thinking is more than just a hopeful outlook; it's a practical approach to improving your life. By focusing on gratitude, maintaining a positive focus, and surrounding yourself with supportive people, you can cultivate a mindset that drives you toward success and fulfillment. Embrace the power of positive thinking and watch how it transforms your approach to challenges and opportunities.

To see ***Stress Management*** in Action

Scan QR Code

1.3.2 Stress Management

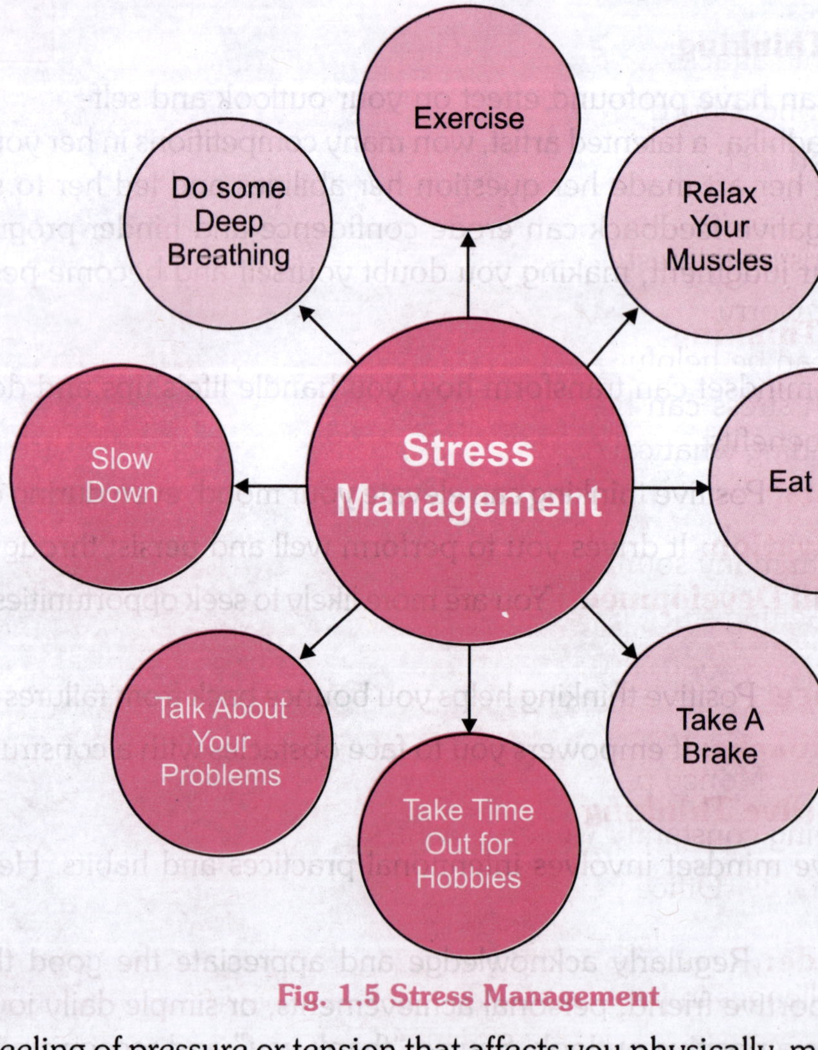

Fig. 1.5 Stress Management

Stress is a feeling of pressure or tension that affects you physically, mentally, or emotionally. It can come from things happening around you, like a busy schedule or a difficult situation, or from inside you, like feeling sick or anxious. In simple terms, stress is what you experience when you're feeling overwhelmed or strained by different factors in your life.

Symptoms of Stress

Stress can show up in various different ways.

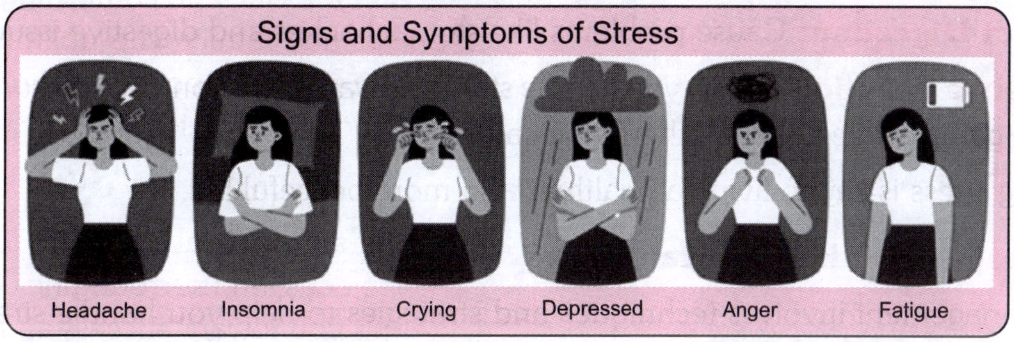

Fig. 1.6 Symptoms of Stress

Common symptoms include

- Feeling irritable or easily upset
- Getting headaches
- Experiencing panic attacks
- Having acidity or heartburn
- Sweaty hands and feet
- Trouble sleeping
- Feeling tired or losing interest in things
- Increased fear or worry

While a little stress can be helpful, like the nerousnes you feel before an exam that pushes you to study, too much stress can hurt your health. It's important to learn how to manage stress by first understanding what causes it.

Causes of Stress

Stress can come from many sources, both big and small. Here are some common causes:

1. **Traffic Jams:** Getting stuck in traffic and being late can be stressful.
2. **Unfair Treatment:** Favouritism or unfairness at work affects your well-being.
3. **Expectations and Pressure:** Pressure from parents or peers can cause stress.
4. **Financial Issues:** Money problems can lead to anxiety and arguments.
5. **Judgement:** Being constantly judged by others can be stressful.
6. **Workplace Politics:** Office politics can create tension.
7. **Relationship Problems:** Issues in personal relationships or marriage can cause stress.
8. **Parenting:** Challenges in parenting can also be a stress factor.
9. **Busy Lifestyles:** A hectic schedule can contribute to stress.

Understanding these causes can help in managing stress effectively.

Effects of Stress

Too much stress is harmful to both your body and mind. It can:

- **Affect Health:** This leads to high blood pressure, heart issues, and a weaker immune system.
- **Impact Digestion:** Cause problems like stomachaches and digestive issues.
- **Influence Reactions:** How you handle stress can vary based on your personality. Some might get frustrated, while others stay calm.

Managing stress is key to living a healthier and more peaceful life.

Stress Management: How to Manage it?

Stress management involves techniques and strategies to help you handle stress better. It means finding out what triggers your stress and using methods to reduce its impact. By finding the right stress management techniques for you, you can improve your ability to deal with stressful situations and lead a healthier, more balanced life.

1. Essential for a Better Life
2. Improves Health
3. Supports Moving on
4. Strengthens Relationships
5. Enhances Work Performance
6. Improves Communication
7. Leads to Growth

Stress management is essential for a better and healthier life. It helps you handle challenges, recover from setbacks, and maintain a positive outlook. Effective stress management improves health by reducing the risk of diseases and slowing aging. It also supports moving on from difficulties, strengthens relationships, enhances work performance, and improves communication. By managing stress well, you can lead a more balanced life and achieve personal and professional growth.

EXERCISE

A. Review Questions

1. What is self-management?
2. Define intrinsic motivation.
3. What is the benefit of positive thinking?
4. Name one symptom of stress.

B. Short Questions

1. How does attitude-based motivation differ from fear-based motivation?
2. What are two causes of stress?
3. How can positive thinking improve your daily life?
4. Explain the impact of stress on health.

C. Long Questions

1. Discuss the different types of motivation and give an example of each.
2. Describe how stress management can enhance personal and professional life.
3. How can understanding your motivations help in setting and achieving personal goals?
4. Analyse the relationship between positive thinking and stress management.

Practical-Based Activities

1. Create a personal stress management plan that includes identifying your main stressors, setting specific goals for stress reduction, and listing at least three techniques you will use to manage stress.
2. Write a reflective essay on a personal goal you achieved. Discuss the types of motivation that drove you, how you managed setbacks, and how positive thinking played a role in your success.

Session-2: The Essence Of Character: Understanding Personality And Its Impact

2.1 Definition

Personality refers to the unique and enduring set of characteristics, traits, and behaviours that define how an individual thinks, feels, and acts. It encompasses a person's patterns of thought, emotion, and behaviour, which are relatively stable over time and across various situations. Personality is shaped by a combination of genetic, environmental, and social factors.

To see ***Personality*** in Action

Scan QR Code

1. Components of Personality:

- **Traits:** Enduring characteristics that influence how individuals respond to different situations.
- **Behaviour:** The actions and reactions that are observable.
- **Cognition:** Patterns of thinking and perception.
- **Emotion:** How an individual experiences and expresses feelings.

2. Personality Influences Others:

(i) Interpersonal Relationships:

- **Social Interactions:** Personality affects how we interact with others, including our approach to friendships, romantic relationships, and professional relationships.
- **Communication Style:** The way we communicate – whether assertive, passive, or aggressive – is influenced by our personality traits.

(ii) Workplace Dynamics:

- **Teamwork:** Personality traits such as openness and agreeableness can impact how well individuals collaborate in a team.
- **Leadership:** Traits like confidence and decisiveness play a role in leadership styles and effectiveness.

(iii) Conflict Resolution:

- **Approach to Conflict:** Personality affects how individuals handle disagreements—some may be more confrontational, while others may avoid conflict.

(iv) Influence on Perception:

- **First Impressions:** Traits such as extraversion or introversion can shape the initial impression one makes on others.
- **Trust and Reliability:** Consistent personality traits contribute to how trustworthy or reliable someone is perceived to be.

3. Basic Personality Traits:

The Big Five Personality Traits:

- **Openness to Experience:** The extent to which an individual is open to new experiences, ideas, and curiosity.
- **Conscientiousness:** How organized, reliable, and responsible an individual is.
- **Extraversion:** The degree of sociability, assertiveness, and enthusiasm in a person.
- **Agreeableness:** How cooperative, compassionate, and friendly an individual is.
- **Neuroticism:** The tendency to experience negative emotions like anxiety, depression, and moodiness.

4. Other Traits:

- **Self-esteem:** The overall sense of self-worth or value.
- **Emotional Stability:** The consistency of one's emotional responses.
- **Locus of Control:** The extent to which individuals believe they have control over their life events.

5. Common Personality Disorders:

To see **Common Personality Disorders** in Action

Scan QR Code

(i) Paranoid Personality Disorder:

- **Description:** Characterized by pervasive distrust and suspicion of others, believing that others have malicious intentions.
- **Symptoms:** Persistent doubts about others' loyalty, reluctance to confide in others, and perceiving benign remarks as threatening.

(ii) Antisocial Personality Disorder:

- **Description:** Marked by a disregard for the rights of others, deceitfulness, and a lack of remorse for harmful actions.
- **Symptoms:** Repeated violations of societal norms, impulsivity, and manipulative behaviour.

(iii) Schizoid Personality Disorder:

- **Description:** Features a lack of interest in social relationships and a tendency to be detached from others.
- **Symptoms:** Preference for solitary activities, emotional coldness, and indifference to praise or criticism.

(iv) Borderline Personality Disorder:

- **Description:** Characterized by instability in moods, self-image, and relationships, often resulting in impulsive actions.
- **Symptoms:** Intense and unstable relationships, fear of abandonment, and a chronic feeling of emptiness.

(v) Narcissistic Personality Disorder:

- **Description:** Involves a grandiose sense of self-importance, a need for excessive admiration, and a lack of empathy for others.
- **Symptoms:** Exaggerated sense of achievement, preoccupation with success and power, and exploitative behaviour.

(vi) Avoidant Personality Disorder:

- **Description:** Marked by extreme shyness, feelings of inadequacy, and hypersensitivity to negative evaluation.
- **Symptoms:** Avoidance of social interactions, fear of criticism, and reluctance to engage in new activities.

(vii) Dependent Personality Disorder:

- **Description:** Characterized by an excessive need to be taken care of, leading to submissive and clinging behaviours.
- **Symptoms:** Difficulty making decisions, fear of separation, and an excessive need for reassurance.

(viii) Obsessive-Compulsive Personality Disorder:

- **Description:** Features a preoccupation with orderliness, perfectionism, and control, often leading to rigidity.
- **Symptoms:** Overemphasis on rules and details, perfectionistic standards, and reluctance to delegate tasks.

Understanding personality is crucial for recognizing how we interact with others and how our behaviours and traits impact various aspects of life. By exploring different personality traits and disorders, students can gain insight into human behaviour, improve interpersonal skills, and foster better relationships.

6. Steps to Overcome Personality Disorders:

Overcoming personality disorders involves a comprehensive approach that includes professional treatment, personal development, and support from others. Here are some steps:

To see ***Overcome Personality Disorders*** in Action

Scan QR Code

(i) Seek Professional Help:

- Engage in therapy with a licensed mental health professional.
- Consider medication if prescribed by a psychiatrist.

(ii) Develop Self-Awareness:

- Recognize and understand recurring patterns of behaviour and thought.
- Engage in regular self-reflection.

(iii) Build Coping Skills:

- Practise stress management techniques.
- Develop problem-solving skills.

(iv) Enhance Communication Skills:

- Practise assertiveness and active listening.

(v) Improve Relationship Skills:

- Set healthy boundaries and develop empathy.

(vi) Engage in Personal Growth:

- Set realistic goals and prioritize self-care.

(vii) Educate Yourself:

- Learn about the specific personality disorder and related resources.

(viii) Practice Patience and Persistence:

- Acknowledge progress and understand the gradual nature of overcoming disorder.

(ix) Regular Review and Adaptation:

- Monitor progress and adjust strategies as needed.

Practical-Based Activities for Students

Case Study Analysis: Personality Disorder:

Case Study: Alex's Struggle

Background: Alex is a 32-year-old marketing manager who has recently been experiencing significant personal and professional challenges. He has a history of unstable relationships, frequent job changes, and intense emotional reactions. Alex's friends and family describe him as highly emotional and unpredictable, often swinging between extreme highs and lows. He frequently feels abandoned and is hypersensitive to criticism.

Symptoms:

- **Interpersonal Relationships:** Alex has difficulty maintaining stable relationships. He tends to idealize people early on, only to become disillusioned and angry when they inevitably disappoint him.
- **Emotional Instability:** He experiences rapid and intense mood swings, from feeling euphoric and overconfident to feeling deeply depressed and hopeless.
- **Impulsivity:** Alex has engaged in impulsive behaviours such as reckless spending and substance abuse during periods of emotional distress.
- **Self-image:** His self-image fluctuates dramatically, and he often feels empty and uncertain about his identity.

Diagnosis: Based on Alex's symptoms, he is likely experiencing **Borderline Personality Disorder (BPD)**. This disorder is characterized by instability in mood, self-image, and relationships, leading to significant emotional distress and difficulties in personal and professional areas.

Answer the following: Case Study Analysis Questions:

1. What specific symptoms in Alex's case are indicative of Borderline Personality Disorder?
2. How do Alex's symptoms impact his behaviour at work and in his relationships?
3. Suggest practical coping strategies which Alex could use to handle his emotional instability and impulsivity. How might these strategies help him in his daily life?
4. How can Alex work on improving his interpersonal relationships? What strategies could he employ to create and maintain healthier relationships?
5. Discuss the role of Alex's support system (friends, family) in his treatment and recovery. How can they contribute to his well-being and stability?

EXERCISE

Review Questions

1. Define personality and list its main components.
2. Explain how traits, behaviour, cognition, and emotion contribute to an individual's personality.
3. How does personality affect interpersonal relationships?
4. Describe the impact of personality on workplace dynamics.
5. Explain how personality traits influence conflict resolution.
6. What are the Big Five Personality Traits? Describe each one briefly.
7. What are the symptoms and characteristics of Borderline Personality Disorder?
8. List and explain the steps involved in overcoming personality disorders.

UNIT 3

INFORMATION AND COMMUNICATION TECHNOLOGY SKILLS–IV

- **Session-1:** Getting Started with Spreadsheet
- **Session-2:** Performing Basic Operations in a Spreadsheet
- **Session-3:** Working with Data and Formatting Text
- **Session-4:** Advanced Features of a Spreadsheet
- **Session-5:** Presentation Software
- **Session-6:** Opening, Closing, Saving and Printing a Presentation
- **Session-7:** Working with Slides and Text in a Presentation
- **Session-8:** Advanced Features Used in Presentation

Session-1: Getting Started With Spreadsheets

1.1 Importance of ICT in the Modern World

To see
Introduction to Information and Communication Technology
in Action

Scan QR Code

Information and Communication Technology (ICT) encompasses a wide range of tools and resources used to communicate, create, store, and manage information, including computers, the Internet, broadcasting technologies, and telephony. ICT converts information into binary format in digital technology or electric pulses in analog technology. UNESCO defines informatics as the science of designing, using, and maintaining information processing systems, including their hardware, software, and organizational aspects. ICT is integral to daily life, enabling tasks like job searching, communication, and information access. Proficiency in ICT is essential for effective communication, business operations, and staying connected in today's digital world.

1.2 Utilizing Spreadsheets for Efficient Calculations in Daily Life and Workplaces

To see
Microsoft Excel
in Action

Scan QR Code

In our daily lives and workplaces, we frequently perform calculations, either manually or using a calculator. For more complex calculations, a scientific calculator is often used. Traditionally, we might have preferred a notebook with rows and columns for easy calculations. Similarly, a spreadsheet is an electronic worksheet, offering a long sheet of rows and columns for performing calculations efficiently.

1.3 Introduction to Spreadsheets

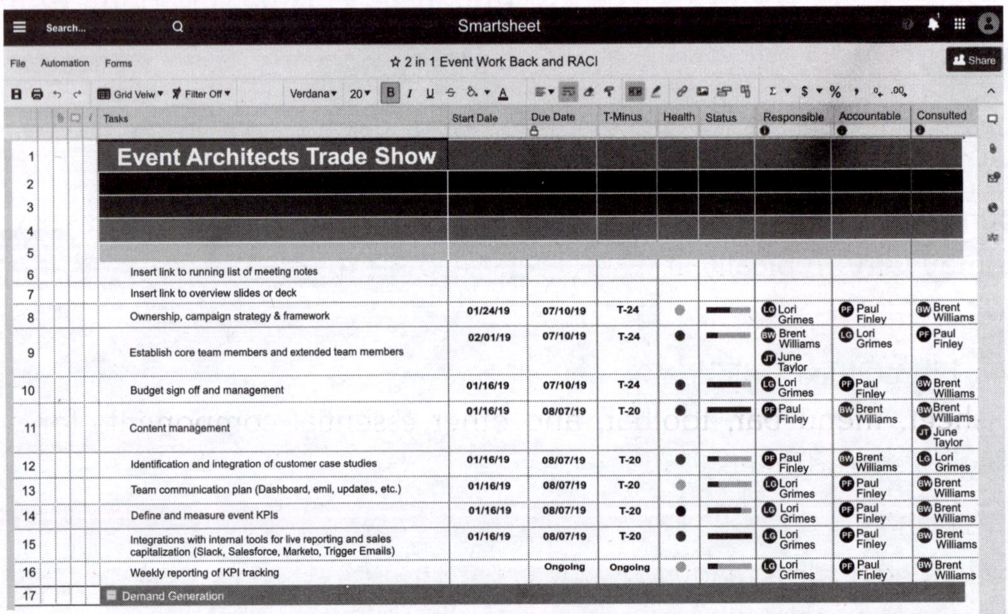

Fig. 1.1 Spreadsheet

- **Definition:** A spreadsheet is a digital tool used to organize, calculate, and analyse data in tabular form.
- **Purpose:** Spreadsheets are commonly used for financial planning, data analysis, record-keeping, and various other applications.
- **Examples of Spreadsheet Software:** Microsoft Excel, Google Sheets, LibreOffice Calc, and OpenOffice Calc.

Spreadsheet Interface:

Worksheet: The area where data is entered, consisting of rows and columns.

Workbook: A file containing one or more worksheets.

Cells: The intersection of a row and column, identified by a unique cell address (e.g., A1).

Rows and Columns:

Rows: Horizontal lines, numbered 1, 2, 3.

Columns: Vertical lines named as A, B, C, etc.

1.4 Loading and Launching LibreOffice Calc: A Step-by-Step Guide

Loading LibreOffice Calc: Refers to the process of starting or opening the LibreOffice Calc application, which is a spreadsheet program within the LibreOffice suite. Here's what it typically involves:

To see **LibreOffice Calc** in Action

Scan QR Code

1. **Launching the Application:**
   - **From the Start Menu (Windows):** Click on the Start button, navigate to the LibreOffice folder, and select "LibreOffice Calc."
   - **From the Applications Folder (macOS):** Open the Applications folder, find the LibreOffice application, and double-click it. Then, choose "Calc" from the opening menu.
   - **From the Dock or Desktop Shortcut:** If you have a shortcut for LibreOffice Calc, double-click it to load the application directly.
2. **Loading Time:**
   - Depending on your system's specifications and the version of LibreOffice, the loading time may vary. Typically, it takes a few seconds for the Calc interface to appear.
3. **Interface Initialization:**
   - When LibreOffice Calc loads, you'll see the user interface, which includes a blank worksheet, menu bar, toolbar, and other essential components for creating and managing spreadsheets.
4. **Ready to Use:**
   - Once loaded, Calc is ready to perform various tasks such as entering data, performing calculations, creating charts, and more.

This process is the first step to start working with spreadsheets in LibreOffice Calc.

1.5 How to Start LibreOffice Calc

Starting LibreOffice Calc, a powerful spreadsheet application, can be done in several ways depending on your operating system.

Here's a simple guide:

1. Starting LibreOffice Calc on Windows:

- **From the Start Menu:**
  - (a) Click the **Start** button (usually located at the bottom-left corner of the screen).
  - (b) Scroll through the list of installed programs or use the search bar to type "LibreOffice."
  - (c) Click on the **LibreOffice** folder to expand it.
  - (d) Select **LibreOffice Calc** to open the application.
- **Using a Desktop Shortcut:**
  - (a) If you have a shortcut for LibreOffice Calc on your desktop, simply double-click the icon.
  - (b) LibreOffice Calc will open directly, ready for use.

2. Starting LibreOffice Calc on macOS:

- **From the Applications Folder:**
  - (a) Open the **Applications** folder on your Mac (you can access this through Finder).
  - (b) Locate the **LibreOffice** application and double-click it.
  - (c) In the LibreOffice start screen, click on **Calc** to open the spreadsheet application.
- **Using the Dock:**
  - (a) If you've added LibreOffice to your Dock, click the LibreOffice icon.
  - (b) Choose **Calc** from the options that appear, or it may open directly into Calc if set as default.

3. Starting LibreOffice Calc on Linux:

- **From the Applications Menu:**
  - (a) Click on the **Applications** menu or equivalent (often found at the top-left or bottom-left of the screen).
  - (b) Navigate to the **Office** or **Productivity** category.
  - (c) Select **LibreOffice Calc** to start the program.
- **Using the Terminal:**
  - (a) Open the **Terminal**.
  - (b) Type libreoffice --calc and press **Enter**.
  - (c) This command will directly open LibreOffice Calc.

4. Starting LibreOffice Calc from a Document:

- **Double-clicking a .ods File:**
  - **(a)** Locate a spreadsheet file (usually with a .ods extension) on your computer.
  - **(b)** Double-click the file, and it will automatically open in LibreOffice Calc.

This process will allow you to start working with spreadsheets in LibreOffice Calc, regardless of your operating system.

1.6 COMPONENTS OF A SPREADSHEET

A spreadsheet is composed of several key components that work together to organize, calculate, and analyse data. Here are the main components:

1. **Workbook:**
   - **Definition:** A file that contains one or more worksheets.
   - **Purpose:** It serves as the container for all data, calculations, charts, and other content within the spreadsheet software.
2. **Worksheet:**
   - **Definition:** A single page within a workbook where data is entered and managed.
   - **Purpose:** It is the area where all the data entry, calculations, and analysis take place. Multiple worksheets can be used for organizing data into separate but related sections.
3. **Cells:**
   - **Definition:** The individual boxes where data is entered, located at the intersection of a row and a column.
   - **Address:** Each cell is identified by a unique cell address (e.g., A1, B5) where "A" represents the column and "1" represents the row.
   - **Purpose:** Cells are the basic building blocks of a worksheet where data, formulas, or functions are stored.
4. **Rows:**
   - **Definition:** Horizontal lines in a worksheet, identified by numbers (1, 2, 3, etc.).
   - **Purpose:** Rows help organize data horizontally and are used in combination with columns to define the location of a cell.
5. **Columns:**
   - **Definition:** Vertical lines in a worksheet, identified by letters (A, B, C, etc.).
   - **Purpose:** Columns help organize data vertically and are used in combination with rows to define the location of a cell.
6. **Range:**
   - **Definition:** A selection of two or more cells that are either adjacent or non-adjacent.

- **Purpose:** Ranges are often used for performing operations like summing data, creating charts, or applying formatting to multiple cells simultaneously.

7. **Formula Bar:**
   - **Definition:** A toolbar at the top of the worksheet where you can enter or edit data, formulas, or functions for the active cell.
   - **Purpose:** It displays the content of the selected cell and allows users to edit or create formulas that perform calculations.
8. **Function:**
   - **Definition:** Predefined formulas that perform specific calculations using the data in the worksheet.
   - **Purpose:** Functions simplify complex calculations like summing values, finding averages, or performing logical tests. For example, = SUM(A1:A10).
9. **Charts:**
   - **Definition:** Visual representations of data, such as bar charts, pie charts, or line graphs.
   - **Purpose:** Charts help to visualize and analyse data trends, making it easier to interpret and present information.
10. **Toolbar and Menu Bar:**
    - **Toolbar:** A set of icons or buttons that provide quick access to commonly used features and tools like formatting, inserting charts, or sorting data.
    - **Menu Bar:** A list of menus (File, Edit, View, etc.) that contain commands and options for managing the spreadsheet.
11. **Status Bar:**
    - **Definition:** A bar located at the bottom of the spreadsheet window, showing information about the current worksheet, such as the sum or average of selected cells.
    - **Purpose:** It provides quick access to common tasks like changing the worksheet view or zoom level.
12. **Gridlines:**
    - **Definition:** The lines that separate the cells, rows, and columns in a worksheet.
    - **Purpose:** Gridlines help to clearly distinguish between different cells, making the data easier to read and organize.
13. **Tabs:**
    - **Sheet Tabs:** Located at the bottom of the worksheet, these tabs allow you to navigate between different worksheets within the same workbook.

- **Purpose:** They help in organizing data into different categories or sections within the same workbook.

Understanding these components is essential for effectively using a spreadsheet to manage and analyse data.

1. A .... is a rectangle shaped box, where a row and a column meet in a spreadsheet. (CBSE Board Paper 2023)
2. In OpenOffice Calc .... contains the Name Box which shows the location of the selected cell. (CBSE Board Paper 2023)

EXERCISE

Fill in the Blanks

1. Information and Communication Technology (ICT) encompasses a wide range of tools and resources used to ...., create, store, and manage information.
2. ICT converts information into .... format in digital technology or electric pulses in analog technology.
3. According to ...., informatics is the science of designing, using, and maintaining information processing systems.
4. A .... is an electronic worksheet offering a long sheet of rows and columns for performing calculations efficiently.
5. In daily life, for more complex calculations, we often use a .... calculator.
6. A spreadsheet is a digital tool used to ...., calculate, and analyse data in tabular form.
7. On macOS, you can start LibreOffice Calc from the .... folder by locating and double-clicking the application.
8. A .... is a file that contains one or more worksheets.

ANSWERS

1. Communicate	2. Digital	3. Ralph M. Williams
4. Spreadsheet	5. Scientific	6. Organize
7. Applications	8. Workbook	

Practical Activities

You have a workbook in LibreOffice Calc with the following data in Sheet 1:

Table. 1.1

Item	Quantity	Price per unit
Apples	10	0.5
Bananas	6	0.3
Oranges	8	0.4

1. Create a formula in the "Total Cost" column to calculate the total cost for each item (Quantity × Price per unit).
2. Use a function to calculate the sum of all total costs.
3. Create a chart to visually represent the quantity of each fruit.

Instructions:

1. Enter the data into the spreadsheet, including columns for "Total Cost" and a row for totals.
2. Apply the formula and function as described.
3. Insert a chart that shows the quantity of each fruit.

Assessment Criteria:

1. Accurate use of formulas to calculate total costs.
2. Correct application of functions to sum total costs.
3. Effective creation and presentation of a chart to visualize data.

Session 2: Performing Basic Operations In A Spreadsheet

2.1 Introduction

In this session, we will explore the fundamental operations that can be performed in a spreadsheet. Understanding these basic operations will help you manage and analyse data efficiently. Spreadsheets, like Microsoft Excel, Google Sheets, and LibreOffice Calc, are powerful tools for organizing information, performing calculations, and creating visual representations of data.

1. **Understanding the Spreadsheet Interface:** Before diving into operations, it is essential to familiarize yourself with the spreadsheet interface:
   - **Workbook:** A file that contains one or more worksheets.

- **Worksheet:** A single page within a workbook where data is entered.
- **Cells:** The individual boxes where data is entered, located at the intersection of rows and columns.
- **Rows and Columns:** Rows are horizontal lines labeled with numbers, while columns are vertical lines labeled with letters.
- **Formula Bar:** Located above the worksheet, it shows the content of the selected cell and allows you to enter or edit formulas.

2. **Basic Data Entry:** To start working with spreadsheets, you need to enter data into cells:
   - Click on a cell to select it.
   - Type your data (e.g., text, numbers) and press Enter to move to the cell below, or Tab to move to the cell to the right.
3. **Basic Calculations:** Spreadsheets are especially useful for performing calculations. Here's how you can use basic arithmetic operations:
   - **Addition:** To add numbers, use the + operator. For example, to add values in cells A1 and A2, type **=A1+A2** in another cell.
   - **Subtraction:** Use the – operator. For example, **=A1– A2.**
   - **Multiplication:** Use the * operator. For example, **=A1*A2.**
   - **Division:** Use the /operator. For example, **=A1/A2.**
4. **Using Functions:** Functions are predefined formulas that simplify complex calculations:
   - **SUM:** Adds a range of numbers. For example, **=SUM(A1:A5)** adds all values from cells A1 to A5.
   - **AVERAGE:** Calculates the average of a range of numbers. For example, **=AVERAGE(A1:A5)**.
   - **MAX:** Finds the highest number in a range. For example, **=MAX(A1:A5)**.
   - **MIN:** Finds the lowest number in a range. For example, **=MIN(A1:A5)**.
5. **Copying and Pasting Data:** To efficiently manage and replicate data:
   - Select the cell or range of cells you want to copy.
   - Right-click and choose "Copy" or use Ctrl + C.
   - Select the destination cell, right-click, and choose "Paste" or use Ctrl + V.
6. **Filling Data:** Use the Fill Handle to quickly fill a series of numbers or dates:
   - Enter the starting value in a cell.
   - Click and drag the small square (Fill Handle) at the bottom-right corner of the cell to extend the series.
7. **Formatting Cells:** Formatting helps make your data more readable:
   - **Font Style:** Change the font type, size, and colour.

- **Number Format:** Adjust how numbers are displayed (e.g., currency, percentage).
- **Cell Borders and Backgrounds:** Add borders or background colours to cells.

8. **Sorting Data:** Sorting helps organize data:
   - Select the range of data you want to sort.
   - Go to the Data tab and choose "Sort."
   - Select the column you want to sort by and choose ascending or descending order.
9. **Filtering Data:** Filtering allows you to display only the rows that meet certain criteria:
   - Select the range of data.
   - Click on the "Filter" button in the Data tab.
   - Use the drop-down menus in the column headers to select your filter criteria.
10. **Creating Basic Charts:** Charts visually represent data:
    - Select the range of data you want to include in the chart.
    - Go to the Insert tab and choose the type of chart (e.g., bar, line, pie).
    - Customize your chart using the Chart Tools.

Mastering these basic operations will make working with spreadsheets much more manageable. By effectively entering data, performing calculations, using functions, formatting, sorting, filtering, and creating charts, you can leverage the full power of spreadsheets to analyse and present data clearly and efficiently. Practices these skills to become proficient and ready to tackle more complex spreadsheet tasks.

EXERCISE

Multiple Choice Questions

1. **What is "Workbook" in a spreadsheet?**
   (a) A single page where data is entered
   (b) A file that contains one or more worksheets
   (c) An individual box where data is entered
   (d) A horizontal line in a worksheet
2. **Which operator would you use to perform division in a spreadsheet formula?**
   (a) + (b) –
   (c) * (d) /
3. **What does the SUM function do in a spreadsheet?**
   (a) Calculates the average of a range of numbers
   (b) Finds the highest number in a range

(c) Adds all values in a specified range

(d) Finds the lowest number in a range

4. How do you fill a series of numbers or dates in a spreadsheet quickly?

(a) Use the Copy and Paste commands

(b) Type each value manually

(c) Use the Fill Handle

(d) Use the Formula Bar

5. What is the purpose of the "Filter" feature in a spreadsheet?

(a) To add visual representations of data

(b) To sort data in ascending or descending order

(c) To display only rows that meet certain criteria

(d) To format text and numbers

ANSWERS

1. (b)	2. (d)	3. (c)	4. (c)	5. (c)

SESSION–3: WORKING WITH DATA AND FORMATTING TEXT

3.1 INTRODUCTION

Welcome to the exciting world of spreadsheets! In this session, we will explore how to work with data and format text effectively. Whether you are creating a budget, analysing survey results, or organizing your school project, mastering these skills will help you present your information clearly and professionally. Let's dive into the basics of data management and text formatting to make your spreadsheets stand out.

To see **Working with Data and Formatting Text** in Action

Scan QR Code

3.1.1. UNDERSTANDING DATA IN SPREADSHEETS

A spreadsheet is like a digital grid where you can enter, organize, and manipulate data. Here's a quick overview of the key components:

- **Cells:** The smallest unit where data is entered. Each cell is identified by a unique combination of a column letter and row number (e.g., A1, B2).
- **Rows:** Horizontal lines of cells. Each row is numbered.
- **Columns:** Vertical lines of cells. Each column is lettered.
- **Worksheets:** Individual sheets within a spreadsheet file where you can enter data.

Example: Imagine that you are tracking your weekly expenses. Each row could represent a different day, and each column could represent different expense categories (e.g., Food, Transport, Entertainment).

3.1.2. Entering and Editing Data

Entering Data:

- Click on the cell where you want to enter data.
- Type the data (text, numbers, or dates).
- Press Enter to move to the next cell.

Editing Data:

- Double-click on the cell containing the data you want to change.
- Make your changes.
- Press Enter to save the changes.

Tips:

- Use descriptive headers for columns (e.g., "Date," "Expense Category").
- Keep your data consistent (e.g., use the same date format throughout).

3.1.3. Formatting Text

Formatting text makes your data easier to read and understand. Here's how you can format text effectively:

Changing Font Style and Size:

- Select the cell or range of cells you want to format.
- Go to the toolbar and choose the font style and size.

Applying Bold, Italics, or Underline:

- Select the text.
- Click on the bold (B), italics (I), or underlined (U) buttons on the toolbar.

Text Alignment:

- Select the cell(s) you want to align.
- Choose from options such as left, center, or right alignment to position your text.

Text Colour and Background Colour:

- Select the cell(s).
- Choose a font colour and background colour from the toolbar to make your text stand out.

Example: If you want to highlight the total expenses in a different colour or bold font, select that cell and apply the formatting options.

3.1.4. Using Number Formats

Different types of data require different formats:

Number Formats:

- **General:** Default format for numbers.
- **Currency:** Displays numbers as monetary values (e.g., $100.00).
- **Percentage:** Shows numbers as percentages (e.g., 25%).

Date Formats:

- Choose from various date formats (e.g., MM/DD/YYYY or DD/MM/YYYY) depending on your preference or regional standards.

Example: When tracking financial data, use the Currency format for monetary values to clearly show the amount.

3.1.5. Working with Formulas and Functions

Formulas and functions help you perform calculations on your data:

Basic Formulas:

- **Addition:** =A1+A2
- **Subtraction:** =A1–A2
- **Multiplication:** =A1*A2
- **Division:** =A1/A2

Using Functions:

- **SUM:** =SUM(A1:A5) adds all numbers in the range A1 to A5.
- **AVERAGE:** =AVERAGE(B1:B5) calculates the average of numbers in the range B1 to B5.

Example: To find the total amount spent on groceries, use the SUM function to add up all grocery expenses in your spreadsheet.

3.1.6. Organizing and Sorting Data

Sorting Data:

- Select the range of cells you want to sort.
- Go to the Data menu and choose Sort.
- Decide the sorting order (ascending or descending).

Filtering Data:

- Select the data range.
- Apply filters to show only the data that meets certain criteria (e.g., showing only expenses greater than $50).

Example: If you have a list of expenses and you want to view only the highest spending categories, use the sorting and filtering options to organize your data.

3.1.7. Practical Applications

Creating a Budget:

- List your income sources and expenses.
- Use formulas to calculate totals and balances.
- Format your spreadsheet to highlight important information.

Analysing Survey Results:

- Enter survey responses in cells.
- Use functions to calculate averages and percentages.
- Format the results for a clear presentation.

Tracking Academic Performance:

- Record grades for different subjects.
- Use formulas to calculate averages and grades.
- Format your spreadsheet to visualize performance trends.

Mastering data entry, formatting, and basic calculations in spreadsheets will enhance your ability to manage and present information effectively. Practise these skills to improve your spreadsheet proficiency and make your data work for you!

EXERCISE

Fill in the Blanks

1. A spreadsheet is organized into rows and ...., where each cell is identified by a unique combination of a column letter and row number.
2. To enter data into a cell, click on the cell, type the data, and press .... to move to the next cell.
3. To format text as bold, select the text and click on the .... button on the toolbar.
4. The .... function in a spreadsheet adds all numbers in a specified range.
5. When you want to display numbers as monetary values, use the .... format.
6. To sort data in descending order, select the range of cells, go to the Data menu, and choose ....
7. When filtering data to show only certain criteria, you should apply .... to your data range.
8. To calculate the average of numbers in a range, use the .... function.

ANSWERS

1. Columns	2. Enter	3. Bold	4. SUM
5. Currency	6. Sort	7. Filters	8. Average

Session–4: Advanced Features Of A Spreadsheet

4.1 Introduction

Spreadsheets are a powerful tool that go beyond basic data entry and calculations. They offer a wide range of advanced features that allow users to analyse data, automate tasks, and create dynamic reports. In this session, we will explore some of these advanced features to enhance your spreadsheet skills.

To see **Advanced Features of a Spreadsheet** in Action

Scan QR Code

1. Conditional Formatting:

Conditional formatting allows you to automatically format cells based on their content. For example, you can highlight cells with values above or below a certain threshold, or apply different colours to cells based on specific criteria.

Key Features:

- Highlight cells based on conditions.
- Create data bars, colour scales, and icon sets.
- Use formulas to apply custom formatting rules.

Example: Apply a green fill to cells where the value is greater than 80.

2. Data Validation:

Data validation helps ensure that the data entered into a spreadsheet meets specific criteria. This feature is useful for preventing errors and maintaining data integrity.

Key Features:

- Restrict data entry to specific types (e.g., numbers, dates).
- Create dropdown lists for data entry.
- Display error messages for invalid entries.

Example: Create a dropdown list of valid options in a cell.

3. Pivot Tables:

Pivot tables are a powerful tool for summarizing, analysing, and exploring large datasets. They allow you to rearrange and filter data to uncover trends and patterns.

Key Features:

- Summarize data by categories and subcategories.
- Calculate sums, averages, counts, and other aggregations.
- Group data by periods or custom categories.
- Drill down into details with interactive fields.

Example: Create a pivot table summarizing sales data by region and product category.

4. Macros:

Macros allow you to automate repetitive tasks by recording a sequence of actions and playing them again with a single click. This feature is handy for complex tasks that need to be performed regularly.

Key Features:

- Record, edit, and run macros.
- Assign macros to buttons or keyboard shortcuts.
- Write custom scripts using Visual Basic for Applications (VBA).

Example: Create a macro to format a report with a specific layout and style.

5. Advanced Formulas and Functions:

Spreadsheets offer a vast array of functions for performing complex calculations and data analysis. Understanding and using advanced formulas can greatly enhance your ability to manipulate data.

Key Functions:

- **LOOKUP, VLOOKUP, HLOOKUP:** Search for values within a range.
- **INDEX and MATCH:** Retrieve data from a specific location.
- **ARRAY FORMULA:** Apply a formula to an entire range of cells.
- **IF, AND, OR:** Perform conditional calculations.
- **SUMIF, COUNTIF, AVERAGEIF:** Aggregate data based on conditions.

Example: Use the VLOOKUP function to find a product's price in a list based on its name.

6. Data Analysis Tools:

Spreadsheet software often includes built-in tools for data analysis, such as Solver, Goal Seek, and Scenario Manager. These tools help you make decisions based on various scenarios and constraints.

Key Tools:

- **Solver:** Optimize values to meet specific goals.
- **Goal Seek:** Find the input value needed to achieve a desired result.
- **Scenario Manager:** Compare different scenarios and their outcomes.

Example: Use Solver to determine the optimal product mix to maximize profit under certain constraints.

7. Charts and Graphs:

Visualizing data through charts and graphs makes it easier to understand and communicate insights. Advanced charting features allow you to create dynamic and interactive visualizations.

Key Features:

- Create various chart types (e.g., line, bar, pie, scatter).
- Customize chart elements (e.g., axis labels, legends, data points).
- Use sparklines to display trends within a single cell.
- Combine different chart types for complex visualizations.

Example: Create a combination chart with a bar and line series to show sales and profit over time.

8. Collaboration Features:

Modern spreadsheet applications often include features for real-time collaboration, making it easier to work with others on shared documents.

Key Features:

- Share spreadsheets with collaborators.
- Track changes and view version history.
- Comment on cells and respond to feedback.
- Set permissions for viewing or editing.

Example: Share a budget spreadsheet with team members and track their changes.

9. Importing and Exporting Data:

Spreadsheets can import and export data from various sources, including databases, text files, and web pages. This feature is crucial for integrating data from different systems.

Key Features:

- Import data from CSV, TXT, XML, and other file formats.
- Connect to external databases and data sources.
- Export data to different formats for use in other applications.

Example: Import sales data from a CSV file into a spreadsheet for analysis.

10. Protecting and Securing Data:

Spreadsheets often contain sensitive information, so it is important to know how to protect and secure your data.

Key Features:

- Protect sheets and ranges with passwords.
- Hide formulas and data from unauthorized users.
- Encrypt the entire workbook for secure sharing.

Example: Protect a worksheet so that only authorized users can edit certain cells.

Mastering the advanced features of spreadsheets can significantly enhance your productivity and data analysis capabilities. By understanding and applying these tools, you will be well-equipped to tackle complex tasks and make informed decisions based on your data.

Practical Session Exercise

1. Create a pivot table from a dataset of your choice and summarize the key findings.
2. Record a macro that formats a spreadsheet in a specific style, then run it on a new sheet.
3. Use conditional formatting to highlight cells that meet certain criteria in a sales report.
4. Import data from a CSV file and create a chart to visualize the information.

SESSION 5: PRESENTATION SOFTWARE

5.1 INTRODUCTION TO PRESENTATION SOFTWARE

To see **Introduction to Presentation Software** in Action

Scan QR Code

Fig. 5.1

Presentation software is a vital tool used to create and display information in the form of slides. It is widely used in educational settings, business meetings, and conferences to visually communicate ideas, data, and concepts.

5.2 KEY FEATURES OF PRESENTATION SOFTWARE

5.2.1 SLIDES AND SLIDE LAYOUTS

Slides: The basic unit of a presentation. Each slide can contain text, images, charts, videos, and other multimedia.

Slide Layouts: Predefined formats for arranging content on slides, such as Title Slide, Two Content, Comparison, etc.

5.2.2 TEXT FORMATTING

Fonts and Styles: Customize the text with various fonts, sizes, colours, and effects.

Bullets and Numbering: Organize text in bullet points or numbered lists to enhance readability.

5.2.3 DESIGN AND THEMES

Themes: Pre-designed colour schemes, fonts, and backgrounds that provide a consistent look across all slides.

Backgrounds: Customize slide backgrounds with colours, gradients, images, or textures.

5.2.4 Multimedia Integration

Images and Graphics: Insert pictures, shapes, SmartArt, and icons to visually represent information.

Audio and Video: Embed sound clips, music, or videos to make the presentation more engaging.

5.2.5 Animations and Transitions

Animations: Apply motion effects to objects like text, images, or charts on a slide to emphasize key points.

Transitions: Control how one slide changes to the next with various transition effects.

5.3 Charts and Graphs

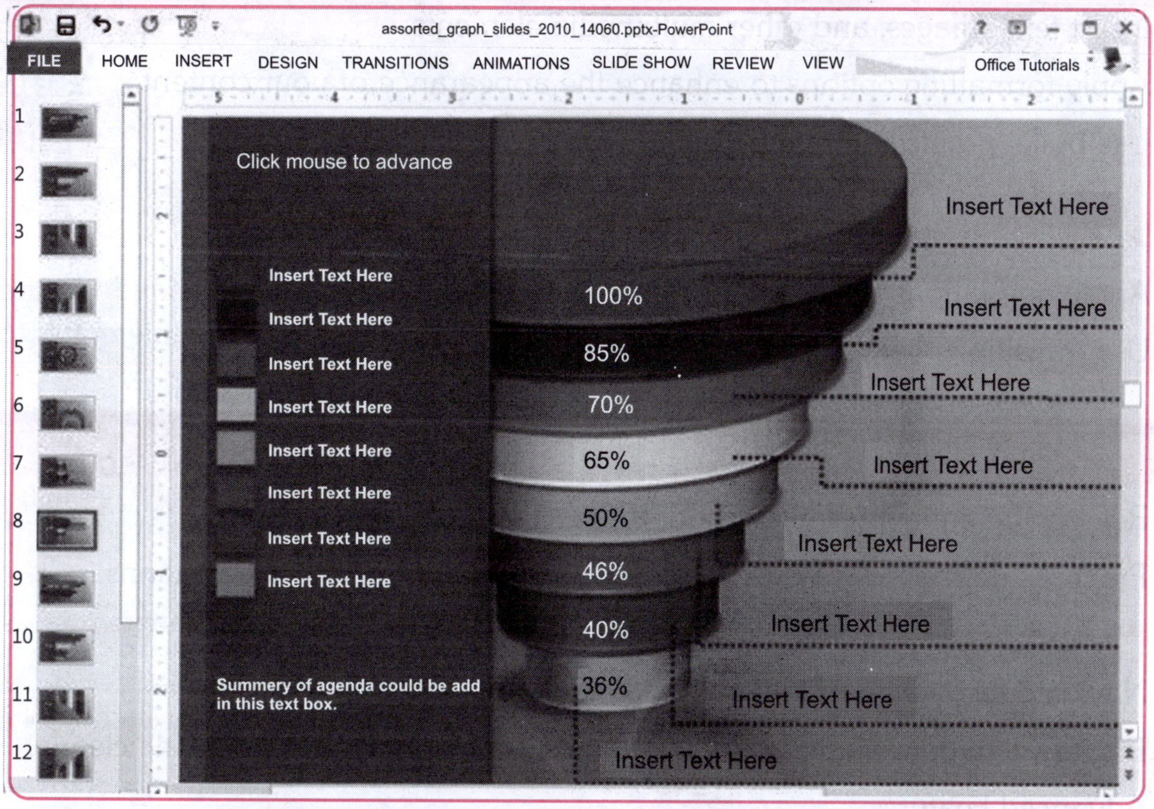

Fig. 5.2 Data Representation

Data Representation: Use charts and graphs to represent numerical data in a visual format, making it easier to understand and analyse.

5.3.1 Hyperlinks and Actions

Hyperlinks: Link to external websites, documents, or other slides within the presentation.

Action Buttons: Interactive buttons that can perform specific actions, such as moving to a particular slide.

Creating a Presentation: Step-by-Step Guide

5.3.2 Planning Your Presentation

- Identify the purpose and audience.
- Outline the key points you want to cover.
- Decide on the structure of your presentation.

5.3.3 Designing the Slides

- Choose a theme that matches the tone of your presentation.
- Create a Title Slide with the presentation's title, subtitle, and your name.
- Add content slides, following your outline, and using appropriate slide layouts.

5.3.4 Adding and Formatting Content

- Insert text, images, and other multimedia elements.
- Apply formatting options to enhance the appearance of your content.
- Use bullet points and numbered lists for clear communication.

5.3.5 Incorporating Animations and Transitions

- Apply animations to important elements to draw attention.
- Use transitions between slides for a smooth flow.

5.4 Finalizing and Reviewing

- Review the entire presentation for any errors or inconsistencies.
- Practices delivering the presentation, focusing on timing and transitions.
- **Presenting:** Use presentation mode to display your slides.
- Navigate through the slides using a remote or keyboard shortcut.
- Engage with your audience by maintaining eye contact and speaking clearly.
- Advanced Features.

Collaborative Editing: Work with others on the same presentation in real-time, using cloud-based software like Google Slides or Microsoft PowerPoint Online.

Slide Master: Customize slide layouts and themes globally across the entire presentation using the Slide Master feature.

Speaker Notes: Add notes to each slide to guide you during the presentation without displaying them to the audience.

Custom Animations: Create complex animations by customizing motion paths, timings, and triggers.

Practical Session Exercise

Task: Create a presentation on a topic of your choice, using at least 10 slides. Incorporate text, images, charts, animations, and transitions. Ensure that your presentation is well-structured and visually appealing.

Deliverables: Present your slides to the class, focusing on clear communication and effective use of presentation software features.

Understanding how to use presentation software effectively is a crucial skill in today's digital world. By mastering the tools and techniques covered in this session, you will be able to create impactful presentations that convey your ideas and engage your audience.

Session 6: Opening, Closing, Saving And Printing A Presentation

6.1 Introduction

Creating presentations is an essential skill for students and professionals alike. This session will guide you through the basic yet important tasks of opening, closing, saving, and printing a presentation. By the end of this session, you'll be confident in managing your presentation files efficiently.

6.1.1 Opening a Presentation

To start working on a presentation, you first need to open it. Here's how:

Locate the File

Use File Explorer (Windows) or Finder (Mac) to navigate to the location where your presentation is saved.

Double-click the File

Simply double-click on the presentation file (usually with a .pptx or .odp extension) to open it. The presentation software installed on your computer (like PowerPoint, Google Slides, or OpenOffice Impress) will automatically launch.

1. Open from the Application:

- Alternatively, open the presentation software first.
- Go to File > Open.
- Browse to the location of your file, select it, and click Open.

2. Closing a Presentation:

After you are done with working on your presentation, it is important to close it properly:

- Save your work.
- Before closing, make sure you have saved your progress (see the next section on saving).

3. Close the File:

Go to File > Close or click on the X at the top-right corner of the application window.

- Exit the Application (Optional):
- If you are finished working with the application, you can also exit the program by clicking on File > Exit or simply closing the window.

4. Saving a Presentation:

Saving your work regularly is crucial to avoid losing any progress. Here's how you can save your presentation:

(a) Save for the First Time:

If you're saving your presentation for the first time:

- Go to File > Save As.
- Choose a location on your computer.
- Enter a name for your presentation.
- Select the file type (usually .pptx for PowerPoint, .odp for OpenOffice).
- Click Save.

(b) Save Updates:

- Once your presentation is saved, you can quickly save updates by going to File > Save or simply pressing Ctrl + S (Windows) or Cmd + S (Mac).

Saving in Different Formats

- To save your presentation in a different format (e.g., PDF, older version).
- Go to File > Save As.
- Select the desired format from the dropdown list.
- Click Save.

5. Printing a Presentation:

- Printing your presentation is useful for sharing handouts or keeping a physical copy. Here's how to do it.

(a) Open the Presentation:

- Make sure your presentation is open and properly formatted for printing.

(b) Go to Print Menu:

- Navigate to File > Print.

(c) Adjust Print Settings:

- Select your printer from the list.
- Choose the number of copies you need.
- Decide which slides you want to print (all slides, selected slides, or a specific range).
- Choose the layout (full-page slides, handouts, notes pages, etc.).

(d) Print:

- Once you are satisfied with the settings, click Print to start printing.

Mastering the basics of opening, closing, saving, and printing presentations ensures that you can manage your work effectively. These skills are fundamental, whether you're preparing for a class project or a professional presentation.

EXERCISE

Multiple Choice Questions

1. What is the first step to open a presentation file on your computer?

(a) Open the application first
(b) Double-click the presentation file
(c) Use Ctrl + O to open the file
(d) Right-click and select "Open"

2. Which command should you use to save your presentation for the first time?

(a) File > Save
(b) File > Close
(c) File > Save As
(d) Ctrl + S

3. How can you quickly save updates to a presentation after it has already been saved once?

(a) File > Save As
(b) Press Ctrl + P
(c) File > Save
(d) Use File > Open

4. What option should you choose if you want to exit the presentation application after closing the file?

(a) File > Save As
(b) File > Exit
(c) File > Close
(d) Press Ctrl + W

5. Which print setting allows you to print multiple slides on a single page?

(a) Notes pages
(b) Full- page slides
(c) Handouts
(d) Selected slides

ANSWERS

1. (b) 2. (c) 3. (c) 4. (b) 5. (c)

Session 7: Working With Slides And Text In A Presentation

7.1 Introduction

Fig. 7.1 Crafting Powerful Presentations

Creating a compelling presentation is an essential skill in both academic and professional settings. The ability to effectively organize and present information using slides and text can significantly impact how your message is received. In this session, we will explore the essential techniques for working with slides and text in a presentation, ensuring that your content is both visually appealing and easy to understand.

7.1.1 Understanding Slide Layouts

A slide layout is the arrangement of elements on a slide, including titles, text, images, and other media. Choosing the right layout is crucial for effectively communicating your message.

Default Layouts:

Title Slide: The first slide in most presentations is used for the presentation title and subtitle.

Title and Content: A versatile layout that includes a title at the top and content (text, images, charts) below.

Section Header: Used to introduce a new section in the presentation.

Two Content: A layout with two placeholders for content side by side.

7.1.2 Customizing Layouts

- **Adding Placeholders:** You can add placeholders for text, images, charts, or other objects to customize a slide layout.
- **Modifying Layouts:** Change the position, size, or formatting of placeholders to fit your needs.

7.1.3 Working with Text

- Text is a fundamental element of any presentation. It is essential to ensure that your text is clear, concise, and well-organized.

7.1.4 Adding Text to Slides

- **Click to Add Text:** Most layouts have text boxes where you can simply click and start typing.
- **Adding Text Boxes:** If a slide layout doesn't meet your needs, you can add additional text boxes by going to Insert > Text Box.

7.1.5 Formatting Text

Font Styles: Choose an appropriate font style that is easy to read. Avoid overly decorative fonts.

Font Size: Ensure that your text is large enough to be readable from a distance, especially in a classroom or conference room.

Text Alignment: Align your text for consistency – left, center, right, or justified alignment can be used depending on the design.

Bullet Points: Use bullet points to break down information into manageable chunks, making it easier for your audience to follow along.

7.1.6 Using Text Effectively

Keep it Concise: Avoid overcrowding slides with text. Use short phrases or bullet points instead of full sentences.

Emphasize Key Points: Use bold, italics, or colour to highlight important information.

Consistency: Maintain consistent text formatting throughout the presentation to create a professional look.

7.1.7 Managing Slides

Managing your slides effectively is key to maintaining a smooth flow in your presentation.

7.1.8 Adding New Slides

Insert a New Slide: To add a new slide, go to Home > New Slide, and choose a layout that suits your content.

Duplicate Slides: If you need multiple slides with the same layout or content, you can duplicate an existing slide by right-clicking on it and selecting Duplicate Slide.

7.2 Rearranging Slides

- **Slide Sorter View:** Use the Slide Sorter view to easily rearrange the order of your slides by clicking and dragging them to a new position.
- **Moving Slides:** In the normal view, you can also move slides up or down by dragging them in the slide navigation pane.

7.2.1 Deleting Slides

- **Remove Unnecessary Slides:** To delete a slide, right-click on it in the slide navigation pane and select Delete Slide. This helps keep your presentation concise and focused.

7.2.2 Inserting and Formatting Images with Text

- Images can enhance your presentation by providing visual support for your message.

(a) Inserting Images

- **From File:** Go to Insert > Pictures to add an image from your computer.
- **Online Images:** You can also insert images from the web by going to Insert > Online Pictures (if supported by your software).

(b) Formatting Images

- **Resizing and Positioning:** Click and drag the corners of the image to resize it. Position it appropriately on the slide to complement your text.
- **Wrapping Text Around Images:** Some presentation software allows you to wrap text around an image, making the slide look more integrated and visually appealing.

7.2.3 Using Images Effectively

Relevance: Ensure that your images are directly related to your content.

Quality: Use high-resolution images to avoid pixelation when projected.

Balance: Don't overcrowd your slides with too many images. Maintain a balance between text and visuals.

7.2.4 Using Themes and Templates

- Themes and templates can give your presentation a consistent and professional look.

Applying a Theme:

- **Choose a Theme:** Go to Design > Themes to select from a variety of pre-designed themes. These themes come with coordinated colours, fonts, and slide layouts.

Customizing Themes: You can customize a theme by changing the background, colours, and fonts to better suit your presentation.

7.3 Using Templates

Pre-designed Templates: Templates are pre-designed presentations with built-in slide layouts, themes, and content suggestions. You can find templates in the New Slide or File > New menu.

Modifying Templates: After selecting a template, you can modify it by adding your content, changing layouts, or customizing the design.

Mastering the art of working with slides and text in a presentation is a fundamental skill that can elevate the quality of your presentations. By understanding how to use layouts, manage text, organize slides, and incorporate images effectively you can create presentations that are not only informative but also visually engaging. Remember, the key to a great presentation is clarity, consistency, and visual appeal.

EXERCISE

Fill in the Blanks

1. A .... layout is typically used for the first slide in a presentation to display the title and subtitle.
2. To add additional text boxes to a slide, go to .... > Text Box.
3. .... fonts should be avoided in presentations to ensure readability.
4. The .... view allows you to rearrange the order of your slides by clicking and dragging them to a new position.
5. To duplicate an existing slide, right-click on it and select .... Slide.

6. To insert an image from your computer, you should go to Insert > ....
7. .... points are used to break down information into manageable chunks, making it easier for your audience to follow along.
8. The .... feature allows you to select from pre-designed themes that come with coordinated colours, fonts, and slide layouts.

ANSWERS

1. Title Slide 2. Insert 3. Overly decorative
4. Slide Sorter 5. Duplicate 6. Pictures 7. Bullet
8. Themes

SESSION–8: ADVANCED FEATURES USED IN A PRESENTATION

8.1 INTRODUCTION

Creating a presentation is more than just adding text and pictures to slides. With advanced features, you can make your presentations more engaging, professional, and effective. This session will guide you through some of the most important advanced features you can use in presentation software.

To see **Advanced Features Used in a Presentation** in Action

Scan QR Code

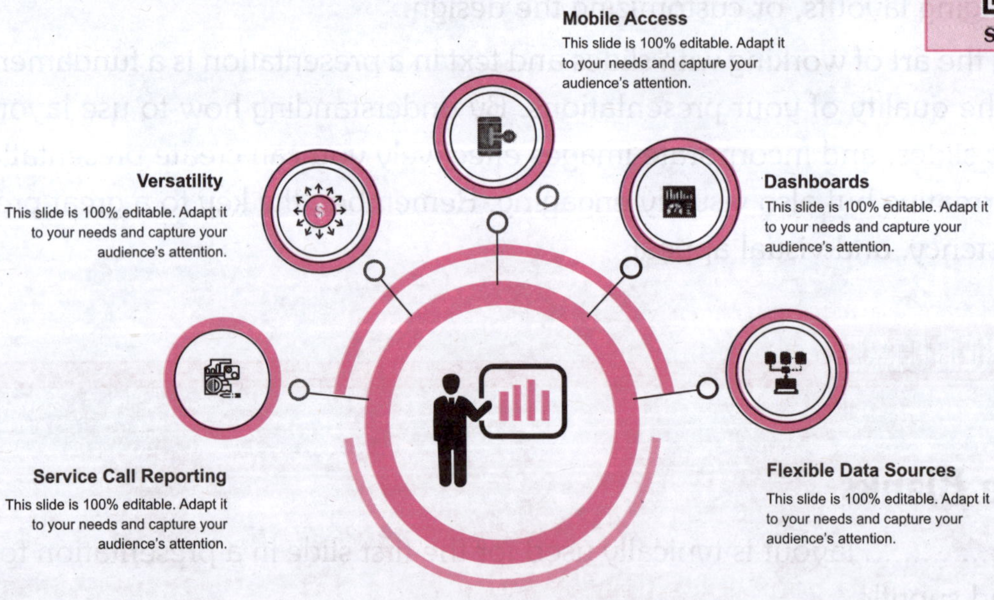

Fig. 8.1 Smart Features for Slides

8.1.1 ANIMATIONS

Animations allow you to add movement to text, images, and other objects on your slides. This can help grab your audience's attention or emphasize key points. Here are some ways to use animations effectively:

Entrance Effects: Make objects appear on the slide in different ways (e.g., fade in, fly in, zoom in).

Emphasis Effects: Highlight important parts of your slide by changing the colour size, or position of objects.

Exit Effects: Make objects disappear from the slide (e.g., fade out, fly out).

Tip: Use animations sparingly to avoid overwhelming your audience.

8.1.2 Transitions

Transitions are effects that occur when you move from one slide to the next. They can make your presentation flow smoothly and look more polished. Common transition effects include:

Fade: The slide gradually appears or disappears.

Slide: The slide moves in from one direction.

Wipe: The new slide replaces the old one with a sweeping motion.

Tip: Choose transitions that match the tone of your presentation – simple transitions for formal presentations and more dynamic ones for creative or informal presentations.

8.1.3 M Integration of Multimedia

Fig. 8.2 Engaging Slides with Media

Adding videos, audio clips, or music to your slides can make your presentation more engaging. Here's how to use multimedia effectively:

Videos: Embed short, relevant video clips to explain a concept or provide a visual demonstration.

Audio: Include sound effects or background music to create a certain mood or to emphasize key points.

Narration: Record your voice to guide your audience through the presentation, which can be especially helpful for online or self-paced presentations.

Tip: Ensure that multimedia elements are relevant and do not distract from the main content.

8.1.4 SmartArt

SmartArt is a feature that allows you to create diagrams, such as flowcharts, organizational charts, and lists, in a visually appealing way.

Use SmartArt to:

- **Visualize Processes:** Show step-by-step processes or workflows.
- **Organize Information:** Group all related information in a structured format.
- **Highlight Relationships:** Show connections between different concepts or items.

Tip: Choose a SmartArt style that fits the type of information you are presenting.

8.1.5 Slide Master

The Slide Master feature helps you create a consistent look across all your slides. It allows you to design a template that can be applied to your entire presentation. With Slide Master, you can:

- **Customize Layouts:** Design custom slide layouts with specific placeholders for text, images, and other content.
- **Apply Consistent Formatting:** Ensure that fonts, colours, and logos are the same on every slide.
- **Create Slide Templates:** Save time by using pre-designed slide templates for future presentations.

Tip: Use Slide Master to maintain a professional and cohesive design throughout your presentation.

8.1.6 Hyperlinks

Hyperlinks allow you to link to other slides, websites, documents, or e-mail addresses directly from your presentation. They can make your presentation more interactive and informative by:

- **Linking to Websites:** Provide additional information or references without cluttering your slides.
- **Navigating Between Slides:** Create a table of contents or a navigation menu to easily move between different sections of your presentation.
- **Linking to Documents:** Attach supporting documents or reports for your audience to access.

Tip: Use hyperlinks thoughtfully to enhance the audience's experience without confusing them.

8.1.7 Custom Shows

Custom Shows allow you to create different versions of your presentation within a single file. You can select specific slides to show based on your audience or the context. This feature is useful when:

- **Presenting to Different Audiences:** Tailor your content to different groups without creating separate presentations.
- **Focusing on Specific Topics:** Highlight particular sections for shorter presentations or in-depth discussions.
- **Preparing Backup Slides:** Have additional slides ready for questions or deeper dives into topics.

Tip: Plan your Custom Shows ahead of time to ensure a smooth presentation flow.

8.1.8 Rehearse Timings

Rehearse Timings allows you to practices your presentation and record the time it takes to deliver each slide. This helps you manage your time effectively during the actual presentation. You can:

- **Practise Delivery :** Get comfortable with your material and pacing.
- **Set Automatic Slide Timings:** If your presentation is self-running, you can set each slide to advance automatically based on your rehearsed timings.
- **Evaluate and Adjust:** Identify areas where you need to speed up or slow down.

Tip: Rehearse your presentation multiple times to ensure that it fits within the allotted time.

Mastering these advanced features will take your presentations to the next level. By using animations, transitions, multimedia, SmartArt, Slide Master, hyperlinks, Custom Shows, and Rehearse Timings effectively, you can create presentations that are not only informative but also engaging and memorable. Practices using these features in your next presentation to see the difference they can make.

EXERCISE

Fill in the Blanks

Complete the following sentences using the correct terms.

1. ________ allows you to add movement to text, images, and other objects on your slides, such as entrance, emphasis, and exit effects.
2. ________ are effects that occur when you move from one slide to the next, including fade, slide, and wipe.
3. Adding ________ like videos, audio clips, or music to your slides can make your presentation more engaging and dynamic.
4. ________ is a feature that allows you to create visually appealing diagrams, such as flowcharts and organizational charts.
5. The ________ feature helps you create a consistent look across all your slides by customizing layouts, applying consistent formatting, and creating slide templates.
6. ________ enable you to link to other slides, websites, documents, or e-mail addresses directly from your presentation.
7. ________ allows you to create different versions of your presentation within a single file, tailoring content for different audiences or contexts.
8. ________ allows you to practices your presentation and record the time it takes to deliver each slide, helping you manage your to presentation time effectively.

ANSWERS

1. Animations 2. Transitions 3. Multimedia 4. SmartArt
5. Slide Master 6. Hyperlinks 7. Custom Shows
8. Rehearse Timings

Formulas and Functions

Formulas and functions are tools commonly used in spreadsheet software (like Microsoft Excel and Google Sheets) for calculations and data analysis.

Formulas: User-defined equations to perform calculations.

Example: =A1+B1 (adds the values of cells A1 and B1).

Functions: Predefined operations to simplify complex tasks.

Examples:

SUM: = SUM(A1:A10) (adds all values in the range A1 to A10).

IF: = IF(A1>10, "Yes", "No" checks if A1 is greater than 10).

VLOOKUP: =VLOOKUP(lookup_value, table_array, col_index, [range_lookup] searches for a value in a table).

COUNT: =COUNT(A1:A10 counts numeric entries in a range).

Password Protection

Password protection is essential for securing sensitive documents, presentations, or files.

For Documents and Spreadsheets:

Microsoft Office:

Go to File > Info > Protect Workbook/Presentation > Encrypt with Password.

Google Sheets/Docs: Use access permissions to restrict editing or sharing.

For PDFs:

Use tools like Adobe Acrobat to set a password under File > Protect Using Password.

For Presentation Files:

PowerPoint allows password protection via File > Info > Protect Presentation.

Software Packages for Presentations

Several software tools are available to create engaging presentations:

Microsoft PowerPoint: A widely used tool with advanced features like animations and templates.

Google Slides: A cloud-based, collaborative presentation tool.

Apple Keynote: A professional presentation tool for macOS users.

Prezi: Focuses on dynamic, non-linear presentations with a zoomable interface.

Canva: Offers design-based presentations with customizable templates.

Zoho Show: A web-based presentation tool with collaborative features.

LibreOffice Impress: A free, open-source alternative for creating presentations.

These tools and practices can help you create, protect, and enhance your documents or presentations effectively.

UNIT 4

ENTREPRENEURIAL SKILLS-IV

- **Session 1:** The Essence of Entrepreneurship
- **Session 2:** Overcoming Obstacles in Entrepreneurship
- **Session 3:** Cultivating an Entrepreneurial Mindset

1.1 INTRODUCTION

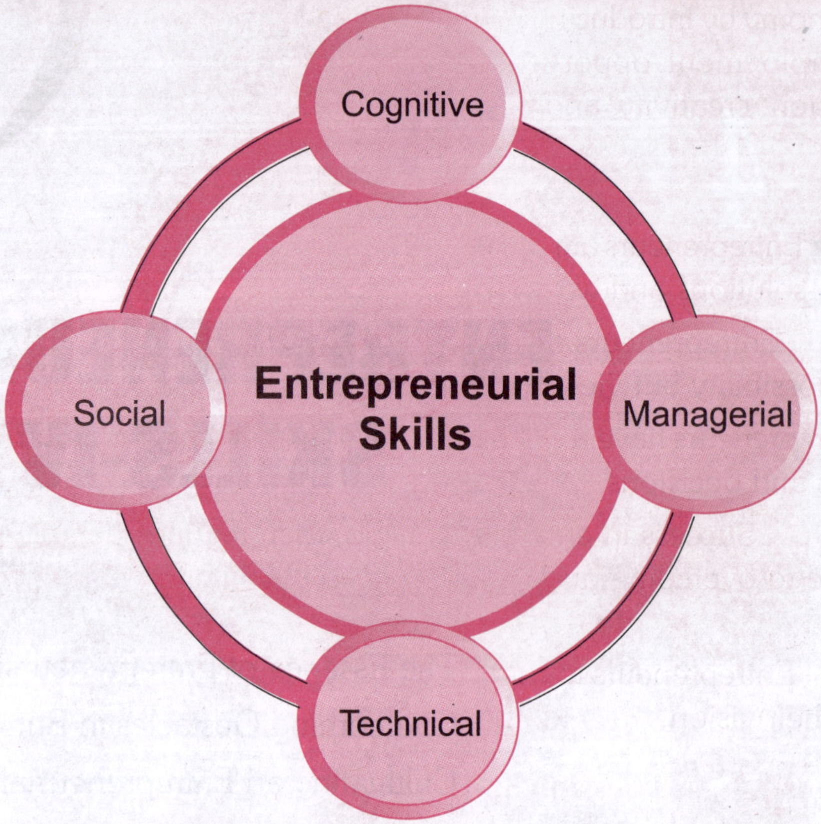

Fig. 1.1 Entrepreneurial Skills

Entrepreneurship is the dynamic process of creating and building something of value from practically nothing. It involves innovation, risk-taking, and the drive to develop an idea into a successful business. Entrepreneurs are the people who undertake these activities, bringing new products, services, or ideas to the market driving economic growth.

Fig. 1.2 Entrepreneurship

1.2 Understanding Entrepreneurship

Entrepreneurship is more than just starting a business; it's about identifying opportunities, solving problems, and creating value. Entrepreneurs play a vital role in the economy by introducing innovations, increasing competition, and providing employment opportunities. They often have a unique combination of vision, creativity, and perseverance.

To see **Understanding Entrepreneurship** in Action

Scan QR Code

1.2.1 Key Characteristics of an Entrepreneur

- **Innovation:** Entrepreneurs are often seen as innovators, continuously seeking new solutions and ways to improve existing products or services.
- **Risk-taking:** Entrepreneurs are willing to take calculated risks. They understand that failure is a possibility but view it as a learning experience.
- **Vision:** Entrepreneurs have a clear vision of what they want to achieve. This vision drives their actions and decisions.
- **Perseverance:** Success in entrepreneurship often requires persistence. Entrepreneurs must be able to overcome obstacles and keep pushing forward even when faced with challenges.
- **Leadership:** Entrepreneurs must be capable leaders, able to inspire and motivate others to share in their vision.

1.2.2 Role of Entrepreneurship in Society: Entrepreneurship Contributes to the Economy in Several Ways

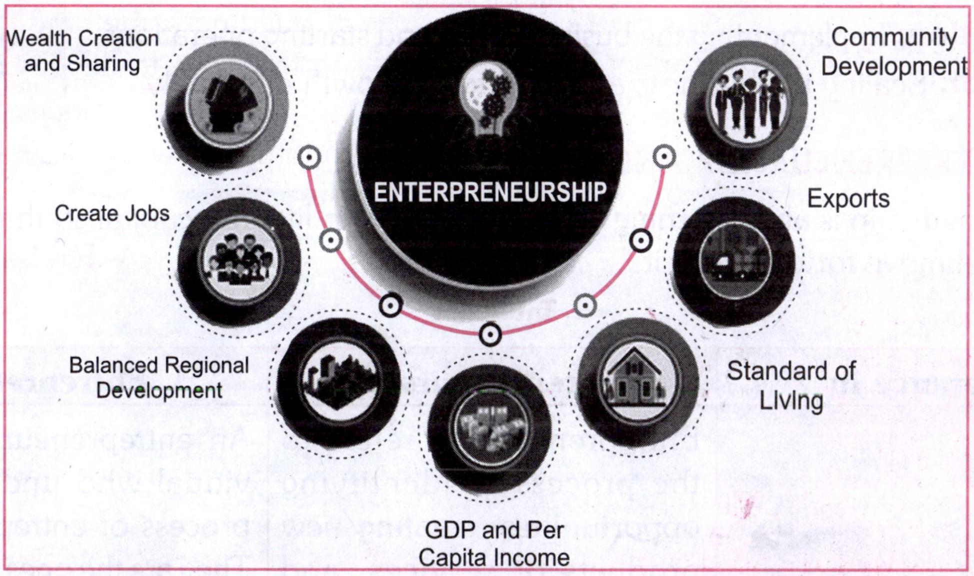

Fig. 1.3 Entrepreneurs Fuel the Economy

- **Job Creation:** Entrepreneurs create jobs by starting new businesses.
- **Innovation:** Entrepreneurs introduce new products, services, and technologies that can improve our quality of life.

- **Economic Growth:** Successful entrepreneurs contribute to economic growth by generating wealth and increasing the flow of capital in the economy.
- **Social Change:** Through innovative ideas, entrepreneurs can address social issues and improve community well-being.

1.2.3 Types of Entrepreneurship

To see **The Entrepreneurial Process** in Action

Scan QR Code

- **Small Business Entrepreneurship:** Most entrepreneurs start small businesses, like local shops, restaurants, or become service providers.
- **Scalable Startup Entrepreneurship:** These entrepreneurs aim to create large, scalable businesses, often in technology or other high-growth industries.
- **Social Entrepreneurship:** These entrepreneurs focus on creating businesses that address social issues or contribute to societal improvement.
- **Corporate Entrepreneurship:** Also known as intrapreneurship, this involves creating new products or services within an existing company.

1.2.4 The Entrepreneurial Process

The entrepreneurial process involves several key steps:

- **Idea Generation:** Identifying a business idea that has potential.
- **Market Research:** Understanding the target market and competition.
- **Business Planning:** Developing a detailed business plan that outlines the strategy, financial projections, and operations plan.
- **Funding:** Securing the necessary financial resources to start the business.
- **Execution:** Implementing the business plan and starting operations.
- **Growth:** Scaling the business and managing growth effectively.

To see **What is an Entrepreneur** in Action

Scan QR Code

1.2.5 Entrepreneurship and Entrepreneur

"Entrepreneurship is about turning what excites you in life into capital so that you can do more of it and move forward with it." **– Richard Branson**

Table.1.1

Difference in	Entrepreneurship	Entrepreneur
Definition	Entrepreneurship refers to the process of identifying opportunities, creating new products or services, and bringing them to the market. It involves innovation, risk-taking, and the ability to manage and grow a business.	An entrepreneur is an individual who undertakes the process of entrepreneurship. They are the ones who identify a market need, create a business plan, take on the financial risk, and work to bring their vision to life.

Conted...

Focus	The focus is on the entire journey of developing an idea into a successful business venture. It includes idea generation, market research, business planning, securing funding, executing the plan, and managing growth.	The focus is on the person who drives the entrepreneurial process. Entrepreneurs are characterized by their vision, creativity, risk tolerance, and leadership abilities.
Example	The process of starting a new tech company to develop and sell a software product is an act of entrepreneurship.	Steve Jobs, who co-founded Apple and led the development of groundbreaking products like the iPhone and Mac, is an example of an entrepreneur.

Entrepreneurship is the process of starting and managing a new business, while an entrepreneur is the individual who undertakes this process is the key player in entrepreneurship, using their skills and vision to turn ideas into reality.

Entrepreneurship is a vital force in the economy, driving innovation, job creation, and social change. Understanding the essence of entrepreneurship helps students appreciate the skills, mindset, and processes involved in turning ideas into successful ventures.

A successful entrepreneur typically possesses a range of qualities that enable them to navigate the challenges of starting and growing a business.

To see **Successful Entrepreneur** in Action

Scan QR Code

Here are some key qualities:

1. **Passion:** A deep enthusiasm for their work drives entrepreneurs to push through obstacles and stay committed to their goals.
2. **Resilience:** The ability to recover quickly from setbacks is crucial, as entrepreneurs often face failures and challenges.
3. **Vision:** Successful entrepreneurs have a clear idea of what they want to achieve and can envision the future of their business.
4. **Creativity:** They think outside the box and come up with innovative solutions to problems.
5. **Risk-taking:** Willingness to take calculated risks is essential, as entrepreneurship often involves venturing into the unknown.
6. **Adaptability:** The ability to pivot and adjust strategies in response to changing circumstances is vital for sustaining growth.
7. **Strong Work Ethic:** Entrepreneurs are often the first to start and the last to leave, demonstrating dedication and commitment.
8. **Leadership:** They can inspire and lead a team towards a common goal, fostering collaboration and productivity.

9. **Problem-solving Skills:** Successful entrepreneurs are adept at identifying problems and devising effective solutions.
10. **Networking:** Building and maintaining relationships with others in the industry, including mentors, investors, and partners, is key to gaining support and resources.
11. **Financial Acumen:** Understanding financial management helps in making informed decisions that contribute to the business's growth.
12. **Customer Focus:** Successful entrepreneurs prioritize understanding and meeting customer needs, as this drives business success.

These qualities often combine to create a strong foundation for entrepreneurial success.

KNOWLEDGE TESTING QUESTIONS

1. Define entrepreneurship in your own words. What makes it different from simply starting a business?
2. List and explain three key characteristics of an entrepreneur. Why are these characteristics important?
3. How does entrepreneurship contribute to economic growth? Provide two examples.
4. What are the different types of entrepreneurship? Provide an example of each.
5. Describe the steps involved in the entrepreneurial process. Which step do you think is the most challenging, and why?
6. Imagine you have an idea for a new product. Outline how you would take this idea through the entrepreneurial process from concept to execution.
7. Discuss the role of innovation in entrepreneurship. Can a business be successful without being innovative? Why or why not?
8. What is social entrepreneurship? How does it differ from traditional entrepreneurship?

FROM THE CBSE BOARD PAPER 2023

1. .... is an economic process, where an idea is generated or an opportunity is created, refined, developed, and implemented, while being exposed to uncertainty, to realize a profit by effective utilization of resources.

   (a) Entrepreneurs (b) Entrepreneurship development
   (c) Entrepreneurship (d) Cluster intervention

2. The act of setting up and running a business and taking risks to earn profits is known as ....

ANSWERS

1. (c) Entrepreneurship 2. Entrepreneurship

Session 2: Overcoming Obstacles In Entrepreneurship

2.1 Factors affecting Entrepreneurship Growth

Entrepreneurs come in all shapes and sizes, but they often share key qualities that help them succeed. While each entrepreneur's motivation and journey to success are unique, they all need to bring their ideas to life. However, this path is not without its challenges.

Entrepreneurship plays a pivotal role in the economic development of regions around the world. Entrepreneurs not only create employment opportunities but also help in addressing issues related to poverty, regional imbalances, and economic stagnation. This is especially significant in developing countries that are heavily reliant on agriculture, as entrepreneurial ventures offer an alternative path to economic diversification and growth.

To see **Factors Affecting Entrepreneurship** in Action

Scan QR Code

Entrepreneurial growth is influenced by a combination of economic and non-economic factors. Understanding these factors is crucial for aspiring entrepreneurs and those interested in economic development.

2.1.1 Economic Factors Affecting Entrepreneurial Growth

Economic factors are essential in ensuring the economic growth and development of a nation. They provide the necessary environment and security for enterprises to flourish. Key economic factors influencing entrepreneurial growth include:

(a) Capital

Capital is the lifeblood of any entrepreneurial venture. It is necessary for acquiring land, materials, machinery, and other essentials required for production. The availability of adequate capital enables entrepreneurs to start and expand their businesses, leading to overall entrepreneurial growth.

(b) Labour

The availability of skilled and inexpensive labour is critical for the success of any business. A productive workforce enhances the efficiency and productivity of the enterprise, contributing to its growth and success.

(c) Raw Material

Access to quality raw materials at affordable prices is another crucial factor. If raw materials are readily available and close to the manufacturing site, production costs decrease, leading to higher profit margins and sustainable growth. However, issues with raw material supply can be mitigated through effective supply chain management, although this might increase production costs.

(d) Market

The market is where producers and consumers interact. For an entrepreneurial venture to succeed there must be a demand for its products or services in the market. Understanding market needs and preferences allows entrepreneurs to create products that fulfill consumer demands, driving sales and business growth.

2.1.2 Non-Economic Factors

While economic factors are fundamental, non-economic factors also play a vital role in entrepreneurial success. These factors include social, psychological, and political influences that shape the entrepreneurial environment.

2.1.3 Social Factors

(a) Social Mobility:

Social and geographical mobility significantly impact entrepreneurship development. Regions with flexible and liberal environments often witness higher entrepreneurial activity. Social mobility allows individuals to access opportunities and resources necessary for starting and growing businesses.

(b) Entrepreneurship Legitimacy:

Society's norms, rules, and regulations create a social environment that can either encourage or hinder entrepreneurship. Entrepreneurs must navigate these social values while pursuing their business objectives to ensure societal acceptance and success.

2.1.4 Psychological Factors

(a) Status Respect:

The desire for social status and recognition can drive individuals to innovate and create new ventures. When people are dissatisfied with their current status, they often seek new opportunities, leading to entrepreneurial growth.

(b) Motivation for High Achievement:

According to D. McClelland's theory of need achievement, the level of motivation is a key determinant of entrepreneurial success. Entrepreneurs and their teams must maintain high levels of motivation to overcome challenges and achieve their goals. Proper training and development can help foster this motivation.

2.1.5 Political Factors

Governments play a significant role in shaping the entrepreneurial landscape. Policies, laws, and regulations are often designed to support and encourage entrepreneurship, recognizing its potential to drive economic growth. Governments may offer incentives such as subsidies, special economic zones, and industrial areas to promote entrepreneurial activities.

Entrepreneurship is influenced by a complex interplay of economic and non-economic factors. For entrepreneurs to thrive, they need support from various stakeholders, including the government, society, and their internal teams. In a country like India, fostering entrepreneurship is particularly important as it can lead to substantial economic benefits and job creation. Understanding these factors is crucial for anyone looking to embark on an entrepreneurial journey.

Common barriers to entrepreneurship include:

To see
Common Barriers to Entrepreneurship
in Action

Scan QR Code

1. **Lack of Capital:** Difficulty in securing sufficient funds to start or grow a business.
2. **Limited Access to Resources:** Difficulty in accessing essential resources such as equipment, technology, or skilled labour.
3. **Regulatory Hurdles:** Complicated legal and regulatory requirements that can be challenging to navigate.
4. **Market Competition:** Intense competition from established businesses or other startups.
5. **Uncertain Economic Conditions:** Economic instability or downturns that affect business prospects.
6. **Risk Aversion:** Fear of failure or financial loss that can deter individuals from taking entrepreneurial risks.
7. **Skill Gaps:** Lack of necessary skills or knowledge to manage and grow a business effectively.
8. **Limited Network:** Difficulty in building a strong professional network for support and advice.

Fear and the Importance of Teamwork in Entrepreneurship:

To see
Importance of Teamwork in Entrepreneurship
in Action

Scan QR Code

Fear is a significant factor for entrepreneurs, often stemming from the risk of failure, financial loss, or the unknown. This fear can hinder decision-making and progress. However, forming a strong team can help alleviate these fears.

A well-chosen team brings diverse skills, experiences, and perspectives, helping to share the load and address challenges more effectively. Teamwork fosters collaboration, innovation, and mutual support, enabling entrepreneurs to tackle problems more creatively and confidently. Building a reliable team not only strengthens the business but also provides a support system that can mitigate the impact of fear and uncertainty.

From The CBSE Board Paper 2023

1. Mention any two common barriers to entrepreneurship.

Test Your Knowledge by Answering These Questions

1. Discuss how economic factors such as capital and labour contribute to the growth of entrepreneurship. Provide examples to illustrate your points.
2. Identify and explain two non-economic factors that can influence entrepreneurial success. How do these factors impact an entrepreneur's ability to start and grow a business?

Session 3: Cultivating An Entrepreneurial Mindset

3.1 Introduction

Entrepreneurial attitudes are the key traits of mindset and behaviour that drive entrepreneurial success. They include risk-taking, where entrepreneurs are willing to embrace uncertainty, which involves seizing opportunities; and innovativeness, the ability to develop creative solutions. Resilience allows entrepreneurs to bounce back from setbacks, while self-motivation keeps them focused on their goals. Adaptability enables them to adjust strategies as needed, and vision provides a clear direction for their ambitions. These attitudes collectively help entrepreneurs navigate the challenges of business and contribute to their overall success and growth.

To see **Entrepreneurial Mindset** in Action

Scan QR Code

Fig. 3.1 Entrepreneurial Mindset

Entrepreneurial competencies are the skills, knowledge, and abilities that enable an individual to start, manage, and grow a business successfully. These competencies are essential for navigating the complexities of entrepreneurship and include a range of personal and professional attributes.

Entrepreneurial competencies include:

To see **Entrepreneurial Competencies** in Action

Scan QR Code

- **Opportunity Recognition:** Identifying and assessing business opportunities.
- **Strategic Planning:** Developing and executing business strategies.
- **Financial Management:** Managing financial resources and budgeting.
- **Marketing and Sales:** Creating and implementing marketing strategies.
- **Leadership and Team Management:** Leading and motivating a team.
- **Problem-solving:** Resolving business challenges.
- **Networking:** Building and maintaining relationships.
- **Decision-making:** Making informed business decisions.
- **Innovation:** Implementing new ideas and processes.

Competence refers to the ability to perform a task or role effectively and efficiently. It encompasses the combination of skills, knowledge, and behaviours required to achieve the desired outcomes in a specific context.

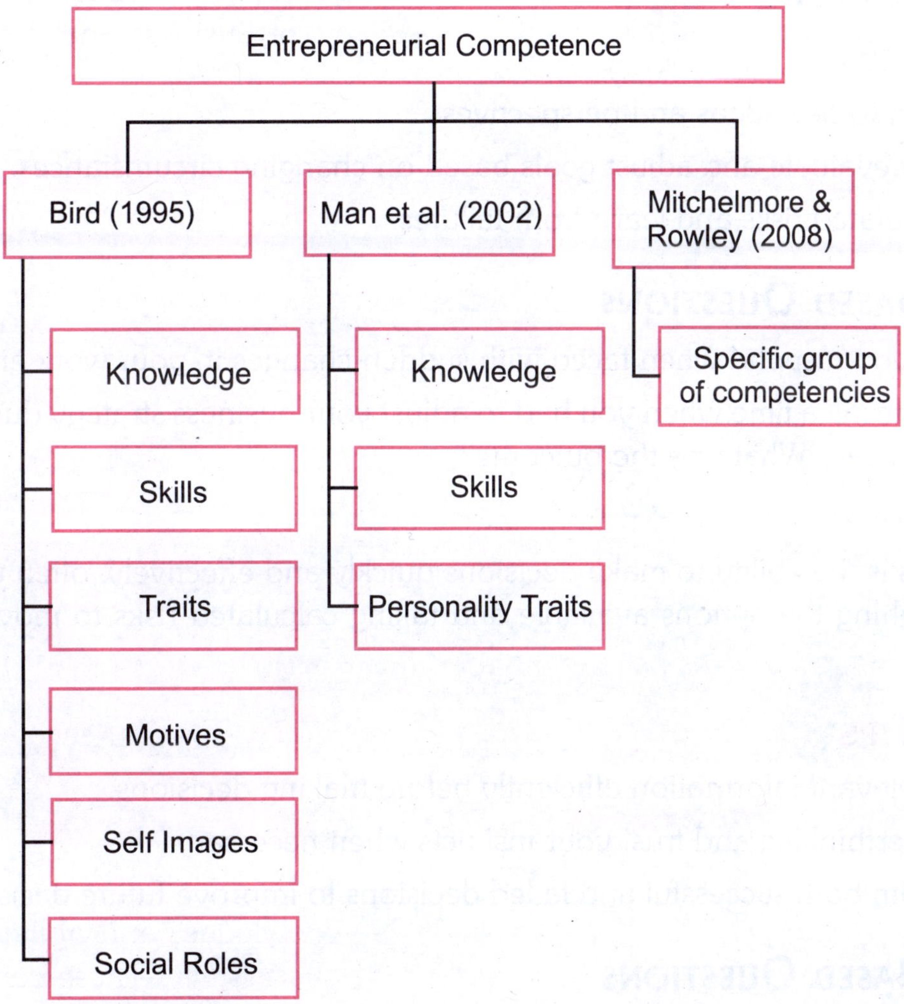

Fig. 3.2 Core Entrepreneurial Competencies

Competence is judged based on several criteria:

- Skill Proficiency
- Knowledge Application
- Performance Outcomes
- Behavioural Traits app
- Problem-solving Ability.
- Adaptability.

3.2 Behavioural and Entrepreneurial Competencies

In today's rapidly evolving world, behavioural and entrepreneurial competencies play a pivotal role in personal growth and professional success. These competencies, which include adaptability, decisiveness, initiative, perseverance, interpersonal skills, organizational skills, stress management, and valuing service and diversity, are essential for thriving in both the workplace and entrepreneurial ventures. This session will explore each competency in detail and offer practical strategies for developing them.

1. Adaptability

Adaptability is the ability to adjust effectively to changing circumstances and new challenges. In the fast-paced world of business and entrepreneurship, this competency is essential for dealing with unexpected obstacles, evolving technologies, and shifting market demands.

Practical Tips

- Stay open to new ideas and perspectives.
- Regularly evaluate and adjust goals based on changing circumstances.
- Take calculated risks and learn from failures.

Practical-Based Questions

(i) How do you respond when faced with sudden changes in your work environment?

(ii) Can you recall a time when you had to adjust your business strategy due to unforeseen circumstances? What was the outcome?

2. Decisiveness

Decisiveness is the ability to make decisions quickly and effectively, often under pressure. It involves weighing the options available and taking calculated risks to move forward with confidence.

Practical Tips

- Gather relevant information efficiently before making decisions.
- Avoid overthinking and trust your instincts when necessary.
- Learn from both successful and failed decisions to improve future decision-making.

Practical-Based Questions

(i) Describe a situation in which you had to make a tough decision quickly. What factors influenced your decision?

(ii) How do you handle situations where you need to make a decision but lack all the information you would prefer to have?

3. Initiative

Initiative refers to the willingness to take proactive steps and act without being prompted. It is about identifying opportunities, addressing problems, and implementing solutions. Entrepreneurs and professionals both need this competency to drive progress.

Practical Tips

- Set personal and professional goals that challenge you to step outside of your comfort zone.
- Volunteer for new projects or responsibilities to demonstrate your commitment.
- Learn to anticipate problems and develop solutions before they arise.

Practical-Based Questions

(i) Can you think of an instance where you took the initiative to solve a problem before it became urgent?

(ii) What new project or responsibility have you taken on recently? What motivated you to do so?

4. Perseverance

Perseverance is the ability to keep going despite challenges, setbacks, or failure. In entrepreneurial ventures, this competency is often the difference between success and failure, as obstacles are inevitable.

Practical Tips

- Develop resilience by embracing challenges as learning opportunities.
- Maintain a long-term vision and break large tasks into smaller, manageable ones.
- Stay motivated and focused on goals even when immediate results are not visible.

Practical-Based Questions

(i) Share a personal story where you faced significant obstacles but continued to pursue your goals. What kept you going?

(ii) How do you stay motivated when your efforts don't produce immediate results?

5. Interpersonal Skills

Interpersonal skills involve the ability to build relationships, collaborate, and communicate effectively with others. Entrepreneurs, leaders, and employees must navigate a variety of personalities and work effectively with diverse teams.

Practical Tips

- Practices active listening and empathy in conversations.
- Be mindful of body language and non-verbal cues.
- Foster positive relationships by offering support and encouragement to others.

Practical-Based Questions

(i) Can you describe a time when you had to resolve a conflict between team members? What approach did you use?

(ii) How do you maintain healthy relationships in a team environment?

6. Organizational Skills

Organizational skills are critical for managing time, resources, and tasks efficiently. Good organization allows you to prioritize effectively, meet deadlines, and achieve desired outcomes.

Practical Tips

- Break large projects into smaller tasks and set clear deadlines for each.
- Use tools like to-do lists, calendars, or project management software to stay organized.
- Regularly evaluate and improve your organizational systems for greater efficiency.

Practical-Based Questions

(i) How do you prioritize tasks when working on multiple projects with tight deadlines?

(ii) What tools or methods do you use to stay organized and ensure nothing slips through the cracks?

7. Stress Management

Stress management is the ability to stay calm and maintain focus during high-pressure situations. Entrepreneurs and professionals both must manage their stress levels to avoid burnout and maintain productivity.

Practical Tips

- Practise mindfulness, meditation, or deep-breathing exercises to reduce stress.
- Take regular breaks to recharge and maintain energy levels.
- Identify stressors early and address them before they escalate.

Practical-Based Questions

(i) How do you handle pressure when faced with tight deadlines or high expectations?

(ii) What activities help you relieve stress and maintain a healthy work-life balance?

8. Valuing Service and Diversity

Valuing service and diversity involves recognizing the importance of providing excellent service to customers and appreciating the diverse perspectives and backgrounds of people around you. This competency is essential for creating inclusive environments and fostering positive relationships with clients, colleagues, and communities.

Practical Tips

- Commit to providing excellent service by understanding and meeting customer needs.
- Encourage diversity in teams and seek out different perspectives.
- Promote an inclusive environment by respecting and valuing differences.

Practical-Based Questions

(i) How do you ensure that the needs of your customers or clients are met?

(ii) Can you give an example of a time when you embraced diversity in your team or business practices?

Mastering these behavioural and entrepreneurial competencies can have a profound impact on personal development and professional success. By developing traits like adaptability, decisiveness, and perseverance, individuals can improve their ability to navigate challenges, seize opportunities, and foster effective relationships. The practical-based questions provided in this session can serve as tools for self-reflection, helping individuals assess their strengths and areas for improvement in each competency.

Competence is typically evaluated through performance assessments, feedback from supervisors and peers, and the successful completion of relevant tasks and projects.

Entrepreneurial competency means having the skills and behaviours needed to start, manage, and grow a business. It also includes handling the risks of running a business. Entrepreneurs need to be good at several things, including:

1. **Risk-taking:** Being willing to take calculated risks.
2. **Creativity:** Thinking outside the box.
3. **Problem-solving:** Finding solutions to challenges.
4. **Initiative:** Starting actions without waiting for instructions.
5. **Persistence:** Keeping at it despite difficulties.
6. **Persuasion and Social Skills:** Influencing others and building relationships.
7. **Business Management:** Handling business operations effectively.
8. **Critical Thinking:** Analysing situations carefully.
9. **Networking:** Making useful connections.
10. **Communication:** Sharing ideas

To encourage these skills in employees, organizations can:

- **Promote Knowledge-sharing:** Make sure information is available and encourage learning.
- **Foster Creativity:** Hold meetings for new ideas and let employees speak up.
- **Allow Ownership:** Give employees the freedom to make decisions and manage their work.
- **Create a Safe Environment:** Make it clear that mistakes are part of learning and won't lead to blame.

By hiring people with an entrepreneurial spirit or investing in training, organizations can help employees develop these valuable skills. Employees with these competencies can greatly benefit the organization by bringing new ideas and driving growth.

EXERCISE

FILL IN THE BLANKS

1. Entrepreneurial attitudes are the key .... and behavioural traits that drive entrepreneurial success.
2. One of the crucial entrepreneurial attitudes is ...., which shows willingness to embrace uncertainty.
3. .... refers to the ability to develop creative solutions to problems.
4. .... allows entrepreneurs to bounce back from setbacks and challenges.
5. .... keeps entrepreneurs focused on their goals and motivates them to achieve them.
6. .... enables entrepreneurs to adjust their strategies as needed in response to changing circumstances.
7. A clear .... provides entrepreneurs with direction for their ambitions.
8. Entrepreneurial competencies are the skills, ..., and abilities necessary to start, manage, and grow a business.
9. Recognition of involves identifying and assessing potential business opportunities.
10. Developing and executing .... is crucial for the strategic direction of a business.

ANSWERS

1. Mindset
2. Risk-taking
3. Innovativeness
4. Resilience
5. Self-motivation
6. Adaptability
7. Vision
8. Knowledge
9. Opportunity
10. Strategic Planning

UNIT 5

GREEN SKILLS–IV

- **Session 1:** Introduction to Green Jobs
- **Session 2:** Importance of Green Jobs
- **Session 3:** Exploring Famous Green Jobs
- **Session 4:** The Role of Green Jobs in Sustainable Development
- **Session 5:** Green Jobs in Action

SESSION 1: INTRODUCTION TO GREEN JOBS

1.1 OVERVIEW OF GREEN JOBS

Green jobs are roles that contribute to preserving or restoring the environment, helping to achieve sustainable development while reducing environmental risks and ecological scarcities. These jobs encompass various sectors, including energy, waste management, agriculture, transportation, and construction. The core focus of green jobs is to improve energy efficiency, reduce greenhouse gas emissions, minimize waste and pollution, protect ecosystems, and support adaptation to climate change.

To see **Green Jobs** in Action

Scan QR Code

1.1.1 KEY AREAS OF GREEN JOBS

1. **Renewable Energy:** Jobs related to solar, wind, geothermal, and bioenergy production. This includes roles in research, manufacturing, installation, maintenance, and project management.
2. **Energy Efficiency:** Roles that involve improving energy use in buildings, appliances, and industrial processes. This includes positions in retrofitting, energy auditing, and designing energy-efficient systems.
3. **Sustainable Agriculture:** Jobs in organic farming, agroforestry, and sustainable fishery practices that focus on reducing environmental impact and enhancing biodiversity.
4. **Waste Management and Recycling:** Roles in waste reduction, recycling, composting, and the development of waste-to-energy technologies. These jobs focus on reducing landfill waste and promoting resource recovery.
5. **Water Conservation:** Positions that work on improving water efficiency, treating wastewater, and developing sustainable water management practices.
6. **Green Construction:** Jobs in designing and constructing environment friendly buildings, using sustainable materials, and promoting energy-efficient building practices.
7. **Public Transport:** Roles focused on developing and managing eco-friendly transportation systems that reduce carbon footprints, such as electric buses, bicycles, and pedestrian-friendly infrastructure.
8. **Conservation and Wildlife Protection:** Jobs that involve protecting natural habitats, conserving biodiversity, and managing protected areas.

1.2 Importance of Green Jobs

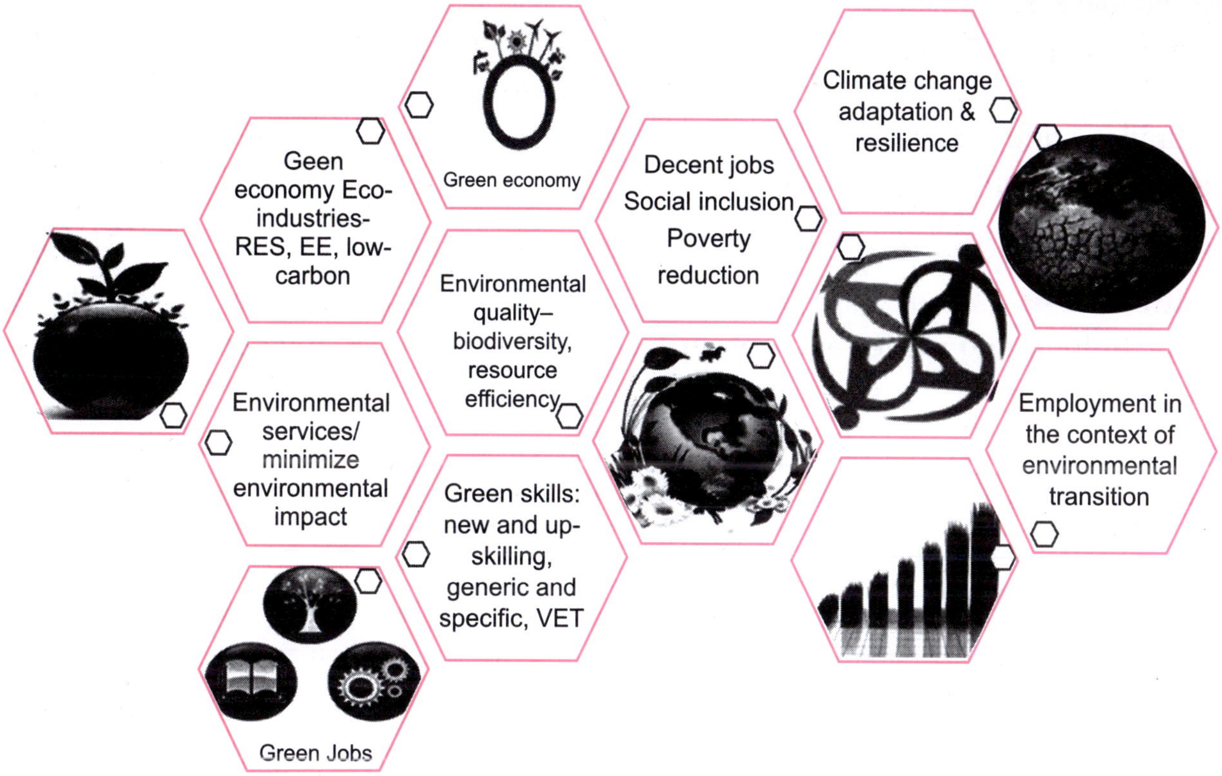

Fig. 1.1 Importance of Green Jobs

- **Environmental Sustainability:** Green jobs contribute directly to environmental preservation and the reduction of harmful practices that degrade ecosystems.
- **Economic Growth:** Green economy is a growing sector that creates new employment opportunities while fostering innovation and sustainable economic development.
- **Social Benefits:** Green jobs can lead to healthier communities by reducing pollution, improving living conditions, and promoting better public health.
- **Climate Change Mitigation:** These jobs play a critical role in addressing climate change by reducing emissions, enhancing resilience, and promoting sustainable practices.

1.2.1 Challenges and Future of Green Jobs

- **Skill Development:** There is a need for education and training programmes to equip the workforce with the necessary skills for green jobs.
- **Policy Support:** Government policies and incentives are crucial to promote green jobs and encourage transition to a green economy.
- **Adoption of Technology:** Integrating advanced technologies, such as smart grids, electric vehicles, and sustainable farming techniques, is essential for the growth of green jobs.

Green jobs are central to building a sustainable future, offering diverse opportunities across multiple sectors while addressing critical environmental challenges.

1.2.2 Importance of Sustainable Employment

To see
Importance of Sustainable Employment
in Action

Scan QR Code

Sustainable employment, also known as green or sustainable jobs, is crucial in fostering long-term economic growth, social equity, and environmental protection. It goes beyond simply providing jobs; it ensures that employment opportunities contribute positively to society and the planet. Here's why sustainable employment is important:

1. Environmental Protection:

Reduction of Carbon Footprint: Sustainable jobs focus on reducing greenhouse gas emissions, minimizing waste, and conserving natural resources, thereby helping to combat climate change.

Preservation of Natural Resources: Sustainable employment promotes practices that protect and restore ecosystems, ensuring that natural resources are available for future generations.

2. Economic Stability:

Long-term Growth: Sustainable employment supports industries and practices that are resilient to economic fluctuations and environmental crises, fostering stable economic growth.

Innovation and Competitiveness: Economic stability drives innovation in green technologies and practices, making industries more competitive and opening new markets for sustainable products and services.

Job Creation: Green economy is a growing sector that generates a wide range of job opportunities, from renewable energy to sustainable agriculture and green construction.

3. Social Equity

Inclusive Growth: Sustainable employment often includes jobs that support marginalized communities, providing fair wages, safe working conditions, and equal opportunities.

Community Well-being: Jobs in sustainable sectors often focus on improving public health, reducing pollution, and enhancing the quality of life in communities.

4. Adaptation to Climate Changes

Developing Resilience: Sustainable jobs contribute to building resilient communities and economies that can better withstand the impacts of climate change, such as extreme weather events and resource scarcity.

Sustainable Infrastructure: Employment in green construction and public transportation helps develop infrastructure that is more resilient to environmental changes.

5. Ethical Responsibility

Corporate Social Responsibility (CSR): Companies that focus on sustainable employment often adhere to CSR principles, ensuring that their business practices are ethical, environment-friendly, and socially responsible.

Global Responsibility: Sustainable employment supports global efforts to meet international climate goals and sustainable development targets, such as the United Nations Sustainable Development Goals (SDGs).

6. Public Health and Safety

Improved Health Outcomes: Jobs that focus on reducing pollution, promoting clean energy, and ensuring safe working conditions contribute to better health outcomes for workers and communities.

Reduction of Environmental Hazards: Sustainable employment in waste management, water conservation, and renewable energy helps reduce environmental hazards, leading to safer living conditions.

7. Future-proofing the Workforce

Skill Development: Sustainable employment encourages the development of new skills and knowledge in green technologies and practices, preparing the workforce for future demands.

Youth Engagement: It offers young people opportunities in emerging sectors, aligning their careers with values of environment stewardship and social responsibility.

1.3 Global Impact

Support for Developing Countries: Sustainable employment can help developing countries grow their economies in environmentally sound ways, reducing poverty and improving living standards without degrading natural resources.

International Cooperation: Promoting sustainable employment fosters global collaboration on environmental protection and economic development.

In essence, sustainable employment is key to creating a balanced, fair, and thriving global economy that respects the environment and meets the needs of all people. It is fundamental to achieving a sustainable future where economic prosperity, social equity, and environmental stewardship are integrated harmoniously.

EXERCISE

Multiple Choice Questions

1. **What is the primary focus of green jobs?**
   (a) Increasing industrial production
   (b) Improving energy efficiency and reducing waste
   (c) Enhancing market competition
   (d) Developing new entertainment technologies

2. Which of the following sectors is NOT typically associated with green jobs?

(a) Renewable Energy (b) Waste Management

(c) Public Transport (d) Entertainment Industry

3. Green jobs contribute to climate change mitigation by:

(a) Increasing fossil fuel consumption (b) Reducing greenhouse gas emissions

(c) Promoting deforestation (d) Enhancing water pollution

4. Which of the following is an example of a job in the renewable energy sector?

(a) Energy auditing (b) Organic farming

(c) Solar panel installation (d) Urban planning

5. Sustainable employment is crucial for:

(a) Short-term economic gains

(b) Long-term economic growth and social equity

(c) Increasing market share of large corporations

(d) Expanding non-renewable resource extraction

6. How does sustainable employment promote social equity?

(a) By providing unequal wages based on region

(b) By focusing only on profitable sectors

(c) By offering fair wages and safe working conditions

(d) By ignoring marginalized communities

7. Which of the following best describes the role of green construction jobs?

(a) Designing energy-efficient buildings

(b) Developing luxury housing projects

(c) Increasing deforestation for urbanization

(d) Manufacturing high-energy appliances

8. What is a significant challenge in the growth of green jobs?

(a) Lack of interest in environmental issues

(b) High availability of skilled workers

(c) Need for education and training programmes

(d) Overabundance of government support

9. How does sustainable employment contribute to public health?

(a) By increasing industrial waste

(b) By focusing on pollution reduction and clean energy

(c) By promoting the use of harmful chemicals

(d) By ignoring environmental regulations

10. Which of the following is a key benefit of sustainable employment in developing countries?

(a) Promotes unsustainable industrial practices
(b) Reduces poverty and improves living standards
(c) Encourages exploitation of natural resources
(d) Focuses solely on urban development

11. The green economy is growing because:
(a) It reduces innovation
(b) It creates new job opportunities in sustainable sectors
(c) It relies on non-renewable energy sources
(d) It only benefits large corporations

12. How does sustainable employment support adaptation to climate change?
(a) By encouraging unsustainable resource use
(b) By building resilient communities and economies
(c) By focusing on short-term economic gains
(d) By reducing renewable energy development

13. Which of the following statements is TRUE about the importance of sustainable employment?
(a) It only focuses on environmental preservation
(b) It ignores social equity issues
(c) It integrates economic growth, social equity, and environmental protection
(d) It promotes unsustainable business practices

14. What is the role of Corporate Social Responsibility (CSR) in sustainable employment?
(a) To maximize profits at all costs
(b) To ensure that business practices are ethical and environment-friendly
(c) To prioritize short-term gains over long-term sustainability
(d) To avoid social and environmental issues

15. Why is skill development important in sustainable employment?
(a) It reduces the need for education
(b) It prepares the workforce for future demands in green technologies
(c) It focuses solely on traditional industries
(d) It ignores the needs of emerging sectors

ANSWERS

1. (b)	2. (d)	3. (b)	4. (c)	5. (b)
6. (c)	7. (a)	8. (c)	9. (b)	10. (b)
11. (b)	12. (b)	13. (c)	14. (b)	15. (b)

These questions and answers will help students grasp the essential concepts related to green jobs and the importance of sustainable employment.

Session–2: Importance Of Green Jobs

Green jobs are employment roles that contribute to preserving or restoring the environment, aiming to achieve sustainable development while reducing environmental risks and ecological scarcities.

Fig. 2.1 Sustainable Development

2.1 Economic And Environmental Significance

Definition: Green jobs, which focus on preserving or restoring the environment, offer significant economic and environmental benefits.

Here's a breakdown of their economic and environmental significance:

2.1.1 Economic Significance

1. Job Creation:

Green jobs contribute to employment growth by creating new roles in renewable energy, energy efficiency, sustainable agriculture, and environmental protection. This helps diversify economies and reduce unemployment.

2. Economic Growth:

Investment in green technologies and industries can stimulate economic growth. For example, advancements in solar and wind energy technology can lead to increased manufacturing and construction activities.

3. Cost Savings:

Green jobs often lead to cost savings for businesses and individuals. Energy-efficient technologies reduce energy consumption and lower utility bills, while sustainable practices can decrease waste disposal costs.

4. Innovation and Competitiveness:

The green sector fosters innovation, leading to the development of new technologies and practices. This can enhance a country's or company's competitiveness in the global market.

5. Economic Resilience:

Green jobs contribute to building resilient economies by focusing on sustainable practices that are less vulnerable to economic shocks. This can include investments in renewable energy that reduce dependence on volatile fossil fuel markets.

2.1.2 Environmental Significance

1. Reduced Pollution:

Green jobs focus on reducing pollution through cleaner technologies and practices. For instance, jobs in renewable energy reduce reliance on fossil fuels, which decreases air and water pollution.

2. Resource Conservation:

Green jobs often involve efforts to conserve natural resources. This includes sustainable agriculture practices that preserve soil and water, and waste management jobs that promote recycling and reduce landfill use.

3. Climate Change Mitigation:

Many green jobs are directly related to combating climate change. For example, roles in renewable energy and energy efficiency help reduce greenhouse gas emissions, which is crucial for mitigating global warming.

4. Biodiversity Protection:

Environmental protection roles, such as conservation and wildlife management jobs, play a crucial role in preserving biodiversity and protecting ecosystems.

5. Sustainable Development:

Green jobs contribute to sustainable development by promoting practices that meet current needs without compromising the ability of future generations to meet their own needs. This includes sustainable building practices, eco-friendly transportation, and green urban planning.

Examples of Green Jobs

- **Renewable Energy Technicians:** Install and maintain solar panels, wind turbines, and other renewable energy systems.
- **Environmental Scientists:** Research and develop solutions to environmental problems.
- **Sustainability Consultants:** Advise businesses on how to implement sustainable practices.
- **Green Building Professionals:** Design and construct energy-efficient and environment-friendly buildings.

To see
Examples of Green Jobs
in Action

Scan QR Code

- **Waste Management Specialists:** Develop and manage recycling and waste reduction programmes.

Overall, green jobs play a vital role in transitioning to a more sustainable economy while offering diverse benefits that extend across environmental protection and economic development.

2.2 Benefits for Communities And Ecosystems

Green jobs play a critical role in fostering healthier communities and more resilient ecosystems. By addressing environmental challenges and promoting sustainable practices, these jobs contribute to the well-being of both people and the planet.

To see **Benefits for Communities and Ecosystems** in Action

Scan QR Code

Green jobs offer numerous benefits for communities and ecosystems.

2.2.1 Benefits for Communities

(i) **Improved Public Health:** Green jobs in areas like renewable energy and waste management can reduce pollution levels, leading to better air and water quality. This contributes to lower rates of respiratory and cardiovascular diseases, benefiting overall community health.

(ii) **Economic Opportunities:** By creating new employment opportunities, green jobs stimulate local economies. This includes job creation in sectors like energy efficiency, sustainable agriculture, and green construction, which can lead to increased local income and economic growth.

(iii) **Enhanced Quality of Life:** Green initiatives often improve the livability of communities. For example, green spaces, such as parks and urban gardens, contribute to recreational opportunities, mental well-being, and a more attractive living environment.

(iv) **Community Resilience:** Green jobs can help communities adapt to climate change and natural disasters. For instance, jobs focused on flood management, disaster preparedness, and resilient infrastructure enhance a community's ability to withstand and recover from environmental challenges.

(v) **Skill Development:** Training and education associated with green jobs can equip individuals with new skills and knowledge, which can be valuable across various sectors. This can increase employability and open doors to diverse career paths.

(vi) **Social Equity:** Green jobs can promote social equity by providing opportunities for under-represented groups in emerging industries. Programes targeting disadvantaged communities can help ensure that the benefits of green economy are shared broadly.

2.2.2 Benefits for Ecosystems

(i) **Ecosystem Restoration:** Green jobs in environmental conservation and restoration help rehabilitate degraded ecosystems. Activities such as reforestation, wetland restoration, and habitat preservation support biodiversity and health of the ecosystem.

(ii) **Biodiversity Conservation:** Jobs focused on wildlife management and conservation efforts protect endangered species and their habitats. This helps maintain ecological balance and supports diverse biological communities.

(iii) **Resource Management:** Sustainable practices promoted by green jobs, such as sustainable forestry and fisheries management, ensure that natural resources are used efficiently and responsibly, preventing overexploitation and preserving ecosystem functions.

(iv) **Climate Regulation:** Green jobs that involve carbon sequestration, such as afforestation and soil management, contribute to mitigating climate change by capturing and storing carbon dioxide from the atmosphere.

(v) **Pollution Reduction:** Jobs in areas like waste management and pollution control reduce contaminants in air, water, and soil. This helps protect ecosystems from harmful effects and maintains ecological health.

(vi) **Sustainable Land Use:** Green jobs related to sustainable land use and urban planning promotes practices that minimize environmental impact. This includes designing green buildings, creating eco-friendly transportation systems, and implementing land use policies that protect natural habitats.

Practical-Based Questions

Imagine your local community is considering implementing a new green initiative aimed at improving public health and environmental sustainability. Your task is to propose a specific green job role that could help achieve these goals.

Instructions:

1. **Identify the Green Job:** Choose a green job role (e.g., renewable energy technician, environmental scientist, sustainability consultant, etc.) that you believe would be effective for your community's initiative.
2. **Describe the Role:** Explain the responsibilities and tasks of this job role. How does this role contribute to both public health and environmental sustainability?
3. **Provide a Justification:** Detail why this job role is particularly suitable for your community. Consider factors such as local environmental issues, existing resources, and community needs.
4. **Outline the Impact:** Discuss the potential short-term and long-term impacts of this green job on the community and the environment. Include how it could lead to improved public health and enhanced environmental conditions.

Session 3: Exploring Famous Green Jobs

3.1 Introduction

Fig. 3.1 CO_2 and Climate Change

As the world increasingly focuses on sustainability and environmental responsibility, green jobs have become a significant aspect of the global workforce. These jobs not only contribute to protecting the environment but also drive economic growth and innovation. This session explores key roles in the green economy and examines successful case studies that highlight the impact of green jobs on various industries and communities.

3.1.1 Key Roles and Examples in Green Economy

To see **Green Economy** in Action

Scan QR Code

1. Renewable Energy Technician:

- **Role:** Renewable Energy Technicians install, maintain, and repair systems that generate energy from renewable sources such as solar panels, wind turbines, and geothermal systems.
- **Examples:**

  (i) Solar Photovoltaic Installer: Installs and maintains solar panels on rooftops and solar farms.

  (ii) Wind Turbine Technician: Ensures the proper functioning of wind turbines and performs repairs and maintenance.

2. Environmental Consultant:

- **Role:** Environmental Consultants assess environmental conditions, provide advice on minimizing environmental impact, and help organizations comply with environmental regulations.

- **Examples:**
  - (i) **Sustainability Consultant:** Advises companies on how to reduce their carbon footprint and implement sustainable practices.
  - (ii) **Ecological Consultant:** Evaluates the impact of development projects on local ecosystems and suggests mitigation measures.

3. Green Building Architect:

- **Role:** Green Building Architects design buildings and infrastructure projects that are energy-efficient, environment-friendly, and sustainable.
- **Examples:**
  - (i) **LEED-certified Architect:** Designs buildings to meet Leadership in Energy and Environmental Design (LEED) standards.
  - (ii) **Passive House Designer:** Creates buildings that maintain a comfortable indoor temperature with minimal energy use.

4. Environmental Educator:

- **Role:** Environmental Educators develop and deliver educational programmes that raise awareness about environmental issues and promote sustainable practices.
- **Examples:**
- **School Environmental Program Coordinator:** Organizes activities and curriculum to educate students about environmental conservation.
- **Community Outreach Specialist:** Conducts workshops and events to engage the public in environmental stewardship.

5. Waste Management Specialist:

- **Role:** Waste Management Specialists develop and implement systems for waste reduction, recycling, and proper disposal to minimize environmental impact.
- **Examples:**
- **Recycling Coordinator:** Oversees recycling programes and educates the community on recycling best practices.
- **Composting Technician:** Manages composting operations to convert organic waste into valuable compost.

Case Studies of Successful Green Job Initiatives

1. The Solar City Project (USA):

- **Overview:** Solar City, now a part of Tesla, is a leading provider of energy services, specializing in solar energy solutions.
- **Success Factors:**
  - (i) **Innovation:** Introduced new technologies for efficient solar panel installation and energy storage.

(ii) **Impact:** Created thousands of green jobs in the solar industry, contributing to significant growth in renewable energy adoption.

2. The Green Roofs Initiative (Germany):

- **Overview:** The Green Roofs Initiative promotes the installation of green roofs on buildings to improve urban sustainability and energy efficiency.
- **Success Factors:**

  (i) **Environmental Benefits:** Green roofs reduce heat island effects, manage storm water, and enhance building insulation.

  (ii) **Impact:** Generated jobs in green roof design, installation, and maintenance while improving urban environmental quality.

3. The Waste-to-Energy Programme (Sweden):

- **Overview:** Sweden's Waste-to-Energy Programme converts municipal waste into energy through incineration, reducing the need for landfill and generating electricity.
- **Success Factors:**

  (i) **Efficiency:** Utilizes advanced technology to minimize emissions and maximize energy recovery.

  (ii) **Impact:** Created jobs in waste management and energy production while significantly reducing the country's reliance on fossil fuels.

4. The Urban Farming Initiative (Kenya):

- **Overview:** The Urban Farming Initiative in Kenya promotes urban agriculture to address food security and environmental sustainability.
- **Success Factors:**

  (i) **Community Engagement:** Involves local communities in growing food in urban areas, improving access to fresh produce.

  (ii) **Impact:** Created jobs in urban farming and provided economic opportunities for local residents while enhancing food security.

5. The Eco-Tourism Project (Costa Rica):

- **Overview:** Costa Rica's eco-tourism industry focuses on promoting sustainable tourism practices that protect natural resources and support local communities.
- **Success Factors:**

  (i) **Sustainable Practices:** Encourages tourism that minimizes environmental impact and supports conservation efforts.

  (ii) **Impact:** Generated employment in eco-tourism and conservation while fostering economic development in rural areas.

Famous green jobs play a crucial role in advancing sustainability and environmental stewardship. Through innovative solutions and successful initiatives, these roles not only contribute to a healthier planet but also create economic opportunities and drive positive change. Understanding these key roles and case studies can inspire future green professionals and highlight the importance of integrating environmental considerations into various career paths.

Case Study: Green Job Initiative—Solar Power Project

Background: In the small town of Greenfield, a community of 5,000 residents was facing challenges related to energy consumption and environmental impact. The local government, concerned about rising electricity costs and the town's carbon footprint, decided to implement a Green Job Initiative focused on solar power.

Objective: The primary objective of the Green Job Initiative was to transition the town's energy source to solar power, reduce greenhouse gas emissions, and create green jobs for local residents.

3.2 Implementation

1. Assessment and Planning:

- **Energy Audit:** Conducted an energy audit to evaluate current energy usage and identify potential for solar energy.
- **Feasibility Study:** Assessed the feasibility of installing solar panels on residential, commercial, and public buildings.
- **Funding:** Secured funding through a combination of government grants, subsidies, and private investment.

2. Community Engagement:

- **Awareness Campaign:** Launched a campaign to educate residents about the benefits of solar power and the upcoming changes.
- **Training Programs:** Offered training sessions for local workers to become certified solar panel installers and maintenance technicians.

3. Installation:

- **Site Preparation:** Prepared sites for installation by evaluating roof conditions and ensuring structural integrity.
- **Panel Installation:** Installed solar panels on selected buildings, including schools, municipal buildings, and residential homes.
- **Monitoring System:** Set up a monitoring system to track energy production and efficiency.

4. Job Creation:

- **Installer Jobs:** Created 30 new jobs for solar panel installers.
- **Maintenance Jobs:** Established 10 positions for ongoing maintenance and support.
- **Administrative Roles:** Created 5 administrative positions to manage the project and liaise with stakeholders.

3.2.1 Results

1. Environmental Impact:

- **Reduction in Carbon Emissions:** The solar power project led to a 40% reduction in the town's carbon footprint.
- **Energy Efficiency:** Reduced dependence on fossil fuels and improved overall energy efficiency.

2. Economic Benefits:

- **Cost Savings:** Residents experienced a 25% reduction in their electricity bills.
- **Job Creation:** The initiative created 45 new green jobs, providing employment opportunities in the town.
- **Local Business Growth:** The increased demand for solar panel installation and maintenance services stimulated local businesses.

3. Community Impact:

- **Increased Awareness:** Raised awareness about sustainable energy practices and their benefits.
- **Enhanced Quality of Life:** Improved air quality and the reduced environmental impact contributed to a higher quality of life for residents.

Challenges:

- **Initial Costs:** High upfront costs of solar panel installation and infrastructure were a significant barrier.
- **Technical Issues:** Some technical issues arose during installation, requiring additional training and support.
- **Public Resistance:** Initial resistance from some community members who were skeptical about the benefits of solar power.

Solutions:

- **Financial Assistance:** Provided financial assistance and incentives to offset initial costs for residents.
- **Ongoing Support:** Established a support system to address technical issues and provide continuous training.
- **Engagement:** Engaged with community leaders and residents to address concerns and highlight the long-term benefits.

The Green Job Initiative in Greenfield demonstrates how a well-planned green project can address environmental and economic challenges while creating new job opportunities. The transition to solar power not only contributed to a more sustainable and eco-friendly community but also fostered local economic growth and job creation. This case study highlights the potential of green job initiatives to drive positive change and serve as a model for other communities aiming to embrace sustainable practices.

Case Study: Solar Energy Technician

Background: Solar energy technicians, also known as solar photovoltaic (PV) installers, play a crucial role in the renewable energy sector. They are responsible for installing, maintaining, and repairing solar panels that convert sunlight into electricity. With the increasing emphasis on sustainable energy solutions, the demand for skilled solar energy technicians is growing.

Case Study Question

Imagine you are a solar energy technician working for a company that has recently been awarded a contract to install solar panels on the rooftops of a large residential complex. The project is expected to provide clean energy to over 200 households. As part of your role, you need to address several key aspects of the installation process.

1. **Planning and Assessment:** Describe the steps you would take to assess the suitability of the residential complex for solar panel installation. What factors would you consider to ensure the system's efficiency and effectiveness?
2. **Installation Process:** Outline the key stages of the installation process for the solar panels. What specific tasks would you perform at each stage, and how would you ensure safety and compliance with industry standards?
3. **Maintenance and Troubleshooting:** After the installation, how would you monitor the performance of the solar panels? What routine maintenance tasks would you perform, and how would you address potential issues or malfunctions?
4. **Environmental Impact:** Discuss the environmental benefits of installing solar panels in the residential complex. How does this green job contribute to reducing the carbon footprint and promoting sustainable energy practices?

Requirements:

- Provide detailed responses to each aspect of the case study.
- Consider both technical and environmental perspectives in your answers.
- Use relevant examples or scenarios to support your responses.

Session 4: Role Of Green Jobs In Sustainable Development

4.1 Green Jobs for a Sustainable Future

Fig. 4.1 Eco Jobs for Earth

4.1.1 Green Jobs in Toxin-Free Homes and Organic Gardening

Toxin-Free Homes:

Green jobs related to toxin-free homes focus on creating environments that are safe from harmful chemicals. These jobs involve working on:

- **Designing and Constructing Safe Homes:** Professionals ensure that homes use non-toxic materials, like paints and finishes that don't release harmful fumes.
- **Improving indoor Air Quality:** Experts work to improve air quality by installing ventilation systems and using air purifiers.
- **Sustainable Renovations of Home:** Jobs in this field also include renovating existing homes to make them safer and more eco-friendly.

4.1.2 Organic Gardening

Organic gardening is another area where green jobs make a big difference. Here, the focus is on growing plants without harmful chemicals. Key roles include:

- **Organic Farm Management:** Managing farms that grow fruits and vegetables using natural fertilizers and pest control methods.
- **Soil Health Specialists:** Ensuring the soil remains rich and fertile without using synthetic chemicals.

- **Education and Advocacy:** Teaching others about the benefits of organic gardening and how to start their organic gardens.

4.1.3 Public Transport, Energy Conservation, and Water Conservation

Public Transport: Jobs in public transport aim to reduce the number of cars on the road, which helps reduce pollution. These include:

- **Transit Planning:** Designing efficient public transport routes to make it easier for people to use buses and trains.
- **Sustainable Transport Solutions:** Developing new methods of transportation that are eco-friendly, like electric buses and bicycles.

Energy Conservation:

Energy conservation jobs focus on saving energy and reducing waste. Important roles are:

- **Energy Auditors:** Inspecting buildings to find ways to use less energy, such as improving insulation and using energy-efficient appliances.
- **Renewable Energy Technicians:** Installing and maintaining systems that use renewable energy sources, like solar panels and wind turbines.

Water Conservation:

Jobs in water conservation work to ensure that we use water wisely. These roles involve:

- **Water Resource Management:** Developing strategies to manage and distribute water efficiently.
- **Water-saving technologies:** Creating and promoting technologies that reduce water wastage, like low-flow faucets and irrigation systems.

4.1.4 Solar and Wind Power, Waste Reduction, and Recycling

Solar and Wind Power: These green jobs focus on harnessing renewable energy from the sun and wind:

- **Solar Panel Installation:** Setting up solar panels in homes and businesses to generate clean energy.
- **Wind Turbine Technicians:** Maintaining and repairing wind turbines that convert wind energy into electricity.

Waste Reduction and Recycling: Jobs in waste reduction and recycling help manage and reduce waste:

- **Recycling Coordinators:** Managing recycling programmes and ensuring that materials are properly sorted and processed.
- **Waste Management Specialists:** Finding innovative ways to reduce waste and improve waste disposal practices, including composting and reducing single-use plastics.

Green jobs play a vital role in creating a healthier and more sustainable world. Whether it is making homes safer, promoting eco-friendly gardening, or improving energy and water use, these careers help protect our environment and conserve natural resources. By learning about these green jobs, you can see how every role contributes to a greener future and how you might find your place in this important field.

Answer the following questions in 40 to 50 words each

1. What are some of the key roles in creating toxin-free homes?
2. How do organic gardeners ensure that the soil remains healthy without synthetic chemicals?
3. What role does education play in organic gardening?
4. What are two important roles in improving public transport?
5. Describe the role of an energy auditor.
6. What are two green jobs related to solar and wind power?
7. Why are green jobs important for creating a sustainable future?
8. In what ways can learning about green jobs help individuals find their place in this field?

Session 5: Green Jobs In Action

5.1 Introduction

Fig. 5.1 Employment Opportunities

Green jobs are essential in our transition to a sustainable future. They involve practices that help reduce our environmental impact, enhance resource efficiency, and contribute to the restoration of ecosystems. This session explores various green jobs in action, focusing on green tourism, building and construction, appropriate technology, and addressing climate change through mitigation, adaptation, and ecosystem restoration.

5.1.1 Green Tourism

Fig. 5.2 Green Tourism

Green tourism, also known as sustainable or eco-tourism, emphasizes environment-friendly travel and hospitality practices. It involves:

(i) **Conservation of Natural Resources:** Green tourism promotes the preservation of natural environments by minimizing waste and pollution and conserving water and energy.

(ii) **Support for Local Communities:** It encourages tourists to engage with and support local economies by choosing accommodations, restaurants, and activities that are environmentally and socially responsible.

(iii) **Sustainable Practices in Hospitality:** Hotels and resorts implement energy-saving measures, water conservation techniques, waste reduction programmes, and the use of local and organic products.

Example: A hotel that uses solar panels for energy, recycles waste, and promotes eco-friendly tours is contributing to green tourism.

5.1.2 Green Building and Construction

Green building and construction involve designing and constructing buildings that are environmentally responsible and resource-efficient.

5.1.3 Key Aspectss

(i) **Energy Efficiency:** Utilizing insulation, energy-efficient windows, and renewable energy sources like solar or wind power to reduce energy consumption.

(ii) **Sustainable Materials:** Use materials that are renewable, recycled are recyclable, and/or have a low environmental impact, such as bamboo, reclaimed wood, or recycled steel.

(ii) **Water Conservation:** Implementing systems that reduce the use of water, such as low-flow fixtures, rainwater harvesting, and greywater recycling.

Example: A building designed with energy-efficient lighting, green roofs, and rainwater harvesting systems is a model of green construction.

5.1.4 Appropriate Technology

Appropriate technology refers to technology that is suitable for its intended purpose, socially acceptable, and environment-friendly.

(i) **Renewable Energy Technologies:** Solar panels, wind turbines, and biogas plants that provide sustainable energy solutions.

(ii) **Water Purification Systems:** Low-cost, locally manageable technologies that provide clean drinking water in areas lacking infrastructure.

(iii) **Sustainable Agriculture Tools:** Tools and methods that enhance farming productivity while maintaining ecological balance, such as drip irrigation systems.

Example: A community using solar-powered water pumps for irrigation and solar cookers for cooking demonstrates the application of appropriate technology.

5.1.5 Enhancing Energy Efficiency and Resource Use

Enhancing energy efficiency means using less energy to perform the same task, thereby reducing wastage of energy.

This can be achieved through:

(i) **Energy-Efficient Appliances:** Devices that consume less electricity, such as LED bulbs, energy-efficient refrigerators, and air conditioners.

(ii) **Resource Optimization:** Techniques like recycling, reusing materials, and reducing waste to make the best use of available resources.

(iii) **Smart Technologies:** Implementing smart grids and metres to monitor and optimize energy usage in homes and industries.

Example: A manufacturing plant that uses energy-efficient machinery and recycles waste materials demonstrates enhanced energy efficiency and resource use.

5.2 Addressing Climate Change

Addressing climate change involves efforts to mitigate its impacts, adapt to changes, and restore ecosystems.

5.2.1 Key Strategies in Addressing Climate Change

(i) **Mitigation:** Reducing greenhouse gas emissions by adopting renewable energy sources, improving energy efficiency, and promoting sustainable transportation.

(ii) **Adaptation:** Adjusting practices to cope with climate impacts, such as building flood defences, developing drought-resistant crops, and implementing early warning systems.

(iii) **Ecosystem Restoration:** Rehabilitating damaged ecosystems through reforestation, wetland restoration, and soil conservation.

Example: A community project that plants trees to restore a deforested area, implements flood-resistant infrastructure, and uses renewable energy sources is actively addressing climate change.

The key takeaways on green skills from this session are:

- Green jobs play a vital role in creating a sustainable future by reducing environmental impact, enhancing resource efficiency, and restoring ecosystems.
- Emphasizes sustainable travel practices, conservation of natural resources, support for local communities, and eco-friendly hospitality. Green tourism involves activities that reduce waste, conserve water and energy, and engage with local economies.
- Focuses on designing and constructing environmentally responsible and resource-efficient buildings. Key aspects include energy efficiency, sustainable materials, and water conservation.
- Refers to socially acceptable and environment-friendly technology suited for its purpose. Examples include renewable energy technologies, water purification systems, and sustainable agriculture tools.
- Involves using energy-efficient appliances, optimizing the use of resources and implementing smart technologies to reduce energy waste and make the best use of available resources.
- Involves strategies such as mitigation, adaptation, and ecosystem restoration. Mitigation focuses on reducing greenhouse gas emissions, adaptation on coping with climate impacts, and ecosystem restoration on rehabilitating damaged environments.
- Understanding and implementing green jobs are crucial for environmental protection and ensuring a better quality of life for future generations. Each sector, whether tourism, construction, technology, or energy, has a role to play in advancing sustainability.

EXERCISE

Review Questions

1. Define green tourism. Which practices are involved in promoting green tourism?
2. What are the key components of green building and construction? Provide examples of materials and technologies used.
3. Explain the concept of appropriate technology. How does it contribute to sustainability?
4. How can enhancing energy efficiency help in reducing environmental impact?
5. Describe the strategies used in addressing climate change through mitigation, adaptation, and ecosystem restoration. Provide real-life examples.

❑❑❑

PART B

SUBJECT SPECIFIC SKILLS

- **UNIT-1:** Overview of Physical Education and Sports Sector
- **UNIT-2:** Assessment of Students
- **UNIT-3:** Emergency Management
- **UNIT-4:** Health and Hygiene in Play Area

UNIT 1

OVERVIEW OF PHYSICAL EDUCATION AND SPORTS SECTOR

- Career Opportunities in Physical Education and Sports
- Importance of Sports and Games
- Importance of Sports in Developing Life Skills

Physical Education (PE) is an integral part of the educational curriculum that focuses on the development of physical fitness, motor skills, knowledge about physical health, and the promotion of lifelong healthy habits. Physical education programmes typically include activities such as sports, exercise routines, games, and fitness education. The primary aim of such programmes is to encourage students to engage in regular physical activity, understand the benefits of a healthy lifestyle, and develop social skills through team sports and cooperative activities. In the field of physical education, various job scenarios exist that cater to different interests, skills, and career aspirations.

Fig. 1.1 Activities

1.1 Career Opportunities in Physical Education and Sports

1.1.1 Teaching in Physical Education

Physical Education Teachers play a pivotal role in educating students about the importance of physical activity, promoting healthy lifestyles, and developing motor skills. Their responsibilities extend beyond just conducting sports and games; they also include planning lessons, assessing student performance, and fostering an inclusive environment where all students can participate and benefit.

1. Required Skills and Qualities

- **Physical Fitness:** PE teachers should themselves maintain a good level of physical fitness to demonstrate exercises and participate in activities.
- **Knowledge of Sports and Activities:** Should understand various sports, exercises, and fitness techniques is essential.
- **Teaching Skills:** Should have the ability to explain concepts clearly, demonstrate techniques, and adapt instruction to meet diverse student needs.
- **Communication Skills:** Have effective verbal and non-verbal communication skills to engage and motivate students.

- **Patience and Empathy:** Working with students of different abilities and backgrounds requires understanding and patience.
- **Organizational Skills:** Planning lessons, managing equipment, and maintaining records require strong organizational abilities.
- **Leadership:** Leading classes, managing groups, and motivating students to participate and perform.

2. Roles and Responsibilities

(i) Curriculum Development

- Designing age-appropriate lesson plans that cover a variety of physical activities.
- Integrating health education topics such as nutrition, wellness, and personal fitness.
- Ensuring that the curriculum aligns with national and state standards for physical education.

To see **Qualitative and Quantitative Assessment** in Action

Scan QR Code

(ii) Instruction

- Teaching students the rules and skills needed for various sports and physical activities.
- Demonstrating exercises and techniques.
- Encouraging students to participate actively and safely.
- Providing individualized support to students with varying abilities.

(iii) Assessment and Evaluation

- Assessing student performance through observations, tests, and physical fitness assessments.
- Providing feedback and setting goals for improvement.
- Maintaining records of students' progress and performance.

(iv) Classroom Management

- Creating a positive and inclusive environment where all students feel comfortable participating.
- Implementing strategies to manage behaviour and ensure safety during physical activities.
- Encouraging teamwork, fair play, and sportsmanship.

(v) Professional Development

- Staying updated with the latest trends, techniques, and research in physical education.
- Participating in workshops, conferences, and continuing education courses.
- Collaborating with colleagues to share resources and strategies.

(vi) Extracurricular Activities

- Coaching the school's sports teams.
- Organizing and supervising extracurricular activities such as sports clubs, fitness programmes, and events.
- Promoting school-wide initiatives for health and wellness.

Fig. 1.2 Physical Fitness

3. Educational Qualifications and Eligibility

Bachelor's Degree in Physical Education or Related Field: Aspiring PE teachers typically need a bachelor's degree in Physical Education, Kinesiology, Exercise Science, or some other closely related field. These programmes cover essential topics such as anatomy, physiology, kinesiology, sports science, and teaching methods.

Institutes for Physical Education Programmes in India

Institute	Location	Courses Offered	Special Features
Lakshmibai National Institute of Physical Education (LNIPE)	Gwalior	B.P.Ed., M.P.Ed., Ph.D., Diploma & Certificate Courses	Established by the Government of India; Focuses on high-quality education and research
Indira Gandhi Institute of Physical Education and Sports Sciences (IGIPESS)	New Delhi	B.P.Ed., M.P.Ed., B.Sc. in Physical Education, Health Education, and Sports, PG Diploma Courses	Affiliated with the University of Delhi; Theoretical and practical training
Tamil Nadu Physical Education and Sports University (TNPESU)	Chennai	B.P.Ed., M.P.Ed., M.Sc. in Sports Coaching and Exercise Physiology, Ph.D., Diploma & Certificate Courses	State university dedicated to physical education and sports; Variety of specialized courses
University of Mumbai—Department of Physical Education	Mumbai	B.P.Ed., M.P.Ed., Ph.D.	Well-established programmes; Experienced faculty; Practical and theoretical education

Contd...

Lovely Professional University—Department of Physical Education	Phagwara	B.P.Ed., M.P.Ed., Ph.D.	Strong emphasis on research and academic excellence
Banaras Hindu University (BHU)—Faculty of Arts, Department of Physical Education	Varanasi	B.P.Ed., M.P.Ed., Ph.D.	Prestigious central university; Focus on research and practical training
Amity School of Physical Education and Sports Sciences (ASPE)	Noida	B.P.Ed., M.P.Ed., Ph.D.	Part of Amity University; State-of-the-art facilities; Experienced faculty
Punjab University—Department of Physical Education	Chandigarh	B.P.Ed., M.P.Ed., Ph.D.	Strong academic programmes and research opportunities; Variety of sports and fitness-related courses

1.1.2 Coaching in Sports

Coaching in sports involves training and developing athletes and teams to achieve their highest potentials. Coaches play a critical role in helping athletes improve their skills, strategies, and overall performance while fostering teamwork, discipline, and sportsmanship.

Required Skills and Qualities

(i) Knowledge of the Sport

- In-depth understanding of the sport, including rules, techniques, and strategies.
- Awareness of current trends and best practices in coaching.

(ii) Communication Skills

- Ability to convey instructions clearly and effectively.
- Strong interpersonal skills to build relationships with athletes and other stakeholders.

(iii) Leadership and Motivation

- Leading by example and inspiring athletes to strive for excellence.
- Creating a positive, motivating environment that encourages hard work and perseverance.

(iv) Analytical Skills

- Ability to analyse performance data and game footage to identify areas for improvement.
- Making informed decisions based on analysis and observations.

(v) Patience and Adaptability

- Patience to work with athletes of varying skill levels and backgrounds.
- Adaptability to adjust coaching methods and strategies to meet individual and team needs.

(vi) Organization and Time Management:

- Efficiently managing time and resources to ensure productive practice sessions and smooth operations.
- Organizing schedules, travel plans, and administrative tasks effectively.

Fig. 1.3 Coaching

Roles and Responsibilities of a Sports Coach

(i) Training and Development

- Designing and implementing training programmes tailored to the needs and abilities of athletes.
- Focusing on skill development, physical conditioning, and mental preparation.
- Conducting practice sessions and drills to improve performance.

To see **Responsibility of Coaches** in Action

Scan QR Code

(ii) Game Strategy and Tactics:

- Developing game plans and strategies based on the team's strengths and weaknesses and the opponents' characteristics.
- Analysing game footage and performance data to refine strategies and improve tactics.
- Making real-time decisions and adjustments during competitions.

(iii) Motivation and Mentorship

- Inspiring and motivating athletes to perform their best.
- Providing guidance and support to help athletes overcome challenges and setbacks.
- Fostering a positive and inclusive team environment.

(iv) Assessment and Evaluation

- Monitoring and assessing athletes' performance and progress.
- Providing constructive feedback and setting goals for improvement.

- Conducting regular evaluations to track development and make necessary adjustments.

(v) Administrative Duties

- Managing team logistics, such as scheduling practices, arranging travel, and organizing competitions.
- Communicating with stakeholders, including athletes, parents, and administrators.
- Ensuring compliance with rules, regulations, and safety standards.

(vi) Personal Development

- Staying updated with the latest coaching techniques, sports science research, and industry trends.
- Participating in professional development opportunities, such as workshops, seminars, and certifications.

Required Skills and Qualities

(i) Knowledge of the Sport

- In-depth understanding of the sport, including rules, techniques, and strategies.
- Awareness of current trends and best practices in coaching.

(ii) Communication Skills

- Ability to convey instructions clearly and effectively.
- Strong interpersonal skills to build relationships with athletes and other stakeholders.

(iii) Leadership and Motivation

- Leading by example and inspiring athletes to strive for excellence.
- Creating a positive, motivating environment that encourages hard work and perseverance.

(iv) Analytical Skills

- Ability to analyse performance data and game footage to identify areas for improvement.
- Making informed decisions based on analysis and observations.

(v) Patience and Adaptabilit

- Patience to work with athletes of varying skill levels and backgrounds.
- Adaptability to adjust coaching methods and strategies to meet individual and team needs.

(vi) Organization and Time Management

- Efficiently managing time and resources to ensure productive practice sessions and smooth operations.
- Organizing schedules, travel plans, and administrative tasks effectively.

Educational Qualifications and Eligibility

(i) Coaching Certification

National Institute of Sports (NIS): In India, the NIS offers various coaching certificate courses in multiple sports. These courses are recognized and respected nationwide.

International Coaching Certification: Certifications from international bodies like the International Coaching Federation (ICF) or sport-specific organizations (e.g., FIFA, FIBA) can also be valuable.

(ii) Sport-Specific Certificates

Governing Bodies: Many sports have their own governing bodies that offer coaching certification programmes. For example, the Board of Control for Cricket in India (BCCI) for cricket, All India Football Federation (AIFF) for football, and Basketball Federation of India (BFI) for basketball.

Levels of Certification: Often, certificates are offered at different levels (beginner, intermediate, advanced) depending on the coach's experience and expertise.

Institutes for Coaching Diplomas in India

Institute	Location	Courses Offered	Special Features
National Institute of Sports (NIS), Patiala	Patiala	Diploma in Sports Coaching	Premier institute for sports coaching in India; Extensive practical and theoretical training
Lakshmibai National Institute of Physical Education (LNIPE)	Gwalior	Diploma in Sports Coaching	Established by the Government of India; Focus on high-quality education and research
Indira Gandhi Institute of Physical Education and Sports Sciences (IGIPESS)	New Delhi	Diploma in Sports Coaching	Affiliated with the University of Delhi; Combination of theoretical and practical training
Tamil Nadu Physical Education and Sports University (TNPESU)	Chennai	Diploma in Sports Coaching	State university dedicated to physical education and sports; Variety of specialized courses
Amity School of Physical Education and Sports Sciences (ASPE)	Noida	Diploma in Sports Coaching	Part of Amity University, State-of-the-art facilities and experienced faculty
Alagappa University College of Physical Education	Karaikudi	Diploma in Sports Coaching	Offers a range of physical education and sports programmes; Emphasis on practical training
Guru Nanak Dev University—Department of Physical Education	Amritsar	Diploma in Sports Coaching	Focus on developing coaching skills; Strong academic and practical components
Swarnim Gujarat Sports University	Gandhinagar	Diploma in Sports Coaching	State university focusing on sports education; Emphasis on modern coaching techniques
University of Mumbai—Department of Physical Education	Mumbai	Diploma in Sports Coaching	Well-established programme with experienced faculty; Practical and theoretical education

1.1.3 Sports Management

Sports Management is a field that combines the principles of business management with the sports industry. It involves planning, organizing, directing, controlling, budgeting, leading, and evaluating within the context of an organization or department whose primary product or service is related to sports and physical activity.

Roles and Responsibilities in Sports Management

(i) Event Management

- Organizing and managing sports events, tournaments, and competitions.
- Coordinating logistics, scheduling, and ensuring compliance with regulations.

Fig. 1.4 Management

(ii) Marketing and Promotions

- Developing marketing strategies to promote sports teams, events, and products.
- Managing public relations, sponsorships, and advertising campaigns.

(iii) Facility Management

- Overseeing the operations of sports facilities such as stadiums, arenas, and fitness centres.
- Ensuring that facilities are well-maintained, safe, and meet regulatory standards.

(iv) Financial Management

- Budgeting, financial planning, and management of funds for sports organizations.
- Managing revenues from ticket sales, sponsorships, and merchandize.

(v) Human Resources

- Hiring, training, and managing staff, including coaches, trainers, and administrative personnel.
- Ensuring compliance with labour laws and organizational policies.

(vi) Legal and Ethical Management

- Navigating legal issues related to sports contracts, negotiations, and compliance.
- Promoting ethical practices and ensuring adherence to codes of conduct.

Required Skills and Qualities

(i) Leadership and Management

- Strong leadership skills to manage teams and projects effectively.
- Ability to make strategic decisions and solve problems efficiently.

(ii) Communication Skills

- Excellent verbal and written communication skills to interact with stakeholders, media, and the public.
- Ability to convey information clearly and persuasively.

(iii) Organizational Skills

- Strong organizational skills to manage multiple tasks and projects simultaneously.
- Attention to detail to ensure all aspects of sports management are handled effectively.

(iv) Analytical Skills

- Ability to analyse data and make informed decisions based on financial and performance metrics.
- Critical thinking skills to evaluate and improve organizational processes.

(v) Marketing and Public Relations

- Knowledge of marketing principles and techniques to promote sports entities.
- Skills in managing public relations and maintaining a positive image.

Required Educational Qualifications and Eligibility

- **Bachelor's Degree:**

  Sports Management or Related Field: Most sports management professionals hold a bachelor's degree in Sports Management, Business Administration, Marketing, or some other related field.
- **Master's Degree (Optional but Beneficial):** Pursuing a master's degree in Sports Management, Business Administration (MBA) with a focus on sports management, or a related field can enhance career prospects.
- **Professional Certificates:** Certificates from organizations like the National Association of Sports Officials (NASO), International Sports Professionals Association (ISPA), or sport-specific governing bodies can add value.

Institutes for Sports Management in India

Institute	Location	Courses Offered	Special Features
Indian Institute of Management (IIM)	Ahmedabad, Bengaluru, Kolkata	MBA with focus on Sports Management	Premier management institute; Comprehensive business education
Symbiosis School of Sports Sciences (SSSS)	Pune	MBA in Sports Management	Focused on sports management; Industry collaborations
Lakshmibai National Institute of Physical Education (LNIPE)	Gwalior	M.A. in Sports Management	Government-established; Specializes in physical education and sports
International Institute of Sports Management (IISM)	Mumbai	BBA and MBA in Sports Management	Dedicated to sports management; Strong industry connections
Tata Institute of Social Sciences (TISS)	Mumbai	M.A. in Sports Management	Renowned institute; Emphasis on social aspects of sports management
Amity School of Physical Education and Sports Sciences (ASPE)	Noida	MBA in Sports Management	Part of Amity University; Modern facilities and faculty
National Academy of Sports Management (NASM)	Mumbai	BBA and MBA in Sports Management	Specialized in sports management education; Practical training focus
Manipal Academy of Higher Education (MAHE)	Manipal	MBA in Sports Management	Prestigious university; Comprehensive curriculum
Swarnim Gujarat Sports University	Gandhinagar	MBA in Sports Management	State university; Emphasis on sports and physical education

1.1.4 Fitness Sector

Fitness Instructorrs are professionals who help individuals and groups to improve their physical fitness through exercise, instruction, and motivation. They design and implement exercise programmes, provide guidance on proper techniques, and offer advice on health and wellness.

To see **Fitness Sector** in Action

Scan QR Code

Roles and Responsibilities

(i) Personal Training

- **Individual Assessments:** To assess clients' fitness levels, goals, and health conditions.
- **Customized Programmes:** To develop personalized exercise programmes tailored to clients' needs, goals, and preferences.

(ii) Group Fitness Instruction

- **Class Design:** To plan and lead group exercise classes, such as aerobics, strength training, yoga, or cycling.
- **Instruction:** To demonstrate exercises, correct form, and ensure safety for all participants.

Fig. 1.5 Fitness Instructor

(iii) Fitness Assessments and Monitoring

- **Progress Tracking:** To monitor clients' progress and adjust programmes as needed.
- **Fitness Testing:** To conduct assessments such as body composition, strength, flexibility, and cardiovascular fitness.

(iv) Health and Wellness Advice

- **Lifestyle Guidance:** To offer advice on nutrition, hydration, and overall wellness to complement exercise routines.
- **Injury Prevention:** To educate clients on injury prevention techniques and proper exercise form.

(v) Administrative Duties

- **Scheduling:** To manage appointment bookings, class schedules, and client records.
- **Client Communication:** To maintain regular communication with clients to address their needs and concerns.

Required Skills and Qualities

(i) Knowledge of Exercise Techniques

- **Fitness Expertise:** In-depth understanding of exercise techniques, anatomy, and physiology.
- **Programme Design:** Ability to design safe and effective exercise programmes for diverse populations.

(ii) Communication Skills

- **Instructional Ability:** Clear and effective communication skills to instruct and motivate clients.
- **Interpersonal Skills:** Skills to build positive relationships with clients to understand their needs and provide support.

(iii) Motivation and Leadership

- **Inspirational:** Ability to inspire and motivate clients to achieve their fitness goals.
- **Encouragement:** Enthuse the trainee to provide consistent encouragement and support to enhance their commitment.

(iv) Organizational Skills

- **Time Management:** Efficiently managing class schedules, client appointments, and administrative tasks.
- **Record-keeping:** Maintaining accurate client records and progress reports.

(v) Adaptability

- **Flexibility:** Adapting programmes and techniques to suit different fitness levels and individual needs.
- **Problem-solving:** Addressing and resolving any issues related to fitness routines or client concerns.

Educational Qualifications and Eligibility

(i) Educational Background

Bachelor's Degree: A degree in Exercise Science, Physical Education, Kinesiology, or a related field is beneficial but not always required.

(ii) Fitness Certificates: Certification from a recognized organization is often required or preferred. Examples include:

- American College of Sports Medicine (ACSM)
- National Academy of Sports Medicine (NASM)
- American Council on Exercise (ACE)
- International Sports Sciences Association (ISSA)

Fitness Centres in India

Institute	Location	Courses Offered	Special Features
Gold's Gym	Various locations	Fitness Instructor Certification	Established gym chain; Practical and theoretical training
American College of Sports Medicine (ACSM)	Online	Certification Programmes	Internationally recognized; Comprehensive fitness certifications
National Academy of Sports Medicine (NASM)	Online	Certified Personal Trainer (CPT)	Well-regarded international certification; Evidence-based programmes

Contd...

International Sports Sciences Association (ISSA)	Online	Certified Fitness Trainer	Global certification; Focus on practical application
K11 School of Fitness Sciences	Mumbai, New Delhi	Fitness Trainer Certification	Dedicated fitness education; Hands-on training and industry connections
Institute of Fitness & Sports Sciences (IFSS)	Delhi	Fitness Instructor Course	Specialized training in fitness and sports sciences
Fitness Training Institute (FTI)	Bengaluru	Certified Fitness Trainer Programme	Comprehensive certification; Emphasis on practical skills
IIT Delhi—Physical Education and Sports	New Delhi	Fitness and Wellness Programmes	Part of a prestigious institute; Research-based approach

1.1.5 Equipment Managers

The role of an Equipment Manager in sports and games is essential for the smooth functioning of a team or organization.

Equipment Maintenance and Management

- Ensures all sports gear (e.g., balls, uniforms, shoes, safety gear) is in good condition.
- Conducts regular checks for wear and tear.
- Manages repair and replacement of damaged equipment
- Maintains an organized inventory of all equipment.
- Tracks issued gear to athletes and ensures timely return.
- Keeps records of equipment usage, stock levels, and procurement needs.
- Works with coaches and management to determine equipment needs.
- Helps create a budget for equipment.
- Purchases new gear within budget limits while ensuring quality
- Oversees cleaning of uniforms and gear, especially in team sports.
- Ensures hygiene standards are maintained to prevent infections or skin diseases.
- Prepares and sets up equipment for practices, games, or tournaments.
- Ensures all required items are packed and transported if the game is away.
- Assists players with last-minute equipment needs.
- Ensures all protective equipment (like helmets, pads, guards) meets safety regulations.
- Educates players on how to use gear properly to avoid injuries.

- Acts as a bridge between players and management for equipment issues.
- Provides timely solutions during games to prevent delays or disruptions.
- Helps tailor equipment to individual athlete needs (e.g., shoe sizes, jersey fits).
- May label gear with names or numbers for easy identification.

1.1.6 Sports Journalism

To see **Media and Sports** in Action

Scan QR Code

Sports journalism focuses on reporting and writing about sports events, athletes, teams, and related issues. It combines the skills of traditional journalism with a deep understanding of sports to deliver compelling stories to audiences through various media platforms.

Fig. 1.6 Sports Journalism

Roles and Responsibilities

(i) Reporting and Writings

- **Event Coverage:** Attending and covering live sports events, games, and competitions. Writing articles, reports, and updates on the events.
- **Feature Stories:** Creating in-depth feature stories on athletes, teams, and sports-related issues.
- **Interviews:** Conducting interviews with athletes, coaches, and other relevant figures.

(ii) Research and Analysis

- **Data Analysis:** Analysing games' statistics, performance data, and trends to provide insightful commentary and analysis.

- **Background Research:** Gathering background information and conducting research to enhance the quality and accuracy of reporting.

(iii) Editing and Proofreading

- **Content Review:** Editing and proofreading the written content to ensure clarity, accuracy, and adherence to journalistic standards.
- **Story Refinement:** Refining stories to make them engaging and informative for the audience.

(iv) Multimedia Production

- **Visual Content:** Creating or overseeing the creation of multimedia content, including photos, videos, and graphics.
- **Digital Media:** Managing and updating content on digital platforms such as websites, social media, and mobile apps.

(v) Audience Engagement

- **Interactive Content:** Engaging with readers through interactive content, such as polls, live chats, and social media interactions.
- **Feedback Management:** Responding to audience feedback and adapting content to meet audience interests and preferences.

Required Skills and Qualities

(i) Writing and Communication

- **Strong Writing Skills:** Ability to write clear, engaging, and accurate articles and reports.
- **Communication:** Effective verbal and written communication skills for interviews, reporting, and interacting with audiences.

(ii) Sports Knowledge

- **In-Depth Understanding:** Comprehensive knowledge of sports, including rules, strategies, and current events.
- **Analytical Skills:** Ability to analyse and interpret sports data and trends.

(iii) Research Skills

- **Investigative Research:** Conducting thorough research to gather accurate information and provide context for stories.
- **Attention to Detail:** Ensuring that all facts are correct and stories are well-researched.

(iv) Multimedia Proficiency

- **Digital Skills:** Proficiency in multimedia tools and digital platforms for creating and managing content.
- **Visual Storytelling:** Ability to use photos, videos, and graphics effectively to enhance storytelling.

(v) Ethical Standards

- **Journalistic Integrity:** Adhering to ethical standards, including accuracy, fairness, and objectivity in reporting.
- **Confidentiality:** Respecting the privacy of sources and subjects.

Educational Qualifications and Eligibility

(i) Bachelor's Degree

- **Degree in Journalism, Communications, or Related Field:** A bachelor's degree in Journalism, Mass Communication, Media Studies, or a related field is commonly required.

(ii) Master's Degree (Optional but Beneficial)

- **Advanced Studies:** A master's degree in Journalism, Sports Management.

Institutes for Journalism in India

Institute	Location	Courses Offered	Special Features
Indian Institute of Mass Communication (IIMC)	New Delhi	PG Diploma in Sports Journalism	Prestigious institute; Focus on journalism with specialized courses in sports
Mumbai University — Department of Journalism	Mumbai	MA in Journalism and Mass Comm-unication	Offers courses with a focus on sports journalism and media studies
Symbiosis Institute of Media and Communication (SIMC)	Pune	MA in Communication Management with Specialization in Sports	Comprehensive media progra-mme with sports specialization
Jain University — School of Journalism and Mass Communication	Bengaluru	BA and MA in Journalism with Sports Journalism Specialization	Focused courses in sports journalism and practical training
Amity School of Commu-nication	Noida	BA and MA in Journalism with Sports Specialization	Part of Amity University; Modern facilities and industry connections
Glamorgan University - Department of Journalism	Cardiff (International Programmes)	MA in Sports Journalism	Offers international perspective and training in sports journalism

Contd...

National Academy of Films Media & Communications (NAFMC)	Delhi	Diploma in Sports Journalism	Specialized diploma with practical and theoretical training
Manipal Academy of Higher Education (MAHE)	Manipal	MA in Media and Communication with Sports Focus	Comprehensive curriculum with a focus on sports media

1.1.7 Photography

The role of photography in sports and games is much more than just capturing action shots—it plays a key role in media, analysis, motivation, and even history.

1. Capturing Key Moments

- Records important events like goals, celebrations, wins, and defeats.
- Freezes intense emotions and dramatic actions in a single frame.
- Creates lasting memories for athletes, fans, and teams

2. Media and Promotion

- Used by newspapers, websites, and sports channels for coverage.
- Helps promote games, tournaments, and athletes through social media.
- Boosts fan engagement with dynamic and eye-catching visuals.

3. Performance Analysis

- Photographs (especially high-speed or sequential shots) help coaches and players study:
  - ➢ Body posture
  - ➢ Movements and techniques
  - ➢ Game strategies
- Useful in correcting form or improving plays.

4. Building Athlete Profiles

- Helps in creating personal branding for players.
- Used in portfolios, sponsorship proposals, and marketing materials.
- Highlights an athlete's journey and achievements.

5. Aesthetic and Emotional Value

- Sports photography turns action into art.
- Captures raw emotion—joy, defeat, focus, teamwork.
- Inspires others and tells powerful stories without words.

6. Historical Documentation

- Archives legendary moments in sports history (e.g., Usain Bolt's victory pose, Maradona's "Hand of God").
- Becomes part of sports museums, documentaries, and retrospectives.
- Helps preserve the culture and evolution of different games.

7. Fan Engagement

- Fans connect more deeply with visual content.
- Creates excitement before and after games through behind-the-scenes shots and highlight photos.
- Enables sharing of personal fan moments (e.g., photos with players, at stadiums).

8. Event Management and Coverage

- Used to assess event arrangements, crowd size, and field conditions.
- Helps sponsors and organizers evaluate the success of the event.

1.1.8 Sports Medicine

Sports Medicine is a specialized branch of medicine that focuses on the prevention, diagnosis, treatment, and rehabilitation of injuries related to sports, exercise, and physical activity. It also aims to enhance athletic performance and overall physical fitness.

1. Injury Prevention

- Designs warm-up, stretching, and fitness programs to reduce injury risk.
- Advises on correct techniques and safe training practices.
- Recommends proper nutrition and hydration.

2. Diagnosis and Treatment of Injuries

- Identifies and treats sports-related injuries like sprains, fractures, ligament tears, etc.
- Uses physical exams, imaging (X-ray, MRI), and medical history to diagnose.
- Provides emergency care during matches or training.

3. Rehabilitation and Recovery

- Plans rehab programs to ensure full and safe recovery.
- Uses physiotherapy, massage, strength training, and mobility exercises.
- Helps athletes return to play with minimal risk of re-injury.

4. Performance Enhancement

- Offers fitness testing and evaluations.
- Advises on safe ways to improve strength, endurance, flexibility, and agility.
- Guides use of supplements and legal performance aids.

5. Mental Health and Motivation

- Addresses mental challenges like stress, anxiety, and pressure.
- Works with sports psychologists to build confidence and focus.

6. Education and Research

- Educates athletes and coaches on injury prevention, first aid, and health.

- Conducts research to develop better treatment methods and training strategies.

Qualifications

Depending on the role (doctor, physiotherapist, trainer), qualifications may vary:

- MBBS (Bachelor of Medicine and Bachelor of Surgery)
- MD or Diploma in Sports Medicine (Postgraduate specialization)
- Optionally, Fellowships in Orthopedics, Sports Rehab, or Exercise Physiology

Course Name	Eligibility	Duration	Level	Offered By / Institutes
MD in Sports Medicine	MBBS	3 years	Postgraduate (MD)	AIIMS Delhi, SAI (Sports Authority of India)
Diploma in Sports Medicine	MBBS or BPT	1–2 years	Diploma	NSNIS Patiala, SAI
BPT (Bachelor of Physiotherapy)	10+2 (Science – PCB)	4.5 years	Undergraduate	DY Patil University, Manipal, Amity University
MPT in Sports Physiotherapy	BPT	2 years	Postgraduate	Guru Nanak Dev University, Jamia Hamdard, SRM University
B.Sc in Sports Science	10+2 (Science)	3 years	Undergraduate	Tamil Nadu Physical Education and Sports University (TNPESU)
M.Sc in Sports Science	B.Sc in relevant field	2 years	Postgraduate	University of Calicut, LNIPE Gwalior
Certificate in Sports Medicine	Varies (MBBS/ BPT preferred)	6 months – 1 year	Certificate Course	ACSM (USA), FIMS, NSNIS Patiala
Fellowship in Sports Medicine	MBBS + PG (Ortho/Physio)	6 months – 1 year	Fellowship	Aspetar (Qatar), Apollo Hospitals, ISMF India

1.1.9 Sports Psychologists

Sports psychologists specialize in helping athletes and teams to enhance their performance and well-being through psychological techniques. They work with individuals and groups to use mental and emotional techniques that impact sports performance by infusing motivation, focus, anxiety, and confidence.

To see **Sports Psychology** in Action

Scan QR Code

Fig 1.7 Sports Psychologists

Roles and Responsibilities

(i) Performance Enhancement

- **Mental Training:** Implementing techniques to improve concentration, motivation, and mental toughness.
- **Goal Setting:** Assisting athletes in setting and achieving performance goals.

(ii) Stress and Anxiety Management

- **Coping Strategies:** Helping athletes to manage stress and anxiety related to competition, training, and performance pressures.
- **Relaxation Techniques:** Teaching methods such as visualization, mindfulness, and breathing exercises to reduce performance anxiety.

(iii) Motivation and Confidence Building

- **Motivational Strategies:** Developing strategies to maintain and enhance motivation and self-confidence.
- **Self-Talk:** Guiding athletes in using positive self-talk and affirmations to boost performance and resilience.

(iv) Team Dynamics and Communication

- **Team Building:** Improving team cohesion, communication, and collaboration.
- **Conflict Resolution:** Addressing and resolving interpersonal conflicts within teams.

(v) Injury Rehabilitation

- **Mental Recovery:** Supporting athletes through the psychological aspects of injury recovery and rehabilitation.

- **Goal Adjustment:** Helping athletes in adjusting their goals and expectations during the recovery process.

(vi) Career Transition and Personal Development

- **Career Counselling:** Assisting athletes in transitioning to post-sport careers and managing life changes.
- **Personal Growth:** Facilitating personal development and life skills beyond sports.

Required Skills and Qualities

(i) Psychological Expertise

- **In-Depth Knowledge:** Strong understanding of psychological principles and techniques relevant to sports.
- **Assessment Skills:** Ability to assess mental and emotional factors affecting performance.

(ii) Communication Skills

- **Effective Listening:** Active listening skills to understand athletes' concerns and needs.
- **Empathy:** Ability to provide empathetic support and build trust with athletes.

(iii) Analytical Skills

- **Problem Solving:** Analysing psychological factors impacting performance and devising effective interventions.
- **Data Interpretation:** Interpreting psychological assessments and feedback to guide interventions.

(iv) Motivational Skills

- **Inspiration:** Ability to inspire and motivate athletes to overcome psychological barriers and achieve their goals.
- **Encouragement:** Providing consistent encouragement and positive reinforcement.

(v) Ethical Standards

- **Confidentiality:** Maintaining strict confidentiality and ethical standards in working with athletes.
- **Professional Integrity:** Adhering to professional guidelines and ethical practices in sports psychology.

Educational Qualifications and Eligibility

(i) Bachelor's Degree

- **Degree in Psychology:** A bachelor's degree in psychology or a related field is typically required as a foundational step.

(ii) Master's Degree

- **Master of Sports Psychology or Clinical Psychology:** A master's degree in Sports Psychology, Clinical Psychology, or a related field is generally necessary.

- **Specialized Training:** Courses in sports psychology, performance enhancement, and mental skills training.

(iii) Doctoral Degree (Ph.D. or Psy.D.)

- **Advanced Studies:** A doctoral degree in Sports Psychology, Clinical Psychology, or Counselling Psychology is often required for advanced practice and academic roles.

(iv) Certification

- **Certification:** Optional certifications from professional organizations, such as the Association for Applied Sport Psychology (AASP), can enhance credibility and career prospects.

Institutes for Sports Psychology in India

Institute	Location	Courses Offered	Special Features
Indian Institute of Sports Science and Research (IISSR)	Delhi	Diploma in Sports Psychology	Focus on sports psychology with practical training
National Institute of Mental Health and Neurosciences (NIMHANS)	Bengaluru	MSc. and MPhil. in Clinical Psychology with Sports Psychology Modules	Renowned for clinical psychology, includes sports psychology training
Tata Institute of Social Sciences (TISS)	Mumbai	MA in Applied Psychology with Specialization in Sports Psychology	Emphasis on applied psychology with sports focus
University of Delhi – Department of Psychology	Delhi	MSc. in Applied Psychology with Sports Specialization	Comprehensive curriculum with sports psychology modules
Manipal Academy of Higher Education (MAHE)	Manipal	MSc. in Clinical Psychology with Sports Psychology Focus	Integrated approach to clinical and sports psychology
Jamia Millia Islamia – Department of Psychology	Delhi	MA in Clinical Psychology with Sports Psychology Electives	Strong focus on clinical and sports psychology
Amity Institute of Psychology and Allied Sciences	Noida	MA in Clinical Psychology with Sports Psychology	Emphasis on clinical and sports psychology
Kolkata Psychological Association (KPA)	Kolkata	Diploma in Sports Psychology	Specialized training in sports psychology
Rishihood University	Sonipat	MA in Sports Psychology	New programme with a focus on contemporary sports psychology practices

1.1.10 Sports Nutritionists

Sports nutritionists specialize in dietary needs and nutritional strategies that enhance athletic performance, support recovery, and improve overall health. They work with athletes and teams to develop tailored nutrition plans that optimize energy levels, muscle recovery, and performance outcomes.

To see **Sports Nutrition** in Action

Scan QR Code

Fig. 1.8 Sports Nutrition

Roles and Responsibilities

(i) Nutrition Planning

- **Customized Diet Plans:** Designing individualized meal plans that meet the specific needs of athletes based on their sport, goals, and dietary preferences.
- **Nutrient Timing:** Advising on optimal timing for nutrient intake to maximize performance and recovery.

(ii) Performance Enhancement

- **Energy Management:** Ensuring that athletes have the right balance of carbohydrates, proteins, and fats to fuel their training and competition.
- **Supplement Guidance:** Providing recommendations on safe and effective use of supplements, if necessary.

(iii) Recovery Support

- **Post-Exercise Nutrition:** Developing strategies for post-exercise nutrition to promote muscle repair and recovery.
- **Hydration Strategies:** Advising on hydration needs and strategies to maintain fluid balance and electrolyte levels.

(iv) Education and Counselling

- **Nutritional Education:** Educating athletes about the importance of nutrition and how it impacts performance and health.
- **Behavioural Counselling:** Helping athletes to develop healthy eating habits and overcome challenges related to diet and nutrition.

Required Skills and Qualities

(i) Nutrition Expertise

- **In-depth knowledge:** Strong understanding of nutrition science, including macronutrients, micronutrients, and metabolism.

(ii) Communication Skills

- **Effective Counselling:** Clear and effective communication skills for providing dietary advice and education to athletes.
- **Interpersonal Skills:** Building rapport with athletes and understanding their individual needs and preferences.

(iii) Analytical Skills

- **Assessment:** Ability to analyse dietary intake, performance data, and body composition.

(iv) Adaptability

- **Customization:** Adapting nutrition plans to fit individual needs, sports demands, and changing conditions.
- **Flexibility:** Adjusting strategies based on new research, feedback, and evolving performance goals.

(v) Ethical Standards

- **Integrity:** Adhering to ethical standards in providing nutrition advice and recommendations.
- **Confidentiality:** Maintaining confidentiality regarding athletes' personal and health information.

Educational Qualifications and Eligibility

(i) Bachelor's Degree

- **Degree in Nutrition, Dietetics, or Related Field:** A bachelor's degree in nutrition, dietetics, or a related field is generally required.

(ii) Master's Degree (Optional but Beneficial)

- **Advanced Studies:** A master's degree in sports nutrition, clinical nutrition, or a related field can enhance career prospects and specialization.

(iii) Certifications

- **Professional Certificates:** Obtaining certificates from recognized organizations can enhance credibility. Examples include:

1. Certified Specialist in Sports Dietetics (CSSD) by the Academy of Nutrition and Dietetics.
2. International Society of Sports Nutrition (ISSN) Certifications.

Institutes for Nutrition in Sports in India

Institute	Location	Courses Offered	Special Features
All India Institute of Medical Sciences (AIIMS)	New Delhi	MSc. in Clinical Nutrition and Dietetics	Renowned institute with focus on clinical and sports nutrition
National Institute of Nutrition (NIN)	Hyderabad	Diploma in Sports Nutrition	Specialized training in sports nutrition
Manipal Academy of Higher Education (MAHE)	Manipal	MSc. in Clinical Nutrition and Dietetics	Comprehensive curriculum with focus on sports and clinical nutrition
Amity Institute of Nutrition and Dietetics	Noida	MSc. in Clinical Nutrition and Dietetics	Focus on practical training and industry connections
K11 School of Fitness Sciences	Mumbai and Delhi	Diploma in Sports Nutrition	Practical and theoretical training in sports nutrition
Symbiosis School of Culinary Arts	Pune	Diploma in Sports Nutrition	Includes culinary skills and nutrition expertise for athletes

1.2 Importance of Sports and Games

Sports and games play a crucial role in personal development, health, and society. They offer a range of benefits that contribute to physical health, mental well-being, and social interactions. Sports and games are integral to a well-rounded and healthy life. They offer numerous physical, mental, social, and economic benefits, enhancing overall well-being and contributing to personal and community development. Participation in sports and games promotes a balanced lifestyle and helps individuals to lead healthier, more fulfilling lives.

1.2.1 Physical Activity

Physical activity is any movement produced by skeletal muscles that results in energy expenditure. This includes all forms of movement, whether incidental or deliberate and contributes to overall health and well-being.

Fig. 1.9 Fitness Activity

Features of Physical Activity

To see
Physical Activity
in Action

Scan QR Code

Broad Scope: Includes all types of movement, ranging from casual to structured.

Intensity Levels: Varies from light (e.g., walking) to vigorous (e.g., running).

Health Benefits: Improves cardiovascular health, muscle strength, flexibility, and overall well-being.

Examples: Walking, gardening, climbing stairs, daily chores.

Types of Physical Activity

- **Lifestyle Activities:** Daily movements such as commuting, cleaning, or shopping.
- **Exercise:** Planned and structured activities aimed at improving or maintaining physical fitness (e.g., gym workouts, jogging).
- **Occupational Physical Activity:** Movement associated with work tasks (e.g., construction work, teaching).

1.2.2 Games

Games are structured activities with specific rules and objectives, usually involving some form of competition or challenge. They can be formal or informal and may or may not involve physical activity.

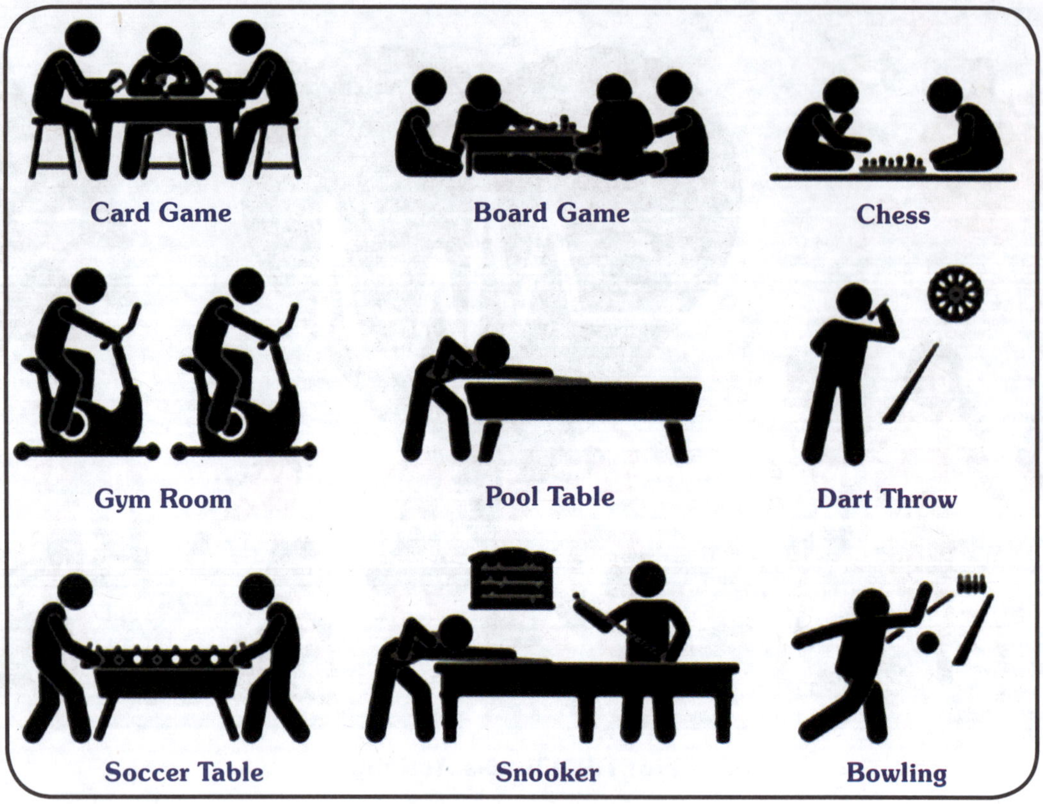

Fig. 1.10 Games

Features of Games

Rules and Objectives: There are defined rules and goals that guide the gameplay.

Variety: Can involve physical activity (e.g., tag) or be non-physical (e.g., chess).

Competitiveness: May be competitive or cooperative.

Examples: Board games, card games, tag, hide and seek.

1.2.3 Sports

Sports are organized, competitive activities with formalized rules, structures, and often professional or amateur leagues. They involve physical exertion and skill.

Features of Sports

Formal Structure: There are established rules, regulations, and often governing bodies.

Competition: Involve competition between individuals or teams.

Skill Development: Require specific training and skill development.

Examples: Soccer, basketball, tennis, swimming.

To see **Recreational Activity** in Action

Scan QR Code

1.2.4 Recreation

Recreation involves activities done for enjoyment, relaxation, and leisure. It encompasses both physical and non-physical activities aimed at enhancing well-being.

Features of Recreation

Leisure-oriented: Pursued primarily for pleasure and relaxation.

Offers Variety: Includes a wide range of activities, both physical and mental.

Promotes Social Interaction: Often involves social interaction and can be done individually or in groups.

Examples: Hiking, playing musical instruments, socializing with friends.

Recreation involves activities done for enjoyment, relaxation, and leisure. It encompasses both physical and non-physical activities aimed at enhancing well-being.

1.3 Importance of Sports in Developing Life Skills

Life skills in sports are crucial for the holistic development of athletes. They encompass a range of competencies that go beyond physical abilities and are essential for success both on and off the field. Here are some key reasons how life skills are developed by sports:

- Sports often require working as part of a team. Learning to cooperate, communicate effectively, and support teammates helps athletes in building strong interpersonal skills.
- Training schedules, practice sessions, and balancing sports with academics or work require discipline and effective time management. These skills are valuable in all areas of life.
- Athletes face setbacks, injuries, and losses. Learning to cope with these challenges builds resilience, teaching them to handle stress and bounce back from adversity.
- Being part of a team or leading it helps athletes in developing leadership skills and a sense of responsibility. They learn to motivate others, make decisions, and take accountability for their actions.
- Setting and working towards goals is a fundamental part of sports. This practice extends to other areas, helping individuals to set, pursue, and achieve personal and professional goals.
- Effective communication with coaches, teammates, and referees is essential in sports. These skills enhance personal and professional relationships.
- Sports teach the importance of playing by the rules, respecting opponents, and practising good sportsmanship. These ethical values are crucial for personal integrity and societal interactions.
- Success in sports builds self-esteem and confidence. These positive self-perceptions contribute to better mental health and overall well-being.
- Participation in sports encourages a healthy lifestyle, including physical fitness, proper nutrition, and avoidance of harmful behaviours.
- Sports often present unexpected challenges that require quick thinking and problem-solving. These cognitive skills are valuable in academic and professional settings.

1.3.1 Sports Help in Dealing with Failure

Sports provide an excellent environment for learning how to deal with failure. This skill is crucial not for athletic success, but for personal and professional resilience as well. Here are some ways in which sports teach individuals to cope with failure:

- In sports, losing is a common experience. Alongside success, athletes regularly face defeat in games, matches, or personal performance goals. This frequency helps to accept failure as a part of the learning process.
- Observing professional athletes handle failure gracefully can provide valuable lessons. Many top athletes have overcome significant setbacks, serving as examples of perseverance.
- Post-game analyses and feedback from coaches help athletes in understanding their mistake and weaknesses. This constructive approach turns failures into learning opportunities.
- By focusing on areas for improvement, athletes learn to see failure as a stepping stone rather than a roadblock.

Fig. 1.11 Success and failure

1.3.2 Importance of Working Hard

Working hard is a fundamental principle that plays a crucial role in achieving success and personal growth in various aspects of life. Working hard is essential for making progress towards goals. Consistent effort and dedication are necessary to reach milestones and achieve desired outcomes. Many successful individuals attribute their achievements to working hard. It is often the difference between mere aspiration and actual accomplishment. Regular effort and practice are key to developing and honing skills. Whether in academics, sports, or professional fields, working hard leads to mastery and competence. Working hard involves persistence, which means learning from mistakes and improving continuously.

Fig. 1.12 Hard work

1.3.3 Sports will Teach you how to be a Team Member

Team members in sports play crucial roles that contribute to the success and overall experience of the game. Team members work together towards common objectives, such as winning games and championships.

They provide emotional and moral support, encouraging each other during difficult times. Effective communication and coordination are essential for executing strategies and plays.

Fig. 1.13 Team game

1.3.4 Learning how to Make Sacrifice

Learning to make sacrifices in sports is a critical aspect of achieving success and personal growth. It involves prioritizing the needs of the team, enduring physical and mental challenges, and sometimes making difficult choices. Making sacrifices in sports is essential for achieving excellence and contributing to the team's success. It builds character, discipline, and a strong work ethic, which are valuable both in sports and in life. Understanding and embracing these sacrifices can lead to personal growth and a deeper appreciation for the sport.

Fig. 1.14 Sacrifices

1.3.5 Learning Discipline

Discipline is a fundamental requirement under rules in sports that influences performance, personal growth, and team dynamics. Learning discipline involves developing self-control, adherence to rules, and a consistent work ethic. One should commit to regular practice sessions, even when it is challenging or inconvenient, and should focus on improving specific skills through repetitive and focused (specific) drills.

Fig. 1.15 Discipline

1.3.6 Time Management

Time management is a crucial skill for athletes and individuals involved in sports. Efficiently managing time helps in balancing training, competitions, personal life, and other responsibilities, and ultimately leads to better performance and overall well-being.

Fig. 1.16 Time management

ACTIVITY

Divide teams in your class to conduct a competition for following sports and observe

(a) Football

(b) Kho-kho

Multiple Choice Questions

1. **What is one of the primary life skills that team sports teach?**
   (a) Selfishness (b) Teamwork
   (c) Isolation (d) Leadership skills
2. **How can participation in sports improve time management skills?**
   (a) By learning to balance practice, games, and personal life
   (b) By focusing only on sports and ignoring other responsibilities
   (c) By practising at one's own convenience
   (d) By skipping practice sessions
3. **Which life skill is developed through regular physical exercise?**
   (a) Procrastination (b) Discipline
   (c) Overeating (d) Time management
4. **How can sports help in developing leadership skills?**
   (a) By avoiding responsibility
   (b By trying to appease everybody
   (c) By leading a team or group and making decisions
   (d) By focusing only on team dynamics
5. **Which life skill is enhanced by handling wins and losses in sports?**
   (a) Entitlement (b) Resilience
   (c) Avoidance (d) Fear
6. **What can be learned about communication through participating in sports?**
   (a) The importance of shouting instructions
   (b) The necessity of clear and effective communication with teammates and coaches
   (c) The value of ignoring feedback
   (d) The benefits of staying silent during play
7. **Why is goal setting an important life skill learned from sports?**
   (a) It helps in setting toughest expectations
   (b) It leads to constant disappointment
   (c) It encourages planning, perseverance, and achieving targets
   (d) It makes one dependent on others

8. **Which skill is developed when athletes learn to respect rules and officials?**
   (a) Leadership (b) Sportsmanship
   (c) Teamwork (d) Strategy

9. **How does participation in sports foster social skills?**
   (a) By isolating individuals from social interactions
   (b) By including antisocial elements
   (c) By creating opportunities to interact, build friendships, and work within a team
   (d) By focusing only on individual achievements

10. **What personal attribute is commonly developed through overcoming challenges in sports?**
    (a) Passivity (b) Low self-esteem
    (c) Confidence and self-efficacy (d) Indifference

11. **Why are sports skills important for personal development?**
    (a) They lead to physical laziness.
    (b) They foster discipline, teamwork, and goal setting.
    (c) They promote avoiding social interactions.
    (d) They encourage unhealthy habits.

12. **Which of the following is a potential career opportunity in sports?**
    (a) Sports journalist (b) Sports scientist
    (c) Sports coach (d) All the above

13. **How can sports skills contribute to mental health?**
    (a) By increasing stress levels
    (b) By promoting anxiety
    (c) By improving mood and reducing anxiety
    (d) By causing depression

14. **What role does sportsmanship play in career opportunities in sports?**
    (a) It is irrelevant to career success
    (b) It enhances reputation and professional relationships
    (c) It promotes cheating and dishonesty
    (d) It discourages fair play

15. **Which career in sports involves providing medical care to athletes?**
    (a) Sports agent (b) Sports physiotherapist
    (c) Sports journalist (d) Sports psychologist

16. Why is teamwork considered a crucial skill in sports?

(a) It leads to constant conflicts.

(b) It promotes individual glory over team success.

(c) It encourages cooperation and collective effort towards a common goal.

(d) It focuses exclusively on communication among players.

17. Which degree is often pursued for a career in sports management?

(a) Bachelor of Arts in machoism

(b) Bachelor of Science in biology

(c) Master of Business Administration (MBA) in Sports Management

(d) Bachelor of Fine Arts

18. What is one key benefit of developing strategic thinking through sports?

(a) It encourages impulsive decisions.

(b) It promotes short-term thinking.

(c) It enhances problem-solving and planning skills.

(d) It leads to overconfidence.

19. Which of the following careers involves analysing athlete's performance and creating training programmes?

(a) Sports agent

(b) Sports analyst

(c) Sports coach

(d) Sports commentator

20. Why is physical fitness important for career opportunities in sports?

(a) It has no impact on career opportunities.

(b) It is required for peak performance and endurance in various sports roles.

(c) It develops the ability to play sports.

(d) It is only necessary for non-sports-related careers.

ANSWERS

1. (b)	**2.** (b)	**3.** (b)	**4.** (c)	**5.** (b)
6. (b)	**7.** (c)	**8.** (c)	**9.** (c)	**10.** (c)
11. (b)	**12.** (d)	**13.** (c)	**14.** (b)	**15.** (b)
16. (c)	**17.** (c)	**18.** (c)	**19.** (c)	**20.** (b)

Long Questions

1. Write all the career options in physical education.
2. Write the roles and responsibilities of a coach.
3. What is the difference between physical activity, games, sports, and recreational activity?
4. Discuss the importance of sports in developing life skills.

UNIT 2

ASSESSMENT OF STUDENTS

- Meaning of Assessment
- Types of Assessment
- Factors that Influence Assessment
- Rubrics
- Benchmark
- Evaluation

2.1 Meaning of Assessment

Assessment is a fundamental aspect of the learning process. Traditionally, its primary aim has been to gauge and report on the knowledge acquired by students.

To see **Assessment** in Action

Scan QR Code

All actions that provide information about students' development and support modifications to teaching and learning strategies are included in assessment. This includes teacher's observation and analysis of the students' work such as homework, tests, essays, reports, practical procedures, and classroom discussions. Students dedicate a significant proportion of their time in school practising the knowledge and skills assessed, ultimately shaping what they acquire. To assess the impact of any innovation on student learning, it is essential for teachers to meticulously plan and execute a comprehensive assessment programme.

Without a clear plan, assessments may become disjointed and lack coherence. Therefore, having a structured approach that integrates all assessment components and provides a holistic view of students' performance is essential. Evaluating how thoroughly students have learned involves assessing their performance against some pre-determined criteria.

2.2 Types of Assessment

2.2.1 Formative Assessment

Formative assessment is an ongoing process used by teachers to evaluate students' understanding, learning needs, and academic progress during a lesson, unit, or course. The primary goal of formative assessment is to provide continuous feedback that can be used by instructors to improve their teaching, and by students to improve their learning.

- **Ongoing Process:** Unlike summative assessments, which are typically administered at the end of a course or unit, formative assessments occur throughout the learning process.
- **Feedback-oriented:** The focus is on providing specific and constructive feedback to students to help them to understand their strengths and areas for improvement.
- **Informal and Flexible:** These assessments are often less formal than summative assessments and can take many different forms, tailored to the needs of the students and the teaching context.
- **Student-centred:** Formative assessment encourages self-assessment and active participation of students, fostering a deeper engagement with the learning material.

Observations

- Teachers observe students during classroom activities to gauge understanding and engagement.
- Notes are taken on students' behaviour, participation, and interactions.

Class Discussions

- Structured or unstructured discussions encourage students to express their understanding of the material.
- Teachers can ask probing questions to elicit deeper responses and clarify misunderstandings.

In-Class Quizzes and Polls

- Short, low-stake quizzes help in assessing students' grasp of the material covered.
- Polling tools can quickly gauge class-wide understanding and provide instant feedback.

Homework Assignments

- Regular tasks for homework give students the opportunity to practise new skills and concepts.
- Teachers can review and provide feedback on these assignments to guide student improvement.

Fig. 2.1 Assignment

2.2.2 Summative Assessment

Summative assessment evaluates students' learning, knowledge, proficiency, or success at the conclusion of an instructional period. This type of assessment is typically more formal and structured than formative assessments and is often used for the purpose of assigning grades or evaluating overall achievement.

End-of-period Evaluation: Summative assessments are conducted at the end of a unit, course, semester, or school year.

Formal and Structured: These assessments are typically standardized and follow a specific format.

High Stakes: Summative assessments often have significant consequences, such as determining final grades, advancement to the next grade level, or eligibility for certain programmes.

Comprehensive: They cover a broad range of contents and skills learned over a specific period.

Comparative: Summative assessments often compare students' performance against predefined standards or benchmarks.

Methods of Summative Assessment

(i) Final Exams

- Comprehensive exams that cover all material taught in a course.
- Can include multiple-choice questions, essays, short answers, and problem-solving tasks.

(ii) Standardized Tests

- Exams are administered and scored in a consistent manner across different schools or districts.
- Examples include SAT, ACT, GRE, and state achievement tests.

(iii) End-of-term Projects

- Long-term projects that students work on throughout a unit or course.
- Can include research papers, presentations, portfolios, or creative work.

(iv) Cumulative Assignments

- Assignments that require students to synthesize and apply what they have learned over a period.
- Examples include capstone projects, theses, and comprehensive case studies.

(v) Performance Assessments

- Tasks that require students to demonstrate their knowledge and skills in practical or real-world contexts.
- Examples include performances, exhibitions, and practical exams in fields like music, art, and physical education.

(vi) Oral Examinations

- Verbal assessments where students answer questions or discuss topics with an examiner.
- Common in language courses, graduate programmes, and certain professional fields

Fig. 2.2 Verbal Assessment

2.2.3 Criterion-Referenced Assessment

Criterion-referenced assessment is a type of evaluation designed to measure students' performance against a fixed set of predetermined criteria or learning standards. Unlike norm-referenced assessments, which compare a student's performance to that of a peer group, criterion-referenced assessments focus on whether each student has achieved specific learning objectives or skills.

(a) Standardized Tests Aligned with Learning Standards

- Tests designed to measure students' performance against state or national educational standards.
- Examples include state achievement tests and common core assessments.

(b) Rubrics

- Detailed scoring guides that describe the criteria for different levels of performance on an assignment or task.
- Evaluate essays, projects, presentations, and other complex tasks.

(c) Unit, or Chapter, Tests

- Tests administered at the end of a unit or chapter that assess students' understanding of the specific content covered.
- Questions are directly aligned with the learning objectives of the unit.

(d) Performance Tasks

- Real-world tasks that require students to apply their knowledge and skills.
- Examples include science experiments, research projects, and oral presentations.

(e) Checklists

- Lists of specific criteria that students must meet to demonstrate proficiency in a skill or knowledge area.
- Often used for skills' assessments in areas like writing, maths, and technical subjects.

(f) Benchmark Assessments

- Periodic assessments throughout the school year that measure students' progress toward meeting standards.
- Used to identify areas where students need additional instruction or support.

Examples of Criterion-referenced Test

(i) **Writing assignments with rubrics:** Essays or research papers evaluated using a rubric that outlines criteria such as clarity of thesis, argument development, and grammar.

(ii) **Maths skill tests:** Tests that measure specific mathematical skills, such as solving quadratic equations or performing geometric constructions, based on curriculum standards.

(iii) **Science lab reports:** Reports evaluated using criteria such as hypothesis formulation, experimental procedure, data analysis, and conclusion.

(iv) **Language proficiency tests:** Assessments that measure language skills like reading comprehension, writing, speaking, and listening, based on language proficiency standards.

(v) **Performance-based assessments:** Tasks like oral presentations, debates, or musical performances evaluated against specific criteria related to content, delivery, and technique.

2.2.4 Performance-Based Assessment

Performance-based assessment in sports and games focuses on evaluating athletes' skills, strategies, physical fitness, and overall performance during training and competition. This type of assessment is particularly effective in sports because it measures practical abilities and real-world applications of skills.

Features of Performance-based Assessment

(a) **Skill demonstration:** Athletes demonstrate specific skills and techniques relevant to their sport.

(b) **Game situations:** Assessments are often conducted in real or simulated game situations.

(c) **Physical fitness:** Evaluates athletes' physical condition, including strength, endurance, speed, and agility.

(d) **Tactical understanding:** Assesses knowledge and application of game strategies and tactics.

(e) **Holistic evaluation:** Looks at both the process (e.g., techniques and decision-making) and the outcome (e.g., performance results).

Methods of Performance-based Assessment

(i) Skill Drills and Tests

- Specific exercises designed to evaluate fundamental skills.
- *Examples:* Shooting accuracy in basketball, dribbling drills in soccer, serving accuracy in tennis.

(ii) Game Play Analysis

- Observation and analysis of performance during actual games or scrimmages.
- *Examples:* Reviewing game footage to assess positioning, decision-making, and teamwork.

(iii) Fitness Testing

- Standardized tests to measure physical fitness components.
- Examples: A 40-yard dash for speed, vertical jump for power, beep test for cardiovascular endurance.

(iv) Performance Metrics

- Quantitative measures of performance.
- *Examples:* Points scored, assists, defensive stops, and turnovers in basketball.

(v) Tactical Assessments

- Evaluation of an athlete's understanding and execution of game strategies.
- *Examples:* Understanding formations in football, executing plays in basketball, or strategy in a chess match.

(vi) Simulated Competitions

- Simulated game situations to assess performance under controlled conditions.
- *Examples:* Practice matches, scrimmages, or situational drills.

(vii) Video Analysis

- Using video recordings to analyse technique and performance.
- *Examples:* Slow-motion review of a golfer's swing, analysing a swimmer's stroke mechanics.

2.2.5 Self-Assessment

Self-assessment is a process where students evaluate their own work and learning progress. It encourages reflection on personal strengths, areas for improvement, and goal setting, fostering independence and self-regulation in learning.

Methods of Self-Assessment

(a) Checklists and Rubrics

- Students use checklists or rubrics to assess their own work against predefined criteria.
- *Examples:* A rubric for evaluating an essay or project, a checklist for completed homework assignments.

(b) Portfolios

- Students compile a portfolio of their work over time, reflecting on their progress and areas needing improvement.
- *Examples:* Art portfolios, writing portfolios, science experiment logs.

(c) Self-Assessment Forms

- Structured forms where students rate their performance on various aspects of a task or project.
- *Examples:* Rating their understanding of a topic, evaluating their participation in a group project.

(d) Peer Reviews

- Students assess each other's work and provide feedback, often reflecting on their own work in the process.
- *Examples:* Peer feedback on presentations, group projects, or written assignments.

(e) Goal Setting and Reflection

- Students set learning goals and regularly reflect on their progress toward achieving those goals.
- *Examples:* Goal-setting worksheets, progress tracking charts.

Peer Assessment

Peer assessment is a learning activity where students evaluate each other's work based on given criteria. Instead of only the teacher grading the work, classmates give feedback, grades, or comments to help each other improve.

Methods of Peer Assessment

There are several ways to carry out peer assessment, depending on the type of task and the learning goals.

1. **Rating Scales or Rubrics:** One of the most common methods is using a rubric or checklist. Teachers provide specific criteria (like clarity, accuracy, creativity, etc.), and students use these to score or rate their peers' work. This helps keep the feedback fair and focused.
2. **Written Feedback:** In this method, students write comments on their peer's work, pointing out what was done well and what could be improved. This helps both the giver and receiver reflect on the learning process.
3. **Oral Feedback:** Sometimes peer assessment is done through discussion. Students present their work and then receive spoken feedback from classmates. This is common in group projects, speeches, or class discussions.
4. **Peer Review:** Especially used in writing or research projects, this involves students reviewing each other's drafts before submission. They give feedback on content, grammar, structure, or arguments, which helps improve the final version.
5. **Questionnaires or Evaluation Forms:** Teachers can prepare forms with specific questions to guide student feedback. These can include both open-ended questions and multiple choice responses.
6. **Group Assessment:** In group work, each member may assess the performance and contribution of the other members. This ensures fairness and accountability in team-based projects.
7. **Performance-Based Feedback:** In activities like sports, drama, or presentations, students observe their peers and provide feedback on their performance, often using structured guidelines.

Teacher Observation

Teacher observation is a method used by educators to monitor and assess student behavior, participation, skills, and learning progress during class activities. It allows the teacher to gather information about how students are engaging, interacting, and developing in real-time. Observations can be formal or informal, and they help teachers make better instructional decisions, provide support, and adjust teaching strategies as needed.

Methods of Teacher Observation

1. **Anecdotal Records:** Teachers write short, descriptive notes about specific events or behaviors observed in class. These are useful for tracking progress over time or noting unusual behavior.
2. **Checklist:** Teachers prepare a list of behaviors, skills, or learning goals and tick off when a student demonstrates them. This method is quick and effective for large groups.
3. **Rating Scales:** Teachers rate students' performance or behavior on a scale (e.g., from 1 to 5) based on criteria like participation, cooperation, or understanding.
4. **Event Sampling:** This method focuses on observing a particular behavior or event whenever it occurs. It's useful for identifying patterns in specific actions, like how often a student asks questions or interrupts.
5. **Time Sampling:** In this method, the teacher observes students at regular time intervals (e.g., every 5 minutes) to note what they are doing. It's great for tracking attention span and engagement.
6. **Narrative Observation:** A more detailed form of note-taking where the teacher writes a continuous description of what the student is doing over a set period. This method captures more context but takes longer.
7. **Video or Audio Recording:** Sometimes teachers use recordings to analyze student behavior or classroom interactions later. This is helpful for reviewing and reflecting without missing real-time events.

Homework

Homework assessment is the process of evaluating students' homework to check their understanding, effort, accuracy, and learning progress outside the classroom. It helps teachers determine how well students have grasped the topic and whether any concepts need to be revisited.

Methods of Homework Assessment

1. **Teacher Review:** The teacher checks each student's homework for correctness, completeness, and presentation. Feedback may be written or oral.
2. **Grading or Scoring:** Homework is given marks or grades based on set criteria such as accuracy, creativity, neatness, and effort.
3. **Peer Assessment:** Sometimes, students review and provide feedback on each other's homework. This encourages critical thinking and collaboration.
4. **Self-Assessment:** Students reflect on their own work using a checklist or rubric, helping them become more independent learners.
5. **Oral Review in Class:** Homework is discussed or solved in class, allowing students to compare their answers and understand mistakes.
6. **Spot Checking:** The teacher checks only a few parts of the homework or randomly selects students' work to assess. This saves time while keeping students accountable.
7. **Homework Quizzes:** Based on homework content, the teacher may give a short quiz to check understanding without collecting the actual homework.

2.2.6 Formal Assessment

Formal assessment refers to structured methods of evaluating students' learning, typically involving standardized procedures and tools. These assessments are planned and implemented systematically to provide reliable and valid measures of students' knowledge, skills, and abilities.

Features of Formal Assessment

Standardized Procedures: Follows consistent methods and conditions for administration and scoring.

Objective Measurement: It is designed to minimize subjectivity in evaluation.

Predefined Criteria: Uses specific criteria or rubrics to evaluate performance.

Data Collection: Collects data systematically to ensure comparability and reliability.

Summative and Formative: Can be used for both summative (end-of-term) and formative (ongoing) purposes.

Methods of Standardized Test

(a) Standardized Tests

- Tests that are administered and scored in a consistent manner across different settings.
- *Examples:* SAT, ACT, GRE, state achievement tests.

(b) Exams and Quizzes

- Structured tests administered at specific points in a course or programme.
- *Examples:* Mid-term exams, final exams, chapter quizzes.

(c) Diagnostic Tests

- Assessments designed to identify students' strengths and weaknesses at the beginning of a course or unit.
- *Examples:* Pre-tests, entry-level assessments.

(d) End-of-Term Projects

- Comprehensive assignments completed at the end of a course or unit to demonstrate understanding and application of the material.
- *Examples:* Capstone projects, final research papers.

(e) Performance Assessments

- Assessments where students perform tasks that demonstrate their knowledge and skills.
- *Examples:* Practical exams in science laboratories, performance tasks in the arts.

(f) Formal Portfolios

- Collections of students' work that are evaluated according to predetermined criteria.
- *Examples:* Portfolios for writing, art, or digital media projects.

(g) State and National Assessments

- Large-scale assessments mandated by educational authorities to measure students' achievement across a wide population.
- *Examples:* National Assessment of Educational Progress (NAEP), state-wide standardized tests.

2.2.7 Informal Assessment

Informal assessment refers to the ongoing, flexible methods used by educators to gauge students' learning and understanding in a less structured way compared to formal assessments. These assessments often occur during regular classroom activities and provide immediate feedback that can guide instruction and support students' development.

1. Features of Informal Assessment

Flexible and Spontaneous: Conducted in a variety of settings and moments, often spontaneously during instruction.

Qualitative Data: Provides qualitative insights into students' understanding and progress.

Embedded in Learning: Integrated into everyday classroom activities rather than being separate, formal events.

Immediate Feedback: Allows for quick adjustments to teaching based on students' responses and needs.

2. Methods of Informal Assessment

(a) Observations

- Teachers observe students during class activities, noting behaviours, interactions and performance.
- *Examples:* Monitoring group work, observing students' participation, and noting their problem-solving approaches.

(b) Questioning

- Asking questions during lessons to assess that students are understanding, and to encourage critical thinking.
- *Examples:* Open-ended questions, quick checks for understanding, and Socratic questioning.

(c) Exit Tickets

- Short, written responses from students at the end of a lesson to assess their understanding of the day's content.
- *Examples:* Brief answers to questions or a quick summary of what has been learnt.

(d) Classroom Discussions

- Engaging students in discussions to gauge their comprehension and ability to articulate their thoughts.

- *Examples:* Think-pair-share, group discussions, and whole-class conversations.

(e) Peer Assessments

- Students assess each other's work and provide feedback, promoting collaborative learning and self-evaluation.
- *Examples:* Peer reviews, group feedback sessions, and collaborative projects.

(f) Self-Assessments

- Students evaluate their own work and learning progress, fostering self-awareness and responsibility.
- *Examples:* Self-reflection journals, checklists, and goal-setting activities.

(g) Anecdotal Records

- Teachers keep informal notes on individual student's progress and observations during class activities.
- *Examples:* Noting instances of significant achievement, behavioural changes, or learning challenges.

(h) Journals and Learning Logs

- Students maintain journals or logs to record their learning experiences, reflections, and questions.
- *Examples:* Reflective writing about a lesson, recording insights from a project, or tracking progress on learning goals.

(i) Interactive Activities

- Engaging activities that allow teachers to assess students' understanding and skills in a dynamic context.
- *Examples:* Educational games, role-playing exercises, and simulations.

2.3 Factors That Influence Assessment

Several factors can influence the assessment process, impacting its fairness, accuracy, and effectiveness.

2.3.1 Student-related Factors

- Students with a strong foundation in the subject matter are likely to perform better.
- Proficiency in specific skills relevant to the assessment (e.g., reading comprehension, mathematical problem-solving) can impact performance.
- Students who are intrinsically motivated are more likely to put effort into assessments.
- External rewards or pressures, such as grades or parental expectations, can also influence performance.

- Students may perform better on assessments that align with their preferred learning styles (e.g., visual, auditory, kinesthetic).
- Students who can adapt to various assessment formats tend to perform better overall.
- Students with physical, cognitive, or emotional disabilities may require accommodations to perform at their best.
- Tailored assessment strategies to meet special educational needs of students can improve performance.
- Chronic illnesses, fatigue, and other health issues can affect concentration and performance.
- Emotional stability and mental health play a crucial role in students' ability to perform well in assessments.

2.3.2 Physical Factors

Physical factors can have a significant impact on the assessment process, affecting students' ability to perform to the best of their abilities.

- Students with chronic health conditions may experience fatigue, pain, or other symptoms that can hinder their performance.
- Temporary illnesses, such as cold or flu, can also affect concentration and cognitive function.
- Students with mobility impairments may require special accommodations to access assessment locations and materials.
- Students with visual or hearing impairments may need adapted assessments, such as braille, large print, or sign language interpreters.
- Adequate and restful sleep is critical for cognitive function, memory, and concentration. Sleep deprivation can severely impact performance.
- Over-exertion from physical activities or other commitments can lead to fatigue, reducing cognitive performance during assessments.
- Students with disabilities may require assistive technologies, such as screen readers, speech-to-text software, or adaptive keyboards, to effectively participate in assessments.
- The assessment venue should be accessible to all students, including those with mobility challenges.
- Ensuring students that they have access to water during assessments can help to maintain hydration, which is important for cognitive function and overall well-being.

Checklist for General Health Condition

Health Aspect	Criteria	Yes/No
Physical Health		
Chronic illnesses	Does the student have any chronic illnesses?	Yes / No
Acute illnesses	Is the student experiencing any temporary illnesses?	Yes / No
Nutrition	Did the student have a nutritious meal?	Yes / No
Hydration	Did the student have enough water?	Yes / No
Sensory Health		
Vision	Does the student have any vision impairments?	Yes / No
Hearing	Does the student have any hearing impairments?	Yes / No
Mental Health		
Stress levels	Is the student experiencing high levels of stress?	Yes / No
Anxiety	Is the student experiencing anxiety?	Yes / No
Fatigue	Is the student feeling overly tired or fatigued?	Yes / No
Sleep and Rest		
Sleep quality	Did the student have sufficient and restful sleep?	Yes / No
Rest breaks	Has the student taken necessary rest breaks?	Yes / No
Physical Comfort		
Comfort of seating	Is the seating comfortable and ergonomic?	Yes / No
Temperature	Is the room temperature comfortable?	Yes / No
Lighting	Is the lighting adequate for reading and writing?	Yes / No
Noise levels	Is the environment quiet and free from distractions?	Yes / No
Medical Needs		
Medication	Does the student have access to necessary medications?	Yes / No
Medical support	Is medical support available if needed?	Yes / No
Accessibility		
Assistive devices	Are necessary assistive devices available and functioning?	Yes / No
Physical accessibility	Is the venue physically accessible for all students?	Yes / No

2.3.3 School Factor

The evaluation is affected by various school-related factors. Understanding the mental, psychological, and physical challenges of the child is essential. The checklist below can be used as a guide for this purpose.

School Assessment Checklist

School Factor	Criteria	Yes/No
Curriculum and Instruction		
Alignment with standards	Is the curriculum aligned with assessment standards?	Yes / No
Instructional quality	Are teaching methods effective and high-quality?	Yes / No
Instructional resources	Are textbooks and learning materials readily available?	Yes / No
School Policies and Practices		
Assessment Policies	Are assessment policies clear and consistent?	Yes / No
Grading Policies	Are grading policies fair and transparent?	Yes / No
Academic Support	Is tutoring and counselling support available?	Yes / No
Teacher Expertise and Development		
Teacher Training	Are teachers put through regular professional development programmes?	Yes / No
Teacher Experience	Do teachers have adequate experience in assessment design?	Yes / No
School Environment		
Classroom Environment	Is the classroom environment positive and supportive?	Yes / No
School Climate	Is the school climate safe and inclusive?	Yes / No
Class Size and Composition		
Class Size	Are class sizes manageable to allow individual attention?	Yes / No
Student Diversity	Are assessments inclusive of diverse student needs?	Yes / No
Technology and Infrastructure		
Access to Technology	Do students have access to necessary technology?	Yes / No
Technical Support	Is technical support available for technology-based assessments?	Yes / No
Parental and Community Involvement		
Scheduling and Timing		
Assessment Timing	Are assessments scheduled at optimal times?	Yes / No
Frequency of Assessments	Is the frequency of assessments appropriate?	Yes / No
Extracurricular Activities		
Balance	Are academic and extracurricular activities balanced?	Yes / No
Support for Extracurriculars	Does the school support a range of extracurricular activities?	Yes / No

2.3.4 Teacher Factor

Every teacher has a unique teaching style, building upon the same foundation of education but employing different tools. Their choice of language, management skills, and interaction with students all have an impact on assessments. Furthermore, the teacher's physical and mental state, their knowledge of the test materials, and their familiarity with the testing environment also influence assessments.

Assessment Tools

Assessment tools are the instruments used to measure and evaluate students' learning, skills, understanding, and performance. Various types of assessment tools can be used, depending on the learning objectives and context.

Creating a comprehensive checklist for assessments that cover pre-assessment, during-assessment, and post-assessment phases ensures a structured and effective evaluation process.

Pre-Assessment Checklist

Pre-Assessment Task	Description	Completed
Define Objectives	Clearly define the learning objectives and outcomes to be assessed.	Yes / No
Select Appropriate Assessment Tools	Choose the right tools and methods to assess the objectives (e.g., tests, projects).	Yes / No
Create Assessment Plan	Develop a detailed plan including timeline, materials needed, and procedures.	Yes / No
Communicate with Stakeholders	Inform students, parents, and other stakeholders about the assessment details.	Yes / No
Prepare Assessment Materials	Ensure that all necessary materials and resources are ready (e.g., test papers, equipment).	Yes / No
Train Assessors	Provide training to teachers or assessors on administering the assessment.	Yes / No
Pilot Testing	Conduct a pilot test to check the assessment's validity and reliability.	Yes / No
Set Up Environment	Arrange the physical or virtual environment to be conducive for assessment.	Yes / No

During-Assessment Checklist

During-Assessment Task	Description	Completed
Adhere to Schedule	Start and finish the assessment as per the planned schedule.	Yes / No
Provide Clear Instructions	Give clear, concise instructions to students about the assessment.	Yes / No
Monitor Environment	Ensure a quiet, distraction-free environment for students to work.	Yes / No
Assist Students as Needed	Be available to clarify any doubts or issues which students might have during the assessment.	Yes / No
Ensure Fairness	Monitor to prevent cheating and ensure that all students are treated equally.	Yes / No

Contd...

Document Any Issues	Keep a record of any issues or irregularities that occur during the assessment.	Yes / No
Collect Materials	Gather all assessment materials and ensure that nothing is lost or left behind.	Yes / No

Post-Assessment Checklist

Post-Assessment Task	Description	Completed
Grade Assessments	Evaluate the assessments according to pre-defined criteria and rubrics.	Yes / No
Analyse Results	Analyse the assessment data to identify trends, strengths, and areas for improvement.	Yes / No
Provide Feedback	Give timely and constructive feedback to students.	Yes / No
Reflect on Assessment Process	Review the assessment process to identify what worked well and what could be improved.	Yes / No
Report Results	Communicate the results to students, parents, and other stakeholders.	Yes / No
Adjust Instruction	Use assessment results to inform and adjust future teaching strategies.	Yes / No
Record Keeping	Document and store assessment results and related materials securely.	Yes / No

2.4 RUBRICS

Rubrics are scoring guides used to evaluate the quality of students' constructed responses. They typically consist of criteria that describe what is expected in each category and the different levels of performance for each criterion. Rubrics provide detailed feedback and ensure consistent and objective assessment.

2.4.1 TYPES OF RUBRICS

(i) Analytic Rubrics

Analytic rubrics break down the assessment criteria into multiple components, each with its own scale. This type allows for detailed feedback on each aspect of the students' performance.

Example

Criteria	Excellent (4)	Good (3)	Fair (2)	Poor (1)
Dribbling	Controls the ball exceptionally well at various speeds.	Controls the ball well but with occasional mistakes.	Has basic control but struggles at higher speeds.	Frequently loses control of the ball.
Shooting	Consistently makes shots with proper technique.	Makes most shots with proper technique.	Makes some shots but with inconsistent technique.	Rarely makes shots and has poor technique.
Passing	Passes accurately and quickly under pressure.	Passes accurately most of the time.	Passes are sometimes inaccurate or slow.	Frequently inaccurate or weak passes.

Contd...

Defence	Maintains strong defensive position and anticipation.	Generally maintains good defence but occasionally lapses.	Sometimes maintains position but often out of place.	Frequently out of position and poor anticipation.

(ii) Holistic Rubrics

Holistic rubrics provide a single score based on an overall impression of a student's performance, combining various criteria into a general assessment.

Score	Description
4	Demonstrates outstanding skill, knowledge, and sportsmanship. Consistently performs at a high level with excellent technique and effort. Engages fully and positively.
3	Shows good skill, knowledge, and sportsmanship. Performs well most of the time with good technique and effort. Participates positively.
2	Shows basic skill and knowledge with acceptable sportsmanship. Performs inconsistently with effort. Participation is adequate but lacks enthusiasm.
1	Lacks skill, knowledge, and sportsmanship. Struggles to perform. Has poor technique and effort. Minimal participation.

(iii) Performance-Based Rubrics

Performance-based rubrics assess students on specific tasks or performances, such as executing a dance routine or completing a fitness test.

Criteria	Excellent (4)	Good (3)	Fair (2)	Poor (1)
Choreography	Executes choreography with precision and creativity.	Executes choreography well but with minor errors.	Executes basic choreography with noticeable errors.	Struggles to execute choreography and lacks creativity.
Rhythm and Timing	Moves are perfectly in sync with the music.	Moves are mostly in sync with the music.	Moves are occasionally out of sync with the music.	Moves are frequently out of sync with the music.
Energy and Expression	Shows high energy and expressive movements.	Shows good energy and expression.	Shows basic energy and minimal expression.	Lacks energy and expression.
Team Coordination	Works seamlessly with team members.	Works well with team members with minor lapses.	Works with team members but has coordination issues.	Struggles to coordinate with team members.

2.5 Benchmark

Just like we need a rubric to evaluate the skill of the student, in the same way to evaluate the performance of the student we need a certain benchmark. There are different benchmarks for different tests. And based on these benchmarks the student gets grades.

Every student has their own capacity and strength, which can increase with the help of regular fitness activities, and decrease with irregular or less physical **Types of Benchmarks in Physical**

Education

1. **Benchmarks of Performance:** Specific targets for physical performance, such as running a certain distance within a time limit or achieving a specific score on a fitness test.
2. **Benchmarks of Skill:** Standards for the proficiency of specific skills, like dribbling a basketball, performing a gymnastics routine, or swimming a particular stroke.
3. **Benchmarks of Behaviour:** Expectations related to students' behaviour, participation, effort, and sportsmanship in PE activities.
4. **Benchmarks of Development:** Milestones that indicate typical physical and motor skill development for different age groups.

Example of a Benchmark Rubric for a Fitness Test

Fitness Component	Benchmark	Exceeds Benchmark (4)	Meets Benchmark (3)	Approaching Benchmark (2)	Below Benchmark (1)
Cardiovascular Endurance	To run 1 mile in less than 8 minutes (boys) / 10 minutes (girls)	Runs 1 mile in less than 7 minutes (boys) / 9 minutes (girls)	Runs 1 mile in less than 8 minutes (boys) / 10 minutes (girls)	Runs 1 mile in 8-9 minutes (boys) / 10-11 minutes (girls)	Runs 1 mile in more than 9 minutes (boys) / 11 minutes (girls)
Muscular Strength	To perform 20 push-ups in one minute	Performs more than 25 push-ups	Performs 20-25 push-ups	Performs 15-19 push-ups	Performs less than 15 push-ups
Flexibility	To reach at least 12 inches on the sit-and-reach test	Reaches 14 inches or more	Reaches 12-13 inches	Reaches 10-11 inches	Reaches less than 10 inches
Muscular Endurance	To complete 30 sit-ups in one minute	Completes more than 35 sit-ups	Completes 30-35 sit-ups	Completes 25-29 sit-ups	Completes less than 25 sit-ups

Example of a Benchmark Rubric for a Fitness Test

2.6 Evaluation

Evaluation in Physical Education (PE) and Sports Sciences is the process of assessing students' performance, skills, knowledge, and attitudes to determine their progress, identify areas for improvement, and provide feedback. Effective evaluation helps educators to tailor instruction, enhance student learning, and promote physical development and lifelong fitness habits.

Types of Evaluation in Physical Education

Evaluation is of many types, namely, formative, summative, diagnostic.

(a) Formative Evaluation

Formative evaluation in Physical Education (PE) is a continuous process of assessing students' learning and progress during instruction. This type of evaluation is designed to provide ongoing feedback to both teachers and students, allowing for adjustments in teaching strategies and learning activities to enhance students' performance and understanding.

Methods of Formative Evaluation

Observations: Regularly observing students during activities to assess their skills, effort, and behaviour.

Skill Checks: Brief assessments of specific skills, such as dribbling, shooting, or passing in basketball.

Fitness Logs: Students to keep logs of their physical activity and fitness progress.

Questioning: Asking questions to gauge students' understanding of rules, strategies, and fitness concepts.

Peer- and Self-Assessment: Encouraging students to assess their own and their peers' performance.

Exit Tickets: Ask students to write brief reflections or answers to questions at the end of a class.

Performance Tasks: Assigning short tasks or activities that require students to demonstrate specific skills or knowledge.

Checklists and Rating Scales: Using tools to systematically assess students' performance on various criteria.

Fig. 2.3 Formative Evaluation

Example of Formative Evaluation (Basketball)

Skill	Criteria	Yes	No
Dribbling	Maintains control while dribbling		
Shooting	Uses proper shooting technique		
Passing	Passes accurately to teammates		
Defence	Maintains defensive position		
Teamwork	Communicates effectively with teammates		

Example of Evaluation for Fitness Progress

Activity	Goal	Current Performance	Progress Notes
Running	Run 1 mile	Takes 9 minutes	Improved from 10 minutes last month
Push-ups	20 push-ups	Does 15 push-ups	Working on upper body strength
Sit-ups	30 sit-ups	Does 25 sit-ups	Improved core strength, aim for 30 next week
Flexibility	Touch toes	Can reach 2 inches from toes	Stretching daily, getting closer to goal

Fig. 2.4 Fitness Evaluation

(b) Summative Evaluation

This is done at the end of a unit, term, or course to evaluate students' learning and achievement.

Summative evaluation in Physical Education (PE) is conducted at the end of an instructional period to assess the students' overall learning, achievement, and performance. This type of evaluation aims to measure how well the students have met the learning objectives and standards set for the course or unit. Summative evaluations provide a comprehensive overview of the students' progress and are often used for grading and reporting purposes.

Methods of Summative Evaluation

Performance Tests: Assess students' abilities to perform specific physical tasks or skills.

Written Exams: Evaluate students' knowledge of rules, strategies, health, and fitness concepts.

Final Projects: Require students to demonstrate their learning through comprehensive projects or presentations.

Fitness Assessments: Measure components of physical fitness, such as endurance, strength, flexibility, and body composition.

Skill Demonstrations: Students perform specific skills or routines to show their proficiency.

Portfolios: Collections of students' work over the course of the term that demonstrate learning and progress.

Examples of Summative Evaluation Techniques

Fig. 2.5 Summative Evaluation

Performance Test in Football

Skill	Excellent (4)	Good (3)	Fair (2)	Poor (1)
Dribbling	Controls the ball exceptionally well at all speeds	Controls the ball well with occasional mistakes	Has basic control but struggles at higher speeds	Frequently loses control of the ball
Shooting	Consistently makes accurate shots with proper technique	Makes most shots with good technique	Inconsistent accuracy and technique	Rarely makes shots; poor technique
Passing	Passes accurately and quickly under pressure	Passes accurately most of the time	Passes are sometimes inaccurate or slow	Frequently inaccurate or weak passes
Defence	Maintains strong defensive position and anticipation	Generally maintains good defence with minor lapses	Sometimes maintains position, often out of place	Frequently out of position, poor anticipation

Fig. 2.6 Dribbling

(c) Diagnostic Evaluation

Diagnostic evaluation in Physical Education (PE) is used to assess students' existing skills, knowledge, and physical abilities before the instruction begins. The primary goal of diagnostic evaluation is to identify students' strengths, weaknesses, and learning needs, which can help educators in tailoring their instructions to meet individual and group needs better.

Methods of Diagnostic Evaluation

Skill Inventories: Assessments that evaluate students' proficiency in specific physical skills, such as running, jumping, or swimming.

Fitness Assessments: Measurements of baseline fitness levels, including cardiovascular endurance, strength, flexibility, and body composition.

Questionnaires and Surveys: Tools to gather information about students' previous experiences, interests, and self-perceived abilities.

Observations: Observing students' performance and behaviour in various physical activities to identify strengths and areas for improvement.

Pre-Tests: Short assessments that measure students' current understanding of rules, strategies, and concepts related to PE.

Interviews: Conversations with students to understand their physical activity history, goals, and concerns.

Performance-Based Evaluation: Assessments that require students to demonstrate specific skills or competencies through practical tasks.

Peer- and Self-Evaluation: Opportunities for students to assess their own performance and those of their peers, fostering reflection and self-improvement.

Fig. 2.7 Back flip

Examples of Diagnostic Evaluation Techniques

Skills Inventory for Gymnastics

Skill	Assessment Method	Criteria	Notes
Balance	Performance Test	Ability to hold balance on a beam for 30 seconds	Check for any wobbles or loss of balance
Vaulting	Observation and Skill Test	Technique and height achieved in vault	Evaluate form and execution
Floor Routine	Performance Test and Observation	Execution of routine components	Assess overall performance and difficulty

Fig. 2.8 Balance

Assessment is also categorized on another parameter— quantitative or qualitative.

(a) Meaning and Step of Qualitative Assessment

Qualitative assessment focuses on understanding the quality of students' performance, behaviours, and attitudes rather than just quantifiable measures. It involves gathering of detailed and descriptive information about students' skills, effort, and progress to provide a richer, more comprehensive view of their learning and development.

Characteristics of Qualitative Assessment

- **Descriptive:** Provides detailed observations and descriptions of students' performance and behaviour.
- **Holistic:** Considers various aspects of students' abilities, including technique, effort, and attitude.
- **Subjective:** Involves personal interpretations and judgments based on observations and interactions.
- **Narrative:** Often involves written or verbal feedback rather than numerical scores.
- **Contextual:** Takes into account the context and conditions under which students perform.

Methods of Qualitative Assessment

Observations: Systematic observation of students during activities to assess their skills, effort, and behaviour.

Journals and Reflections: Students write about their experiences, progress, and challenges.

Interviews and Discussions: Conversations with students to gain insights into their understanding, attitudes, and experiences.

Teacher's Anecdotes: Detailed notes from teachers about individual students' performance, progress, and participation.

Peer Assessments: Feedback from peers on skills, effort, and teamwork.

Portfolios: Collections of students' work, including reflections and examples of their performance over time.

The qualitative assessment table for students' skills (shown here) provides detailed feedback, and assesses various aspects of students' performance.

Qualitative Assessment Table for Students' Skills

Skill	Observation Criteria	Description/ Examples	Strengths	Areas for Improvement	Next Steps/ Recommendations
Dribbling (Basketball)	Control and Technique	Observe how well the student dribbles while moving and changing directions.	Consistently maintains control of the ball; smooth changes in direction.	Struggles with dribbling at high speeds; occasionally loses control.	Practise dribbling drills focusing on speed and control.
Passing (Soccer)	Accuracy and Timing	Evaluate the accuracy of passes and the timing of when they are made.	Makes precise passes to teammates, good timing in game situations.	Sometimes misses targets or makes passes too late.	Work on passing drills and quick decision-making exercises.
Running Form	Technique and Endurance	Assess the student's running posture, stride, and stamina over distance.	Maintains proper form; shows good stamina throughout the run.	Poor posture or inconsistent stride; fatigue affects performance.	Focus on form drills and endurance training.
Balance (Gymnastics)	Stability and Coordination	Observe the student's ability to maintain balance on apparatuses or during routines.	Demonstrates excellent balance and coordination during routines.	Wobbles or loses balance during complex movements.	Practise balancing exercises and core strengthening activities.
Teamwork (Group Activities)	Communication and Cooperation	Evaluate how well the student's works with others, communicates, and contributes to group tasks.	Actively participates, communicates effectively, and supports team members.	Hesitant to communicate or cooperate with team members.	Encourage more active communication and collaborative tasks.
Fitness (General)	Effort and Progress	Observe the students' effort during fitness activities and their progress over time.	Shows consistent effort and noticeable improvement in fitness levels.	Inconsistent effort or slow progress in fitness activities.	Develop a personalized fitness plan and set specific goals.

Fig. 2.9 Coordination

(b) Meaning and Step of Quantitative Assessment

Quantitative assessment involves measuring and evaluating students' performance, skills, and knowledge using numerical data and statistical methods. This type of assessment is objective, providing measurable and comparable results. Common quantitative assessments include tests, quizzes, fitness assessments, and performance metrics.

Physical fitness refers to attributes that contribute to overall health and well-being. These components are critical for preventing diseases and promoting long-term health. The primary components of physical fitness include cardiovascular endurance, muscular strength, muscular endurance, flexibility, and body composition. Each component can be evaluated using specific tests and measurements.

Elements of teaching process\Ongoing evaluation success factors for imparting high quality physical education Organizing an evaluation plan.

Fig. 2.10 Qualitative Assessment

Elements of Teaching Process

Teaching games and sports is more than just showing how to play—it's a structured process that helps learners develop skills, knowledge, and the right attitude.

1. Planning/Preparation

- The teacher or coach sets clear objectives.
- Selects appropriate games, drills, and equipment.
- Plans the session based on age, skill level, and goals.
- Ensures safety measures are in place.

2. Presentation/Introduction

- The teacher introduces the activity or skill to be taught.
- Explains the rules, techniques, and importance of the activity.
- Demonstrates the skill or tactic clearly and slowly.

3. Explanation and Demonstration

- The teacher explains how and why a skill is done.
- Uses verbal cues and visual demonstration to help understanding.
- May show the skill step-by-step and from different angles.

4. Practice and Participation

- Students actively practice the skill through drills or small games.
- The practice may be individual, pair, or team-based.
- Encourages repetition for improvement and confidence-building.

5. Observation and Supervision

- The teacher observes each student's performance.
- Checks for correct technique, posture, and movement.
- Ensures safety and correct use of equipment.

6. Feedback and Correction

- The teacher gives positive and constructive feedback.
- Corrects mistakes immediately to avoid bad habits.
- Encourages students to reflect and self-correct.

7. Evaluation and Assessment

- Assesses student progress using observation, checklists, or skill tests.
- Evaluates not just physical skills, but also teamwork, discipline, and attitude.
- Helps in setting goals for improvement.

8. Revision and Reinforcement

- Reviews previously learned skills in future lessons.
- Adds variety to keep students engaged.
- Reinforces key concepts through games, drills, or peer teaching.

Ongoing Evaluation

Ongoing evaluation is a continuous process used in education (including sports and games) to assess the progress and development of students over time. Unlike a one-time exam or assessment, ongoing evaluation involves regularly gathering information about students' performance, understanding, skills, and behaviour. This helps teachers, coaches, and trainers make informed decisions about instruction and support.

Factors of Ongoing Evaluation

1. Continuous Monitoring

- Instead of waiting for a final exam or assessment, ongoing evaluation happens throughout a course, training, or activity.
- Teachers or coaches observe performance, participation, and effort during every lesson or practice.

2. Formative Feedback

- Provides feedback to students or athletes on what they are doing well and what needs improvement.
- Helps in adjusting teaching methods, drills, or tactics to better suit the learner's needs.
- Encourages self-reflection, which helps learners adjust their strategies.

3. Holistic Approach

- Evaluates not just academic or physical performance, but also effort, attitude, and behavior.
- Takes into account skills, communication, teamwork, and problem-solving.

4. Flexible and Adaptive

- Adjusts according to the individual's progress or needs.
- Allows for the modification of teaching or training methods to ensure better outcomes.

5. Encourages Growth and Development

- Motivates learners by providing them with regular feedback on their improvement.
- Helps students focus on their personal progress rather than comparing themselves to others.

6. Non-judgmental and Supportive

- Focuses on growth rather than grades. The goal is to encourage continuous improvement.
- Builds trust and reduces the pressure associated with a single final assessment.

Key Success Factor for Imparting High Quality Physical Education

The key success factors for imparting high-quality physical education focus on creating an engaging, effective, and sustainable learning environment that benefits students in both physical and mental aspects.

1. **Qualified and Passionate Educators**
   - **Expertise and Certification:** Teachers should have a strong academic background in physical education, sports science, or related fields, along with practical experience.
   - **Passion for Teaching:** Passionate educators inspire students and create a positive learning atmosphere.
   - **Ongoing Professional Development:** Teachers should continuously update their skills and knowledge to stay current with trends in physical education.
2. **Comprehensive and Well-Structured Curriculum**
   - **Balanced Content:** A diverse curriculum that incorporates various activities, from team sports and individual exercises to fitness training and health education.
   - **Developmental Appropriateness:** The curriculum should cater to the physical, emotional, and cognitive development of students at different age levels.
   - **Clear Learning Objectives:** The program should be goal-oriented, with measurable objectives and outcomes for skill development, fitness, and health.
3. **Safe and Accessible Environment**
   - **Proper Facilities:** Access to safe, well-maintained sports fields, gymnasiums, swimming pools, or courts is essential.
   - **Safety Protocols:** Ensuring students follow proper warm-up and cool-down routines, and having first-aid measures in place for emergencies.
   - **Inclusive Environment:** Activities should be accessible for all students, regardless of their physical abilities, gender, or background.
4. **Active Student Participation**
   - **Engagement:** Ensuring all students are actively involved, with minimal downtime, and encouraging full participation in physical activities.
   - **Motivation:** Fostering intrinsic motivation through positive reinforcement, goal-setting, and celebrating individual and team achievements.
   - **Variety and Choice:** Offering a variety of activities and sports that cater to diverse interests and abilities, helping to keep students engaged and motivated.
5. **Use of Innovative Teaching Methods**
   - **Interactive Learning:** Incorporating games, hands-on activities, and cooperative learning to make physical education more engaging.
   - **Technology Integration:** Using modern technologies like fitness trackers, mobile apps, and video analysis tools to enhance teaching and monitor student progress.
   - **Differentiated Instruction:** Tailoring teaching methods to accommodate the diverse learning styles, abilities, and needs of students.

6. Comprehensive Health and Wellness Focus

- **Physical Fitness:** Developing students' physical fitness through regular exercise routines and fitness assessments.
- **Health Education:** Teaching students about the importance of nutrition, hydration, mental health, sleep, and stress management to promote overall well-being.
- **Lifestyle Choices:** Encouraging students to adopt a healthy, active lifestyle both in and out of school, which contributes to lifelong health and fitness habits.

7. Regular and Constructive Feedback

- **Continuous Assessment:** Providing regular formative assessments to track individual progress and give feedback that focuses on effort, growth, and improvement.
- **Positive Reinforcement:** Emphasizing effort and perseverance over perfection, and celebrating achievements regardless of the outcome.
- **Goal Setting:** Encouraging students to set personal fitness or skill development goals and monitoring their progress.

Organizing an Evaluation Plan

An evaluation plan is a structured outline that explains how, when, and what will be assessed during a program or course. It helps track learner progress, measure program success, and guide future improvements.

Set Clear Objectives

- Define what you want to evaluate.
- Objectives can be based on:
  - ➢ Knowledge (theory)
  - ➢ Skills (practical performance)
  - ➢ Attitudes (behavior, teamwork)
  - ➢ Fitness or personal development (in PE)

Decide the Timeframe

- Determine when the evaluation will take place:
  - ➢ Daily or weekly
  - ➢ Mid-term or end of term
  - ➢ After a specific unit or activity
- Use ongoing (formative) and final (summative) assessments.

Select Assessment Methods

Choose appropriate tools based on the objectives:

- Observation (skills, behavior)
- Practical Demonstration (sports techniques, drills)

- Written Tests or Quizzes (theory, rules, fitness knowledge)
- Peer or Self-Assessment
- Performance Rubrics
- Fitness Tests (in PE)

Prepare the Tools

- Checklists
- Rating scales
- Rubrics
- Worksheets
- Question papers
- Progress logs or journals

Record and Track Results

- Keep detailed records of each student's performance.
- Use forms, spreadsheets, or software to track progress.
- Track both individual performance and group/team outcomes.

Provide Feedback

- Give constructive feedback after each evaluation.
- Highlight strengths and offer tips for improvement.
- Involve students in self-reflection where possible.

Parent teacher Meeting

Parent- Teacher Meetings (PTMs) are an essential aspect of the educational process, fostering communication and collaboration between parents and teachers. These meetings help to ensure that students receive the necessary support both at school and at home to succeed academically and personally.

Objectives of a Parent-Teacher Meeting

1. **Review Student Progress:** Discuss academic performance, behavioural development, and social interactions.
2. **Identify Strengths and Weaknesses:** Highlight the student's strengths and areas needing improvement.
3. **Set Goals:** Establish short-term and long-term goals for the student.
4. **Address Concerns:** Provide a platform for parents and teachers to address any concerns or issues.
5. **Collaborate on Strategies:** Develop strategies to support the student's learning and development at home and school.

Managing Parent-Teacher Meetings

Managing a Parent-Teacher Meeting (PTM) effectively involves careful planning, clear communication, and a structured approach.

(a) Schedule Meetings

- **Select Dates and Times:** Choose dates and times that accommodate the schedules of most parents.
- **Send Invitations:** Notify parents well in advance through multiple channels (e-mails, newsletters, school portals).

(b) Organize Information

- **Collect Data:** Gather academic records, behaviour reports, attendance records, and samples of students' work.
- **Prepare Reports:** Create concise progress reports highlighting key areas of performance, strengths, and areas for improvement.

(c) Set an Agenda

- **Outline Key Points:** Identify the main topics to be discussed, such as academic progress, behaviour, goals, and strategies for improvement.
- **Time Allocation:** Allocate time for each item in the agenda to ensure that all important points are covered.

(d) Environmental Set-up

- **Private and Comfortable Space:** Arrange a quiet, private space for the meeting where discussions can be held without interruptions.
- **Resources Ready:** Ensure that all necessary resources (students' files, progress charts, seating arrangements) are prepared in advance.

Fig. 2.11 Parents Interaction

Interaction with Parents Post Assessments

Interaction with parents after the assessment activity is important as it facilitates:

(a) Understanding and Clarity

- **Detailed Explanation:** Parents gain a clear understanding of their child's assessment results, strengths, and areas needing improvement.
- **Addressing Confusion:** Helps to clarify any questions or concerns that parents may have about the assessment process or findings.

(b) Collaborative Planning

- **Individualized Support:** Facilitates the development of a personalized action plan or Individualized Education Programme (IEP) tailored to the child's unique needs.
- **Goal Setting:** Engages parents in setting realistic and achievable goals for their child's development and education.

(c) Empowering Parents

- **Informed Decisions:** Provides parents with the information needed to make informed decisions about their child's education and support.
- **Active Participation:** Encourages parents to take an active role in their child's learning and development.

Aspect	Importance
Understanding and Clarity	Provides clear explanation of assessment results. Addresses parents' questions and concerns.
Collaborative Planning	Develops a personalized action plan or IEP. Involves parents in setting realistic and achievable goals.
Empowering Parents	Informs parents for better decision-making. Encourages active participation in child's education.
Building Trust and Relationship	Strengthens relationship with educators. Fosters a supportive partnership essential for the child's success.
Resource Allocation	Informs parents about available resources. Helps in effective utilization of support services.
Ongoing Monitoring and Adaptation	Sets up progress tracking and plan adjustments. Creates a feedback loop for timely support adjustments.
Building Confidence	Boosts parents' confidence in supporting their child. Contributes to the child's overall success and well-being.

Explanation of Performance Evaluation

Evaluating sports skills and performance in children can help in organizing the assessment process and makes it easier to track progress over time.

Sports Skills Performance Evaluation Chart

Evaluation Component	Description	Assessment Methods	Performance Metrics
Skill Assessment	Evaluates proficiency in specific sports skills	Observations, Skill Drills	Accuracy, Technique Quality
Technical Skills	Ability to perform specific techniques (e.g., dribbling, serving)	Drills, Skill Tests	Execution, Consistency
Tactical Skills	Understanding and application of game strategies	Game Situations, Scrimmages	Decision-making, Execution of Strategies
Physical Fitness	General fitness and physical abilities	Fitness Tests, Agility Drills	Strength, Endurance, Speed
Strength and Conditioning	Muscular strength and endurance	Strength Tests, Conditioning Drills	Performance in Strength Tests
Agility and Speed	Quickness and ability to change direction	Speed Drills, Agility Tests	Time, Reaction Speed
Coordination and Balance	Control of movements and balance	Coordination Drills, Balance Tests	Accuracy, Stability
Performance Metrics	Measures of skill execution and effectiveness	Game Performance, Skill Assessments	Accuracy, Speed, Timing
Accuracy and Precision	How well skills are executed	Skill Drills, Game Situations	Error Rate, Success Rate
Speed and Timing	Speed of skill execution and game timing	Speed Tests, Game Performance	Time, Reaction Time
Game Performance	Application of skills in real game situations	Competitions, Scrimmages	Overall performance, Effectiveness
Behavioural and Psychological Aspects	Motivation, attitude, and sportsmanship	Observations, Interviews	Attitude, Sportsmanship
Motivation and Attitude	Enthusiasm and willingness to practise	Self-assessment, Coach Feedback	Engagement Level, Attitude
Sportsmanship	Behaviour towards teammates and opponents	Observations, Peer Feedback	Respectfulness, Teamwork
Self-Assessment	Child's own evaluation of performance	Self-Reflection, Interviews	Self-Perception, Goal Setting
Feedback from Coaches	Insights from coaches on performance and progress	Coach's Report, Feedback Sessions	Observations, Recommendations
Feedback from Peers	Insights from teammates or other players	Peer Feedback, Observations	Team Dynamics, Interactions
Overall Evaluation	Summary of child's performance and progress	Comprehensive Review, Summary Report	Strengths, Areas for Improvement
Action Plan	Plan for skill development and improvement	Goal Setting, Training Plan	Specific Goals, Training Activities
Follow-up	Regular review of progress and adjustment of plans	Follow-up Meetings, Reassessments	Progress, Plan Adjustments

Steps to Improve Performance of Slow Learners

Improving the performance of slow learners in sports involves a tailored approach that considers their unique needs and learning styles.

(a) Assess Individual Needs

- **Evaluate Skills:** Conduct a thorough assessment of the child's current skills, strengths, and areas needing improvement.
- **Identify Challenges:** Determine specific challenges the child faces, such as coordination issues, understanding of game strategies, or physical limitations.

(b) Customize Training Programmes

- **Set Realistic Goals:** Establish short-term and long-term goals based on the child's current abilities and potential.
- **Personalized Drills:** Design drills and exercises that target the child's specific areas for improvement.
- **Incremental Progress:** Break down complex skills into smaller, manageable steps to facilitate gradual improvement.

(c) Foster a Positive Learning Environment

- **Encourage and Motivate:** Provide positive reinforcement and celebrate small achievements to boost confidence and motivation.
- **Create a Supportive Atmosphere:** Ensure that training environment is supportive and inclusive, encouraging the child to participate without fear of criticism.

(d) Adapt Teaching Methods

- **Use Visual and Verbal Instructions:** Combine visual demonstrations with clear verbal instructions to cater to different learning styles.
- **Provide Hands-on Practice:** Allow plenty of opportunities for practice with immediate feedback and correction.
- **Simplify Instructions:** Break down complex tasks into simpler components and gradually increase difficulty as the child improves.

(e) Incorporate Fun and Engaging Activities

- **Game-based Learning:** Integrate games and activities that make learning enjoyable and less stressful.
- **Varied Drills:** Use a variety of drills to maintain the child's interest and engagement.

(f) Focus on Physical Conditioning

- **Improve Basic Fitness:** Incorporate exercises to enhance general physical fitness, including strength, flexibility, and endurance.
- **Develop Coordination:** Include drills that improve hand-eye coordination, balance, and agility.

(g) Provide Individual Attention

- **One-on-one Coaching:** Offer individual coaching sessions to provide personalized guidance and support.
- **Adjust Pacing:** Allow the child to progress at their own pace without pressure.

(h) Encourage Consistent Practice

- **Regular Training:** Establish a consistent practice schedule to build and reinforce skills.
- **Home Practice:** Suggest exercises or drills which the child can practise at home to reinforce skills learned during training sessions.

(i) Utilize Supportive Tools

- **Adaptive Equipment:** Use equipment designed to assist with specific challenges, such as modified balls or training aids.
- **Technology:** Incorporate technology, such as video analysis, to provide visual feedback on performance.

(j) Involve Parents and Caregivers

- **Communicate Regularly:** Keep parents informed about their child's progress and suggest them strategies to support practice at home.
- **Encourage Support:** Motivate parents to be supportive and positive, reinforcing the child's efforts and progress.

(k) Monitor and Adjust

- **Regular Assessments:** Conduct regular assessments to monitor progress and adjust training programmes as needed.
- **Adapt Strategies:** Modify training methods and goals based on the child's development and changing needs.

(l) Promote Social Interaction

- **Team Activities:** Encourage participation in team sports or group activities to build social skills and teamwork.
- **Peer Support:** Foster positive interactions with peers to enhance motivation and enjoyment of the sport.

After completing this session, you should be able to:

- Describe the various types of assessment and the purpose of evaluation.
- Qualitative and quantitative assessment.
- Organize assessment and evaluation of students.
- Demonstrate the knowledge of organizing interaction with parents.

ACTIVITIES

Props and equipment: As mentioned in the above session.

1. Conduct on-ground skill and fitness assessment with the props available and relate the use to age-appropriateness.
2. Organize a role play on the following topics:
   (a) PTM explaining the norms and the grading to the students playing as parents.
   (b) Explain the steps involved in skill assessment.
3. Discuss on the importance of assessment and evaluation.
4. Group discussion on factor influencing assessment.
5. Preparation of chart on type of assessment.
6. Draw a chart showing the step of qualitative assessment.
7. Group discussion on qualitative and quantitative assessment.

Subjective Questions

1. Describe assessment and name different types of assessment.
2. What are the different factors influencing assessments?
3. Describe any two important assessment tools.

UNIT 3

EMERGENCY MANAGEMENT

- Heat Stroke
- Allergies
- Asthma
- Sudden Cardiac Arrest
- Cardiopulmonary Resuscitation (CPR)
- First Aid—The Concept
- DRABC Of First Aid
- Heat Exhaustion
- Breathing Difficulties
- Basic Sports Injuries
- Concept of First AID KIT
- Area Inspection For Safety
- First Aid Procedures

During any emergency, normal activities and procedures get interrupted and take the back seat, and actions and measures of immediate requirement (management) need to be taken up urgently to prevent a disaster. Disaster management is a related term but should not be equated to emergency management.

Meaning of Emergency Response

Emergency response is sometimes a cyclical process, involving continuous assessment, planning, action and review. It begins with an initial evaluation and can be started by the catastrophic occurrence on its own, or authorities might approve the mobilization of personnel and resources.

Fig. 3.1 Heat Stroke

Emergency Action Plans are essential to manage injuries and illnesses in physical education and sports properly. However, most literature discusses Emergency Action Plans in the athletic arena instead of physical education. In this unit we will try to examine physical education instructors' experiences on students' illness and injury, discuss the steps of an Emergency Action Plan, and provide a template for physical educators to develop a customized Emergency Action Plan at their schools.

Need and Importance of emergency response.

3.1 HEAT STROKE

Definition: Heat stroke is a severe heat-related illness that occurs when the body's temperature regulation system fails, and the body temperature rises to dangerous levels, typically above 104°F (40°C). It is a medical emergency that requires immediate attention.

To see **Heat Stroke** in Action

Scan QR Code

1. Causes

Prolonged Exposure to High Temperatures: Staying in hot environments for extended periods, especially with high humidity.

Strenuous Physical Activity: Intense exercise or physical labour in hot weather.

Dehydration: Inadequate fluid intake, which impairs the body's ability to sweat and cool down.

Clothing: Wearing heavy or tight clothing that inhibits evaporation of sweat.

Pre-existing Conditions: Certain medical conditions and medications that affect the body's ability to regulate temperature.

2. Symptoms

High Body Temperature: Core body temperature of 104°F (40°C) or higher.

Altered Mental State or Behaviour: Confusion, agitation, slurred speech, irritability, delirium, seizures, or coma.

Hot, Dry Skin: Lack of sweating despite the heat.

Nausea and Vomiting: Feeling sick to the stomach or vomiting.

3. Emergency Response Needed to Deal with Heat Stroke

(i) Rapid Intervention:

- **Need:** Heat stroke can cause severe damage to internal organs and the brain within minutes.
- **Importance:** Quick response can prevent complications such as organ failure, permanent brain damage, or death.

(ii) Effective Treatment

- **Need:** Proper medical treatment is essential to lower the body's temperature safely.
- **Importance:** Trained responders can administer cooling techniques like ice packs, cold water immersion, or IV fluids, which are crucial for recovery.

(iii) Minimizing Long-term Health Effects

- **Need:** Prolonged heat stroke can lead to long-term health issues.
- **Importance:** Early intervention reduces the risk of permanent damage, ensuring better health outcomes for the affected individual.

(iv) Public Safety and Awareness:

- **Need:** Educating the public on the signs and risks of heat stroke is vital.
- **Importance:** Awareness campaigns can help to prevent heat stroke by encouraging behaviours such as staying hydrated, avoiding extreme heat, and recognizing early symptoms.

(v) Support Systems:

- **Need:** A robust emergency response system ensures that help is available when needed.

  Importance: Communities with effective emergency response systems are better prepared to handle cases of heat stroke, lowering the mortality rates.

(vi) Resource Allocation:

- **Need:** Proper planning and resource allocation are crucial for managing multiple heat stroke cases during extreme heat events.
- **Importance:** Ensuring that emergency services are adequately equipped and staffed helps in managing large-scale emergencies more effectively.

(vii) Training and Preparedness:

- **Need:** Emergency responders must be trained to recognize and treat heat stroke efficiently.
- **Importance:** Regular training and drills ensure that responders are prepared to handle heat stroke cases promptly and effectively.

(viii) Community Resilience:

- **Need:** Communities need to be resilient in the face of increasing heatwaves due to climate change.
- **Importance:** A strong emergency response system contributes to overall community resilience, helping communities in recovering and adapting to extreme heat conditions.

3.2 ALLERGIES

Allergies occur when the immune system reacts to a foreign substance (allergen) that is typically harmless to most people. These substances can include foods, pollen, pet dander, insect stings, medications, and more.

3.2.1 TYPES OF ALLERGIES

Fig. 3.2 Allergies

(a) Mild to Moderate Allergies:

- Sneezing
- Runny or stuffy nose
- Itchy, watery eyes
- Hives or skin rash
- Itching in the mouth or throat
- Stomach cramps, diarrhoea (food allergies)

(b) Severe Allergies (Anaphylaxis):

- Swelling of the lips, tongue, or throat
- Difficulty in breathing or shortness of breath
- Rapid or weak pulse
- Drop in blood pressure
- Dizziness or fainting
- Severe skin reactions
- Nausea or vomiting

3.2.2 EMERGENCY RESPONSE NEEDED TO DEAL WITH ALLERGIES

To see **Allergies** in Action

Scan QR Code

(i) Saving Lives:

- **Need:** Severe allergic reactions, known as anaphylaxis, can be life-threatening and requires immediate medical intervention.
- **Importance:** Quick and effective emergency response can prevent fatal outcomes by administering life-saving treatments such as epinephrine.

(ii) Preventing Severe Complications:

- **Need:** Allergic reactions can escalate rapidly causing obstruction of airways cardiovascular collapse, or severe asthma attacks.

- **Importance:** Prompt emergency treatment can prevent these severe complications, resulting in better health outcomes, reducing long-term impacts.

(iii) Rapid Symptom Relief:

- **Need:** Allergic reactions can cause intense discomfort and distress, including symptoms like hives, swelling, and difficulty in breathing.
- **Importance:** Emergency response provides rapid relief from these symptoms, improving the affected individual's immediate condition and providing comfort.

(iv) Education and Awareness:

- **Need:** Many people may not recognize the signs of severe allergic reactions or know how to respond appropriately.
- **Importance:** Emergency responders can educate the public and individuals about recognizing symptoms and the proper use of emergency treatments, such as epinephrine auto-injectors.

(v) Preparedness and Planning:

- **Need:** Individuals with regular and chronic allergies need to have a clear action plan in place for potential exposure to allergens.
- **Importance:** Emergency response systems help in ensuring that these plans are extremely useful and effective and that individuals, schools, workplaces, and public spaces are prepared to handle allergic emergencies.

(vi) Support Systems:

- **Need:** Comprehensive emergency response involves support from various sectors, including healthcare providers, emergency responders, and the community.
- **Importance:** Coordinated efforts enhance the efficiency and effectiveness of managing allergic reactions, providing a network of support for individuals with allergies.

(vii) Minimizing Economic Impact:

- **Need:** Severe allergic reactions can lead to hospitalizations and costly medical treatments.
- **Importance:** Quick and effective emergency response can reduce the need for prolonged medical care and hospitalization, minimizing healthcare costs for individuals and the healthcare system.

(viii) Enhancing Quality of Life:

- **Need:** Fear of severe allergic reactions can limit individuals' activities and social interactions.
- **Importance:** Knowing that effective emergency response systems are in place can give those with allergies and their families peace of mind, enhancing their overall quality of life.

(ix) Community Resilience:

- **Need:** Communities must be prepared to handle allergic emergencies, especially in public places like schools, restaurants, and workplaces.

- **Importance:** A well-prepared community can respond promptly to allergic emergencies, reducing the risk of severe outcomes and ensuring a safer environment for everyone.

(x) Reducing Anxiety and Stress:

- **Need:** Individuals with severe allergies often live with the constant worry of exposure to allergens.
- **Importance:** Knowing that emergency response systems are effective can reduce anxiety and stress, helping individuals to have confidence.

3.3 Asthma

Asthma is a chronic respiratory condition which is characterized by inflammation and narrowing of the airways, leading to difficulty in breathing. It can vary in severity and often involves episodes of wheezing, shortness of breath, chest tightness, and coughing.

To see **Asthma** in Action
Scan QR Code

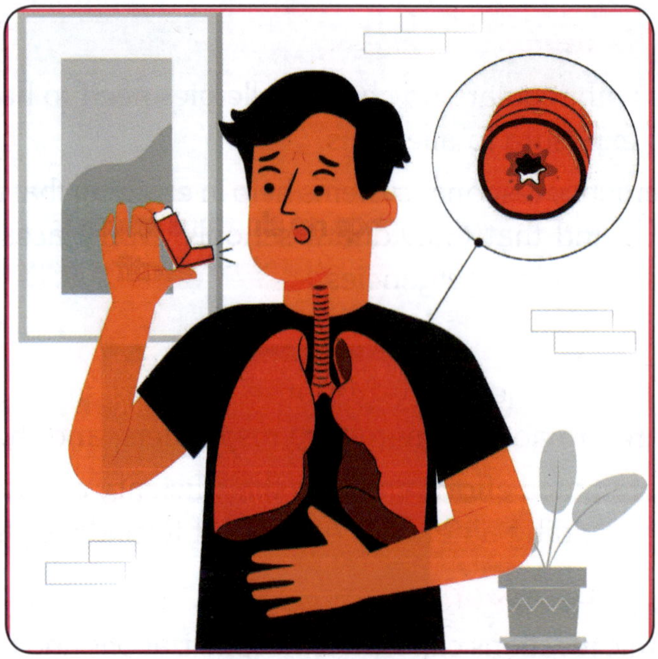

Fig. 3.3 Asthma

3.3.1 Causes

- **Genetic Factors:** A family history of asthma or other allergic conditions increases the risk.
- **Environmental Triggers:** Exposure to allergens (pollen, dust mites, pet dander), air pollution, smoke, and strong odours.
- **Respiratory Infections:** Infections like colds or flu can trigger symptoms of asthma.
- **Physical Activity:** Exercise-induced asthma occurs during or after physical activity.
- **Weather Conditions:** Cold air or sudden changes in weather can provoke asthma.
- **Emotional Stress:** Stress and strong emotions can trigger symptoms of asthma.

3.3.2 Symptoms

- **Wheezing:** A whistling or squeaky sound when breathing.
- **Shortness of Breath:** Difficulty breathing or feeling out of breath.
- **Chest Tightness:** A feeling of pressure or constriction in the chest.
- **Coughing:** Often worse at night or early morning, and during or after exercise.
- **Difficulty Sleeping:** Due to coughing, wheezing, or shortness of breath.

3.3.3 Emergency Response Needed for Dealing with Asthma

(i) Rapid Symptom Relief:

- **Need:** Asthma attacks can cause sudden and severe breathing difficulties, which can be life-threatening.
- **Importance:** Quick and effective emergency response provides immediate relief, often through the administration of bronchodilators, which open the airways and restore normal breathing.

(ii) Preventing Severe Complications:

- **Need:** Without prompt treatment, asthma attacks can lead to respiratory failure, requiring intensive medical intervention.
- **Importance:** Emergency response can prevent severe complications, ensuring that individuals receive the necessary care to stabilize their condition.

(iii) Saving Lives:

- **Need:** Severe asthma attacks can be fatal if not treated promptly.
- **Importance:** Emergency response is crucial in saving lives by providing quick medical intervention during critical asthma attacks.

(iv) Minimizing Hospitalization:

- **Need:** Asthma attacks can lead to emergency room visits and hospital admissions if not managed promptly.
- **Importance:** Effective emergency response can manage symptoms quickly, reducing the need for hospitalization and the associated healthcare costs.

(v) Education and Awareness:

- **Need:** Many people, including asthma patients and their families, may not recognize the signs of a severe asthma attack or know how to respond appropriately.
- **Importance:** Emergency responders can educate individuals on recognizing symptoms, use of a proper inhaler, and following asthma action plans, improving overall management of asthma.

(vi) Support Systems:

- **Need:** Asthma patients require a support network, including healthcare providers, emergency responders, and community resources.

- **Importance:** Coordinated emergency response systems ensure that patients receive comprehensive care and support, enhancing their ability to manage asthma effectively.

(vii) Improving Quality of Life:

- **Need:** Frequent asthma attacks and fear of severe episodes can significantly impact an individual's daily life and activities.
- **Importance:** Knowing that effective emergency response is available can reduce anxiety, improve confidence in managing asthma, and enhance overall quality of life.

(viii) Community Preparedness:

- **Need:** Public places, such as schools, workplaces, and recreational facilities, must be well-prepared to handle emergencies related to asthma.
- **Importance:** A well-prepared community can respond promptly to asthma attacks, ensuring the safety and well-being of individuals with asthma in various settings.

(ix) Reducing Economic Impact:

- **Need:** Asthma-related emergencies can cause significant expenses on healthcare, including emergency room visits and hospital stays.
- **Importance:** Quick and effective emergency response can reduce these costs by managing symptoms early and preventing the need for extensive medical care.

(x) Enhancing Emergency Response Systems:

- **Need:** Effective management of emergencies in asthma requires well-trained responders, proper equipment, and clear protocols.
- **Importance:** Investing in robust emergency response systems ensures that asthma patients receive timely and appropriate care, improving overall outcomes and reducing the burden on healthcare systems.

3.4 Sudden Cardiac Arrest

Sudden Cardiac Arrest (SCA) is a condition where the heart stops beating suddenly and unexpectedly, leading to stoppage of blood flow to the brain and other vital organs. It is a medical emergency that, if not treated immediately, can result in death within minutes.

To see **Cardiac Arrest** in Action

Scan QR Code

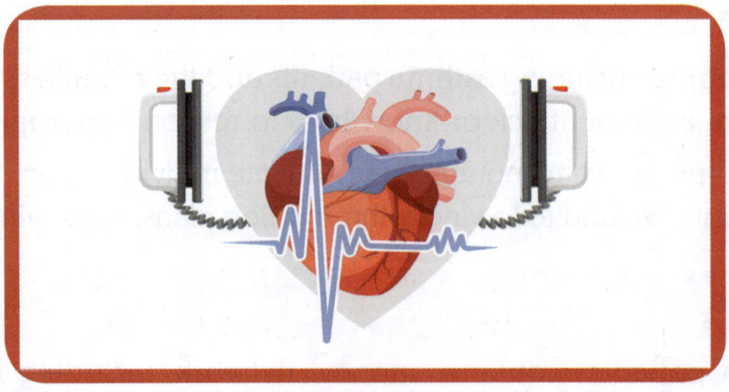

Fig. 3.4 Heart

3.4.1 Emergency Response

(i) Immediate Recognition:

- **Need:** Recognizing SCA quickly is critical for survival.
- **Importance:** Immediate recognition allows for the rapid initiation of life-saving measures. Sooner it is recognized, the better it is.

(ii) Calling Emergency Services:

- **Need:** Professional medical help is essential for advanced life support.
- **Importance:** Dialling emergency services ensures that paramedics can arrive quickly to provide necessary care.

(iii) Cardiopulmonary Resuscitation (CPR):

- **Need:** CPR maintains circulation and oxygenation of the brain and vital organs until professional help arrives.
- **Importance:** Early and effective CPR can double or triple the chances of survival. This has been described in detail in Section 3.5.

(iv) Defibrillation:

- **Need:** Defibrillation is needed to restore a normal heart rhythm.
- **Importance:** Using an Automated External Defibrillator (AED) can significantly improve survival rates within minutes.

(v) Advanced Medical Care:

- **Need:** Hospital care is required for further treatment and stabilization.
- **Importance:** Advanced care includes medications, therapeutic hypothermia, and interventions like angioplasty or surgery.

3.4.2 Importance of Emergency Response

(i) Saving Lives:

- **Need:** Without intervention, SCA can be fatal within minutes.
- **Importance:** Quick and effective emergency response significantly increases the chances of survival.

(ii) Preventing Brain Damage:

- **Need:** Lack of oxygenated blood flow to the brain for more than a few minutes can cause irreversible brain damage.
- **Importance:** Immediate CPR and defibrillation help in maintaining blood flow and oxygenation, protecting brain function.

(iii) Community Readiness:

- **Need:** Public places and communities must be prepared to handle SCA emergencies.

- **Importance:** Training in the use of CPR and AED(automated external defibrillator), and the availability of AEDs in public places, enhance community's readiness and response.

(iv) Education and Awareness:

- **Need:** Many people are unaware of how to recognize or respond to SCA.
- **Importance:** Public education campaigns and training programmes increase awareness and preparedness, improving outcomes.

(v) Chain of Survival

- **Need:** A coordinated series of actions increases the likelihood of survival and recovery.
- **Importance:** The chain of survival includes early recognition, early CPR, early defibrillation, and advanced medical care, all of which are crucial for successful resuscitation. Importance is on early action.

(vi) Support Systems

- **Need:** Comprehensive emergency response involves coordination between lay responders, emergency services, and healthcare providers.
- **Importance:** Effective systems ensure that individuals receive timely and appropriate care at each stage of the emergency response.

3.5 Cardiopulmonary Resuscitation (CPR)

Cardiopulmonary Resuscitation, or CPR, is a lifesaving technique used in emergencies of sudden cardiac arrest to manually keep blood circulation and oxygenation going when a person's heart and breathing have stopped.

Steps for Performing CPR

1. Check for the Safety around

- Ensure that the area is safe for both you and the person needing help.

2. Check the Person's Responsiveness

- Tap the person's shoulder and shout, "Are you okay?" Look for signs of responsiveness, such as movement or verbal response.

3. Check for Breathing

- Tilt the person's head back slightly and look, listen, and feel for signs of breathing for up to 10 seconds. If they are not breathing normally, proceed with CPR.

4. Perform Chest Compressions

- Place the heel of one hand on the centre of the person's chest (between the nipples).
- Place your other hand on top and interlock your fingers.
- Position yourself vertically above the person's chest and perform chest compressions:
    - ❖ Push down firmly and quickly, compressing the chest about 2 inches (5 centimetres) deep.

- ❖ Perform compressions at a rate of about 100-120 compressions per minute. Let the chest rise completely between compressions.

5. Rescue Breaths (if trained and willing)

- After 30 compressions, give 2 rescue breaths. Ensure that the airway is open (head tilted back, chin lifted).
- Pinch the person's nose closed, place your mouth over theirs, and give 2 full breaths, each lasting about 1 second and causing the chest to rise.
- Continue cycles of 30 compressions and 2 breaths until help arrives or the person starts breathing on their own.

6. Continue the CPR

- Continue performing cycles of chest compressions and rescue breaths until:
  - ❖ Emergency help arrives and takes over.
  - ❖ The person shows signs of life, such as breathing normally.
  - ❖ You are too exhausted to continue (if possible, have someone else take over).

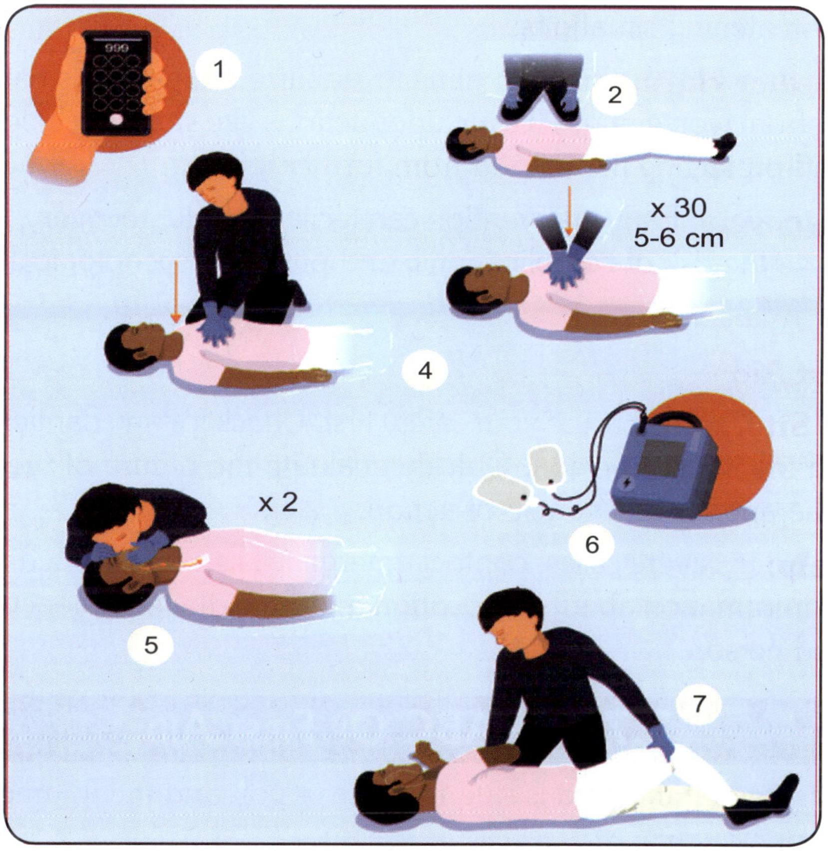

Fig. 3.5 CPR

3.6 First Aid—The Concept

First aid is the immediate care provided to a person who has been injured or suddenly taken ill, before professional medical assistance is available. The primary goal of first aid is to prevent the condition from worsening, promote recovery, and preserve life.

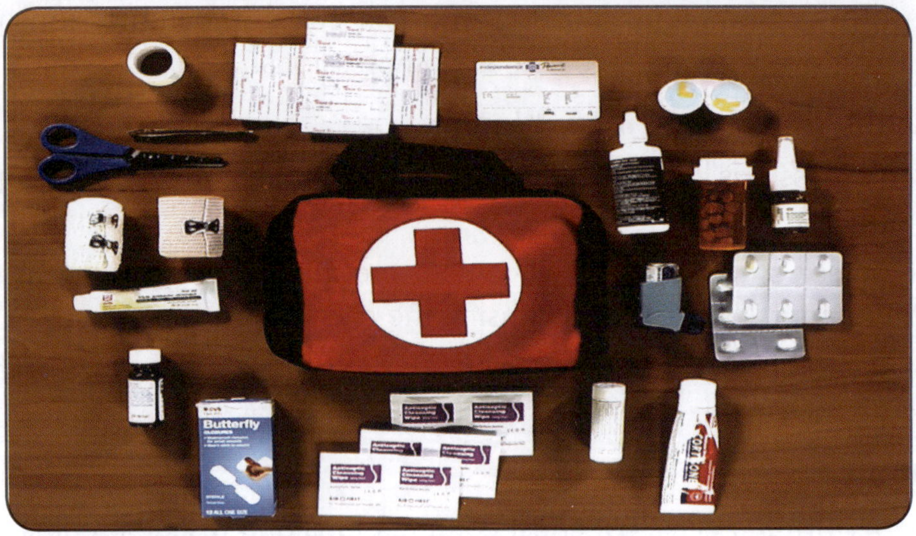

Fig. 3.6 First AID

Purpose of First Aid

(i) **Preserve Life:** The primary objective is to save the affected life by providing immediate care in life-threatening situations.

(ii) **Prevent Further Harm:** First aid aims to stabilize the patient's condition, preventing the situation from worsening. This includes actions like stopping bleeding, immobilizing fractures, and protecting the injured from further injury.

(iii) **Promote Recovery:** Early intervention can facilitate faster recovery. First aid can reduce pain, minimize the risk of complications, and provide psychological reassurance to the patient.

Principles of First Aid

(a) **Assess the Situation:** Ensure your safety first. Check for any dangers or hazards before approaching the injured person. Quickly evaluate the nature of the injury or illness to determine the appropriate course of action.

(b) **Call for Help:** In severe cases, contact emergency services immediately. Provide clear and concise information about the location, nature of the emergency, and the condition of the injured person.

3.7 DRABC Of First Aid

- **Danger:** Ensure that the area is safe for both— you and the injured person.
- **Response:** Check if the person is responsive by gently shaking them and asking if they are okay.
- **Airway:** Ensure that the airway is open and clear. If necessary, perform the head-tilt, chin-lift manoeuvre.
- **Breathing:** Check for normal breathing. Look, listen, and feel for breaths.
- **Circulation:** Check for signs of circulation, such as movement, coughing, or normal breathing. If absent, begin the CPR.

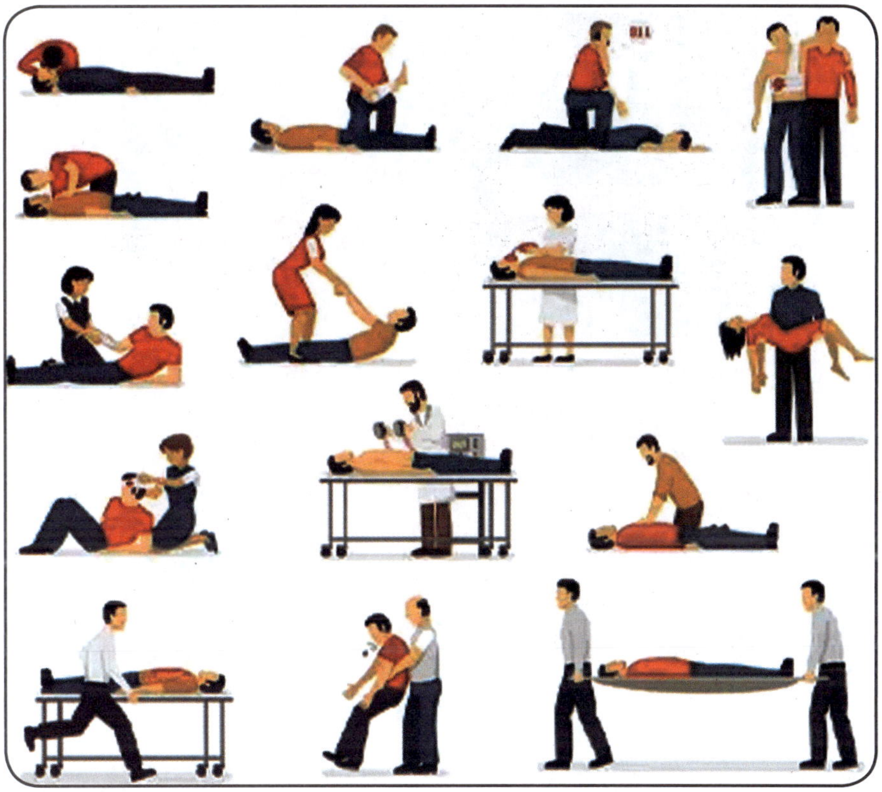

Fig. 3.7 DRABC

Perform a Secondary Survey: Once immediate life-threatening conditions are addressed, conduct a more thorough check for other injuries or medical issues. Check the vital signs, look for bleeding, fractures, burns, or other injuries, and gather information about the person's medical history, if possible.

First AID - Purpose and Basic Principles

1. **Rest:** Minimize movement of the bruised area to prevent further injury and promote healing.
2. **Ice pack:**
   - Apply an ice pack or a cold compress to the bruised area for 15-20 minutes every hour for the first 24-48 hours.
   - Use a cloth to wrap the ice pack to protect the skin.
3. **Compression:**
   - Apply a compression bandage to the area if it is swollen, but ensure that it is not too tight as to restrict the blood flow.
4. **Elevation:**
   - Raise the bruised area above the level of the heart, if possible, to reduce swelling.
5. **Pain Relief:**
   - Over-the-counter pain relievers, such as acetaminophen or ibuprofen, can help to manage pain and reduce inflammation. Follow the dosage instructions on the packing.

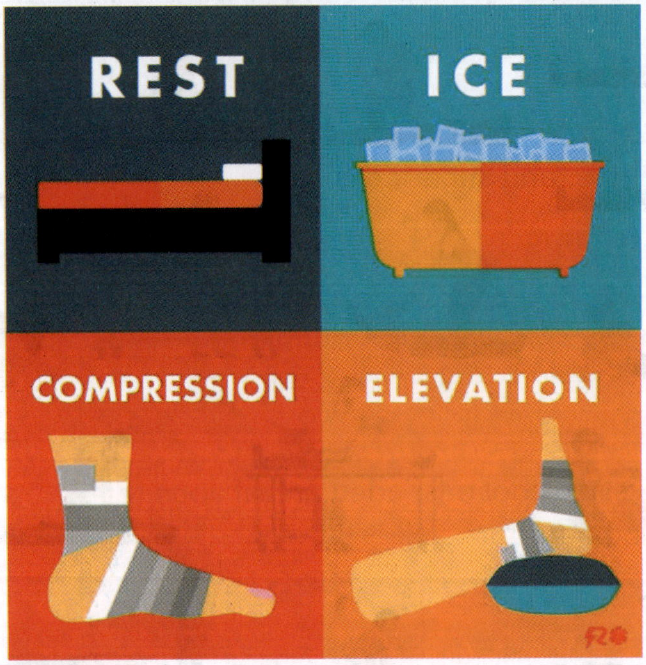

Fig. 3.8 RICE

3.8 Heat Exhaustion

It is a heat-related illness that can occur after being exposed to high temperatures, often combined with high humidity and strenuous physical activity. It is important to recognize the signs and symptoms of heat exhaustion to prevent it from progressing to heat stroke, which is a more severe and life-threatening condition.

Signs and Symptoms of Heat Exhaustion

1. Heavy Sweating:

- Excessive sweating, often accompanied by moist, cool skin.

2. Weakness or Fatigue:

- Feeling weak, tired, or fatigued, often with a sense of being overwhelmed.

3. Dizziness or Fainting:

- Light-headedness, dizziness, or even fainting spells.

4. Nausea or Vomiting:

- Feeling nauseous or vomiting.

5. Muscle Cramps:

- Painful muscle cramps, especially in legs, arms, or abdomen.

6. Headache:

- Throbbing headache.

7. Rapid Heartbeat:

- Fast but weak pulse.

Prevention of Heat Exhaustion

1. Stay Hydrated:

- Drink plenty of fluids, especially water— before, during, and after outdoor activities. Avoid alcohol, caffeine, and sugary drinks, which can contribute to dehydration.

2. Wear Appropriate Clothing:

- Wear lightweight, loose-fitting and light-coloured clothing to help your body stay cool. A wide-brimmed hat and sunglasses can provide additional protection.

3. Take Breaks:

- Take frequent breaks in a cool or shaded area if you are working or exercising outdoors. Take rest regularly and avoid overexertion.

Fig. 3.9 Heat Exhaustion

4. Avoid Peak Sun Hours:

- Limit your outdoor activities to the cooler parts of the day, such as early morning or late evening. Avoid strenuous activities during the hottest part of the day, typically between 10 a.m. and 4 p.m.

3.9 Breathing Difficulties

Breathing difficulties can range from mild shortness of breath to severe respiratory distress. They can be caused by various factors, including medical conditions, environmental factors, and physical exertion. Recognizing the signs and symptoms and knowing how to provide first aid can be critical.

Causes of Breathing Difficulties

1. **Asthma:** Chronic condition where airways get inflamed and become narrow.
2. **Chronic Obstructive Pulmonary Disease (COPD):** Includes chronic bronchitis and emphysema, which obstruct airflow.
3. **Allergic Reactions:** Can cause swelling of the airways.
4. **Infections:** Such as pneumonia or bronchitis.
5. **Heart Conditions:** Including heart failure or heart attack.
6. **Anxiety or Panic Attacks:** Can lead to hyperventilation.
7. **Obstructions:** Choking of throat by some food item or foreign objects.
8. **Environmental Factors:** Exposure to smoke, pollutants, or allergens.

Signs and Symptoms of Breathing Difficulties

1. **Shortness of Breath:** Feeling like you are unable to get enough air.
2. **Rapid Breathing:** Breathing faster than usual.
3. **Laboured Breathing:** Using extra muscles to breathe, indicated by the chest or abdomen moving more than usual.

4. **Wheezing:** A high-pitched sound that accompanies breathing.
5. **Coughing:** Persistent or severe coughing.
6. **Chest Tightness:** A feeling of constriction in the chest.
7. **Cyanosis:** Bluish tint on lips, face, or fingernails due to lack of oxygen.
8. **Fatigue:** Feeling unusually tired.
9. **Confusion:** Difficulty in thinking clearly due to lack of oxygen.
10. **Anxiety:** Feeling panicked or anxious about not being able to breathe.

First Aid for Breathing Difficulties

1. Assess the Situation

- Determine the cause of the breathing difficulty, if possible.
- Check for any obvious signs of airway obstruction, allergic reactions, or injury.

2. Help the Person to a Comfortable Position:

- Often, sitting upright or leaning slightly forward can improve breathing.
- Avoid laying down the person flat on their back.

3. Loosen Tight Clothing:

- Loosen any tight clothing around the neck and chest to help with breathing.

4. Encourage Slow and Deep Breaths:

- If the person is hyperventilating, encourage them to breathe slowly and deeply. Using a paper bag to breathe into can help if the person is hyperventilating due to anxiety.

5. Use Medications, if Available:

- If the person has a prescribed inhaler or medication for a known condition (like asthma), assist them in using it.

6. Monitor and Reassure:

- Stay with the person and keep them calm. Anxiety can worsen breathing difficulties.

7. Perform CPR, if Necessary:

- If the person stops breathing, be prepared to perform CPR. Ensure that the airway is open and begin chest compressions and rescue breaths as needed.

Preventive Measures

1. Avoid Triggers:

- Identify and avoid known triggers for conditions like asthma or allergies.

2. Use Medications as Prescribed:

- Take medications regularly and as prescribed for chronic conditions.

Fig. 3.10 Breathing

3. Stay Hydrated:

- Drink plenty of fluids to keep mucus thin and easier to clear from the airways.

4. Maintain a Healthy Lifestyle:

- Exercise regularly to strengthen the respiratory system and maintain a healthy weight.

5. Avoid Smoking and Pollutants:

- Avoid smoking and exposure to second-hand smoke and other pollutants.

3.10 Basic Sports Injuries

1. Sprains

- **Description:** Stretching or tearing of ligaments (the tissue connecting bones to each other). (First aid on sprains is described in detail in Section 3.12).
- **Common Areas:** Ankles, knees, wrists.
- **Symptoms:** Pain, swelling, bruising, and limited ability to move the affected joint.

To see **Common Sports Injuries** in Action

Scan QR Code

2. Strains

- **Description:** Stretching or tearing of muscles or tendons (the tissue connecting muscles to bones).
- **Common Areas:** Hamstrings, back, shoulders.
- **Symptoms:** Pain, muscle spasms, swelling, and limited muscle movement.

3. Fractures

- **Description:** Breaks in the bone.
- **Common Areas:** Arms, legs, feet, hands.

- **Symptoms:** Severe pain, swelling, bruising, and inability to move the affected area.

4. Dislocations

- **Description:** Bones forced out of their normal position in the joint.
- **Common Areas:** Shoulders, fingers, knees.
- **Symptoms:** Visible deformity, intense pain, swelling, and immobility of the joint.

5. Concussions

- **Description:** Traumatic brain injuries caused by a blow to the head or body, shaking the brain inside the skull.
- **Symptoms:** Headache, confusion, dizziness, nausea, and sometimes loss of consciousness.

6. Tendinitis

- **Description:** Inflammation of a tendon.
- **Common Areas:** Elbows (tennis elbow), shoulders, knees (patellar tendinitis).
- **Symptoms:** Pain and tenderness along a tendon, especially near joints.

7. Bursitis

- **Description:** Inflammation of the bursae (small sacs of fluid that cushion the bones, tendons, and muscles near joints).
- **Common Areas:** Shoulders, elbows, hips, knees.
- **Symptoms:** Pain, swelling, and reduced range of motion in the affected joint.

8. Shin Splints

- **Description:** Pain along the shin bone (tibia), often due to overuse.
- **Symptoms:** Tenderness, soreness, or pain along the inner side of the shin bone and mild swelling in the lower leg.

9. Achilles Tendon Injuries

- **Description:** Injuries to the tendon connecting the calf muscles to the heel bone, including tendinitis and ruptures.
- **Symptoms:** Pain and stiffness along the Achilles tendon, especially in the morning, and swelling or thickening of the tendon.

10. Runner's Knee (Patellofemoral Pain Syndrome)

- **Description:** Pain around the kneecap often due to overuse, misalignment, or damage to the cartilage.
- **Symptoms:** Pain around or behind the kneecap, especially when bending the knee, walking downstairs, or sitting for long periods.

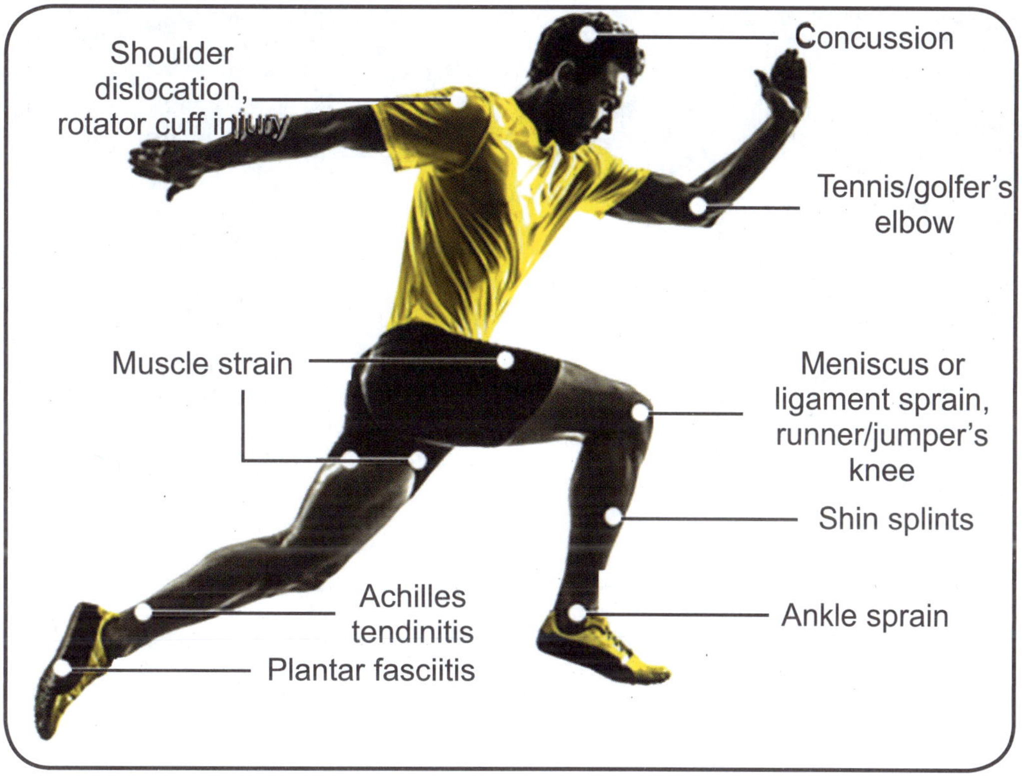

Fig. 3.11 Basic Injuries

Instruction for RICE

First aid for sprains is essential to reduce pain, swelling, and prevent further injury. The RICE method is commonly recommended

Rest

- **Action:** Avoid putting weight on the injured area.
- **Reason:** Resting prevents further injury and allows the healing process to begin.

Ice

- **Action:** Apply ice to the injured area for 15-20 minutes every 2-3 hours during the first 48 hours.
- **Reason:** Ice reduces swelling and numbs the pain. Do not apply ice directly to the skin; use a cloth or towel as a barrier.

Compression

- **Action:** Use an elastic bandage to wrap the injured area.
- **Reason:** Compression helps to reduce swelling and provides support. Ensure that the bandage is snug but not so tight that it restricts blood flow.

Elevation

- **Action:** Elevate the injured limb above heart level.
- **Reason:** Elevation helps to reduce swelling by allowing fluids to drain away from the injured area.

Fig. 3.12 ICE Implementation

3.11 Concept of First AID KIT

A first aid kit is a collection of essential supplies and equipment used to provide initial medical treatment for injuries or illnesses. It is important to have a well-stocked first aid kit when participating in outdoor activities or sports, and even at home and in your car. Here are the key concepts and components of a basic first aid kit:

Components of a Basic First Aid Kit:

- Adhesive bandages (various sizes)
- Sterile gauze pads
- Rolled bandages (e.g., conforming gauze)
- Triangular bandage (for slings or wraps)
- Antiseptic wipes or solution (e.g., alcohol pads, iodine solution)
- Antibiotic ointment (e.g., Neosporin)
- Sterile gloves
- Scissors
- Tweezers (for splinter removal)
- Thermometer
- CPR face shield or mask
- Splint (e.g., SAM splint for stabilizing fractures)
- Pain relievers (e.g., acetaminophen, ibuprofen)

- Antihistamine (for allergic reactions)
- Aspirin (if recommended by a healthcare provider for heart conditions)
- Adhesive tape
- Safety pins
- Emergency contact information and first aid manual
- Flashlight with extra batteries
- Personal medications and medical supplies (if needed)

3.12 Area Inspection For Safety

Area inspection for safety is a vital part of ensuring a secure environment in sports, physical education classes, playgrounds, or any physical activity setting. It involves a thorough check of the facilities, equipment, and surroundings to prevent accidents, injuries, and hazards.

3.12.1 Playing Surface

- Check for cracks, holes, uneven ground, or slippery surfaces
- Ensure there are no sharp objects, glass, or debris
- Surfaces (indoor/outdoor) must be clean and properly marked

3.12.2 Sports Equipment

- Inspect balls, nets, racquets, goalposts, cones, mats, etc.
- Ensure there are no broken, rusted, or damaged items
- All equipment must be age-appropriate and safe to use

3.12.3 Gymnasium/Indoor Area

- Floors must be dry, clean, and non-slippery
- Adequate lighting and ventilation
- Emergency exit routes clearly marked and accessible
- Equipment stored safely to prevent tripping hazards

3.12.4 Playground and Outdoor Fields

- Check swings, slides, bars for loose parts or rust
- Ensure soft ground cover (like sand or rubber) is present to reduce injury risk
- Look for signs of animal waste, insect nests, or dangerous plants

3.12.5 Roles and Responsibilities Of First Responder

A first responder is the first person present at the scene of an emergency who is trained to provide immediate care before advanced medical help arrives. This can be a teacher, coach, trainer, or staff member trained in basic first aid and CPR.

1. Ensure Scene Safety

- Check if the environment is safe for you, the injured person, and others.
- Look out for dangers like fire, sharp objects, traffic, or crowding.
- Prevent further injuries by clearing the area if needed.

2. Assess the Situation Quickly

- Determine the nature and severity of the injury or illness.
- Use the Primary Survey (DR ABC):
    - **D:** Danger – Is the scene safe?
    - **R:** Response – Is the person conscious?
    - **A:** Airway – Is the airway clear?
    - **B:** Breathing – Is the person breathing normally?
    - **C:** Circulation – Is there any bleeding?

3. Call for Help

- Call emergency services immediately (e.g., 911 or local number).
- Provide clear, accurate details:
    - Location
    - Nature of the injury
    - Number of injured persons
    - Current condition of the injured

3.13 First Aid Procedures

First Aid is the **immediate care** given to someone who is injured or suddenly ill **before professional medical help arrives**. It helps to:

- Save lives
- Prevent the condition from worsening
- Promote recovery

Basic Procedures

Stay Calm and Ensure Safety

- Check the area—make sure it's safe for you and the injured person.
- Don't rush—stay calm and focused.

Check the Person's Response (DR ABC)

Use the Primary Survey (DR ABC) method:

Letter	Meaning	What to Do
D	Danger	Check for danger to you or the victim. Remove if safe.
R	Response	Tap their shoulder and ask loudly: "Are you okay?"
A	Airway	Tilt the head back, lift chin to open airway.
B	Breathing	Look, listen, and feel for normal breathing for 10 seconds.
C	Circulation	Check for bleeding, pulse, signs of life.

Call for Help

- Dial emergency number (e.g., 911 / 112 / local number).
- Give details: location, condition, what happened.

Personal Hygiene and Kit Inspection, especially useful for schools, sports teams, and physical education

After completing this session, you should be able to:

- Describe emergency response
- Identify and respond to emergencies in play field
- Prepare an emergency action plan

ACTIVITY

Materials Required

Props and equipment: As mentioned in the above session.

1. Organize an emergency drill/ response under the guidance of a teacher for the following situations:
   (a) Drill assuming that a child falls and breaks his leg and also bleeding due to a small cut on his hand.
   (b) Drill to give CPR to a patient.
   (c) Preparation of an emergency plan

Subjective Questions

1. What is the importance of first aid?
2. What is the first aid for heat stroke?
3. Write the steps of CPR?
4. Explain the ABC of first aid?

UNIT 4

HEALTH AND HYGIENE IN PLAY AREA

- Hygiene and Safety
- General Rules of Hygiene and Sanitation
- Maintenance of Hygiene in Play Area

4.1 Hygiene and Safety

To see
Athlete & Staff Hygiene
in Action

Scan QR Code

Hygiene involves maintaining cleanliness for both yourself and your surroundings, especially to prevent the spread of disease. Practising good personal hygiene is essential for leading a healthy lifestyle and is the first step to ensuring good health. Not that it only safeguards you from poor health but also protects those around you from illnesses caused by unhygienic habits. Although habits like handwashing, bathing, and brushing may seem mundane, they are all integral to good personal hygiene. They promote a sense of well-being and help to keep you free from bacteria, viruses, and illnesses. To safeguard your health, it is crucial to clean your body, hair, mouth, and teeth, and wear clean clothes regularly.

Maintenance of Player's Health and Hygiene

The maintenance of a player's health and hygiene is a critical aspect of their overall well-being, both during their active career and in retirement. This unit explores the importance of preventive measures to avoid the occurrence or worsening of various health conditions in players, with a focus on eight key health domains. These domains include detraining, injuries, osteoarthritis, nutrition, mental health symptoms, medical history, physical examination, and assessments.

Maintenance of Health

1. Regular Medical Check-ups:

- Ensure periodic health assessments to monitor physical condition and catch potential issues at an early stage.
- Include assessments for cardiovascular health, bone density, and muscle condition.

2. Nutrition:

- Follow a balanced diet that is rich in proteins, carbohydrates, fats, vitamins, and minerals.
- Stay hydrated by drinking plenty of water before, during and after games and practice sessions.
- Consider working with a sports nutritionist to develop personalized meal plans.

3. Physical Conditioning:

- Engage in regular strength training, flexibility exercises, and cardiovascular workouts.
- Incorporate sport-specific drills to improve agility, endurance, and performance.
- Allow adequate recovery time to prevent overtraining and injuries.

4. Mental Health:

- Promote a supportive environment to address stress, anxiety, and other mental health concerns.
- Encourage relaxation techniques such as meditation, yoga, and deep-breathing exercises.
- Access to mental health professionals, such as sports psychologists, can be beneficial.

Maintenance of Hygiene

1. Personal Hygiene:

- Maintain regular bathing and showering routine, especially after games and practice sessions.
- Use appropriate skincare products to prevent infections and maintain healthy skin.
- Keep nails trimmed and clean to avoid injuries and infections.

2. Equipment Hygiene:

- Clean and disinfect sports gear, including uniforms, shoes, and protective equipment regularly.
- Ensure proper storage of equipment to prevent moulds, bacteria, and unpleasant odours.
- Replace worn-out or damaged equipment promptly to ensure safety and hygiene.

3. Facility Hygiene:

- Ensure that locker rooms, showers, and restrooms are cleaned and sanitized regularly.
- Provide adequate handwashing stations and hand sanitizers in training areas.
- Maintain playing surfaces clean and safe to reduce the risk of injuries and infections.

4. Management of the Injury:

- Clean and dress the wounds properly to prevent infections.
- Follow appropriate protocols for treating injuries, including icing, compression, and elevation.
- Ensure access to first aid kits and medical supplies during practices and games.

Preventative Measures

1. Vaccinations:

- Stay updated on all necessary vaccinations, including those for flu and other common illnesses.
- Consider vaccinations relevant to the sport, such as tetanus for those prone to cuts and scrapes.

2. Education on Hygiene:

- Educate players on the importance of personal and equipment hygiene.
- Conduct workshops or training sessions on proper hygiene practices.

4.2 General Hygiene and Sanitation Rules

The consequences of neglecting hygiene and sanitation rules can be severe. For instance, tinea pedis, also known as athlete's foot, can spread through contaminated surfaces, leading to itchy, burning, and cracked feet. Additionally, MRSA, a type of bacteria that can cause serious infections, can also spread in sports facilities if proper cleaning and disinfection measures are not taken.

To prevent the spread of infectious diseases, it is essential to maintain equipment and facilities clean. This includes regularly disinfecting surfaces, providing proper ventilation, and encouraging athletes to practice good personal hygiene.

Maintaining proper hygiene and adopting sanitation practices are crucial for athletes to prevent infections, ensure overall health, and enhance performance.

4.2.1 Personal Hygiene

1. **Regular Bathing:** Take a shower before and after training sessions and games to remove sweat, dirt, and bacteria.
2. **Handwashing:** Wash hands frequently with soap and water, especially before eating, after using the restroom, and after any contact with potentially contaminated surfaces.
3. **Nail Care:** Keep nails trimmed and clean to avoid harbouring dirt and bacteria.
4. **Oral Hygiene:** Brush teeth at least twice a day, floss daily and consider using mouthwash to maintain oral health.
5. **Hair Care:** Keep hair clean and tied back if it is long so as to prevent it from blocking vision, interfering with activities or getting caught.

4.2.2 Equipment Hygiene

1. **Clean Gear:** Regularly clean and disinfect all sports equipment, including helmets, pads, gloves, and shoes.
2. **Laundry:** Wash uniforms, towels, and other clothing after each use with appropriate detergent.
3. **Personal Equipment:** Avoid sharing personal items such as water bottles, towels, and clothing to prevent the spread of germs.

Facility Hygiene

1. **Locker Rooms:** Ensure that locker rooms are clean and dry. Disinfect benches, lockers, and other surfaces regularly.
2. **Showers:** Use antimicrobial soap and wear shower shoes to prevent fungal infections like athlete's foot.
3. **Restrooms:** Keep restrooms clean and stocked with soap, paper towels, and hand sanitizers.

Injury and Health Management

1. **Wound Care:** Clean and cover any cuts, scrapes, or blisters promptly to prevent infection.
2. **Sick Policy:** Stay at home if feeling unwell so as to avoid spreading illness to teammates.
3. **Hydration:** Drink plenty of water and use only personal water bottles to avoid sharing.

Environmental Sanitation

1. **Clean Environment:** Keep the playing area free from trash and debris.
2. **Proper Disposal:** Dispose of waste materials, such as bandages and tissues, in appropriate receptacles.

3. **Field Maintenance:** Regularly maintain and sanitize artificial turf and other playing surfaces to reduce contamination.

Additional Tips

1. **Hydration and Nutrition:** Maintain a balanced diet and stay hydrated to support overall health and immune function.
2. **Rest and Recovery:** Ensure adequate sleep and rest to allow the body to recover and maintain a strong immune system.

Hygiene Tips

Wash Hands Frequently

- Always wash your hands **before eating, after using the toilet**, and after playing.
- Use **soap and water** for at least **20 seconds**.
- Use **hand sanitizer** when water isn't available.

Brush Your Teeth Twice a Day

- In the **morning** and **before bed**.
- Use toothpaste and brush for **2 minutes**.
- Don't forget to clean your **tongue and floss** too.

Bathe Daily

- Take a **shower or bath every day**, especially after sweating or sports.
- Use **soap** to clean your body and **shampoo** for hair.

Wear Clean Clothes

- Change into **fresh clothes** every day.
- Don't wear the same socks or undergarments for more than a day.
- Wash sweaty sportswear after every use.

Keep Hair and Nails Neat

- Wash your hair regularly to prevent dandruff or lice.
- Trim your nails weekly to avoid dirt buildup and infection.

Practice Cough & Sneeze Etiquette

- Cover your mouth with a **tissue or elbow** when sneezing or coughing.
- Throw tissues in the bin and **wash hands immediately**.

Use Deodorant

- Helps to control **body odor**, especially after physical activity.

Keep Feet Clean

- Wash your feet daily and dry them well.
- Change socks every day and wear breathable shoes.

Keep Your Belongings Clean

- Clean your **water bottle, lunch box**, and **sports gear** regularly.
- Don't share personal items like towels or combs.

Maintain a Clean Environment

- Keep your **room, school bag, and study area clean**.
- Avoid clutter and remove trash regularly.

4.2.3 Inspection and Maintenance of Sports Facilities and Kits

Effective facility design is crucial for sports performance facilities to meet the varying goals and objectives of each programme. A key aspect of this is delivering a high-quality Strength and Conditioning (S&C) provision in the short, medium, and long term. This requires careful programme analysis to determine the current state of the programme, where it has to reach and how to get there. Feasibility study is the first step in this phase. It should involve a small group of individuals from the overall planning committee. Risk management is of paramount concern during the design process.

Fig. 4.1 Construction Inspection

Low-frequency Inspection

The focus typically shifts towards detecting material flaws, wear and tear, or structural issues that could impact the safety and performance of the equipment. The term "low-frequency" in this context would generally refer to the use of slower or deeper methods of inspection, possibly employing acoustic or vibration-based techniques.

High Frequency Inspection

Inspection of high-frequency sports equipment refers to techniques that use very precise, sensitive tools to detect small, subtle defects or wear in equipment, ensuring the safety and optimal performance of the gear. These inspections are crucial for high-performance sports gear, where even the smallest imperfection could affect safety, comfort, or functionality.

Outlining the Inspection and Maintenance Procedures for Sports Facilities and Kits

Item	Frequency	Inspection Tasks	Maintenance Tasks
Locker Rooms	Daily	Check for cleanliness, proper ventilation, and functioning lights	Clean floors, disinfect surfaces, empty trash bins, and refill soap dispensers
Showers	Daily	Inspect for moulds, mildew, and proper drainage	Clean and disinfect shower areas, ensure that showerheads are functional, replace shower curtains if needed
Restrooms	Daily	Check for cleanliness, stocked supplies, and functioning fixtures	Clean and disinfect toilets and sinks, refill soap and paper products, repair any leaks
Playing Fields	Weekly/Daily (as needed)	Inspect for debris, holes, and uneven surfaces	Remove debris, fill holes, mow the grass, and ensure proper marking of field boundaries
Artificial Turf	Weekly	Check for wear and tear, loose seams, and cleanliness	Brush and clean the turf, repair any damaged areas, disinfect as needed
Gym Equipment	Daily/Weekly	Inspect for damage, proper functioning, and dirt	Clean and disinfect equipment, tighten loose parts, and repair or replace damaged items
Protective Gear	Weekly	Check for wear and tear, proper fit, and dirt	Clean and disinfect gear, repair or replace damaged items
Uniforms and Towels	After each use	Inspect for damage, stains, and dirt	Wash and disinfect, repair any tears or damages
Footwear	Weekly	Check for wear and tear, proper fit, and dirt	Clean and disinfect, replace worn-out insoles or laces
Helmets	Monthly	Inspect for cracks, proper padding, and dirt	Clean and disinfect, replace damaged padding or straps
Pads and Gloves	Weekly	Check for wear and tear, proper fit, and dirt	Clean and disinfect, repair or replace damaged items
Water Bottles	After each use	Inspect for any stains and any damage	Clean and disinfect, replace damaged bottles
Benches and Bleachers	Weekly	Check for stability, cleanliness, and damage	Clean and disinfect, repair any loose or damaged parts
First Aid Kits	Monthly	Inspect for completeness and expiry dates of supplies	Refill supplies, replace expired items
Storage Areas	Weekly	Inspect for how well they are organized, their cleanliness, and pest control	Clean and organize, implement pest control measures if needed
Lights and Electrical Systems	Monthly	Check for proper operation and any exposed wiring	Replace burnt-out bulbs, repair any electrical issues, ensure that all wiring is safe
HVAC Systems	Quarterly	Inspect for proper operation and cleanliness	Clean filters, check for any issues with heating or cooling systems, schedule professional maintenance as needed
Swimming Pools	Daily/Weekly	Check water quality, chemical levels, and cleanliness	Clean pool, balance chemicals, inspect and maintain filtration systems

Sports providers have a legal duty of care to protect the welfare of practitioners and ensure that they are not exposed to risk in any aspect of sports delivery. For this reason, sports facilities and equipment should meet the standard requirements for safety of the particular sport. This must be evaluated by a risk assessment and reduced to a tolerable level according to standard regulation ISO/TC 83. A preventive maintenance programme and a system for removal of damaged or broken equipment are essential for ensuring the safety of athletes and should aim to implement ISO standards to provide a truly safe environment for members and staff, with a focus on maintenance, cleaning, and disinfection tasks that should be done on a daily and weekly basis.

Personal Item and Kits Inspections

Personal Hygiene and Kit Inspection, especially useful for schools, sports teams, and physical education

Item	Frequency	Inspection Tasks	Maintenance Tasks
Mouthguards	**After each use**	**Check for hygiene and any damage**	**Clean and disinfect, replace if damaged**
Gym Bags	Weekly	Check for hygiene and any damage	Clean inside and outside, repair any tears or replace if necessary
Wristbands and Headbands	After each use	Check for hygiene and elasticity	Wash and disinfect, replace if worn out
Eyewear (Goggles, Glasses)	Weekly	Check for scratches, proper fit, and cleanliness	Clean lenses and frames, replace if damaged
Fitness Trackers and Watches	Weekly	Inspect for proper functioning and hygiene	Clean and disinfect, charge if necessary, replace batteries if needed
Personal First Aid Kits	Monthly	Check for completeness and expiry dates of supplies	Refill supplies, replace expired items
Socks and Undergarments	After each use	Check for hygiene and any damage	Wash and disinfect, replace if worn or damaged
Headphones and Earbuds	Weekly	Check for hygiene and proper functioning	Clean earpieces, ensure proper functioning, replace if damaged
Yoga Mats and Personal Exercise Mats	Weekly	Check for wear and tear, cleanliness	Clean and disinfect, replace if damaged
Swimwear and Swim Caps	After each use	Check for wear and tear, proper fit, and cleanliness	Rinse with clean water, wash and disinfect, replace if worn out

4.3 Maintenance of Hygiene in Play Area

Maintaining hygiene in public play areas and play school is crucial for children's health and well-being. Guidelines recommend regular hand hygiene, such as washing hands before eating, after toilet use, and after playing outside. However, studies show that adherence to these guidelines is often low, with overall adherence at 31% and adherence after toilet use and playing outside at 48%. In contrast, hands were less frequently washed before eating, with guideline adherence at 15%. In many playrooms, adequate hand washing facilities were lacking, with 38% having no soap within reach of children and 17% having no towel facilities.

Fig. 4.2 Hygiene

IGIN Tech– (IGIN) is an NGO set up to create and develop World-Class Green Sustainable cities in India. IGIN is a membership driven NGO set up to develop and carry out nation-wide environmental education programmes and activities

Designing safe and hygienic playgrounds is essential for maintaining children's health and preventing injuries. Playground designs should ensure that they do not cause lacerations, puncture wound injury, aspiration, ingestion, amputation, or other injuries. The design requirements for community-built playgrounds include separation of the infant from contaminated soil, physical safety for the infant, visibility into the enclosure, accessibility for caregivers, space for infants to crawl and walk, and reflection of the community context.

Fig. 4.3 Playground

Maintaining hygiene in public playgrounds during the pandemic is a critical challenge. While some suggest closing playgrounds, others recommend enhanced cleaning measures, limiting the number of kids on the playground, providing hand washing stations, and hiring someone to regularly wipe the equipment. Clear posted guidelines for numbers, availability of hand sanitizer at playgrounds, and clearer guidelines for children playing. Information on risks and safety are also important.

Fig. 4.4 Public Park

Fig. 4.5 Sports Field

Safe While Playing

1. Always supervise children and inexperienced swimmers. An adult should always be present to monitor activities in and around the pool.
2. Encourage swimmers to always swim with a buddy, even if they are experienced swimmers.
3. Enroll children and inexperienced swimmers in swimming lessons to teach them how to swim and handle themselves in the water.
4. Always have trained lifeguards on duty.
5. Install a fence around the pool area with a self-latching gate to prevent unsupervised access, especially by young children.
6. Consider installing pool alarms that alert you if someone enters the pool area.
7. Use non-slip materials around the pool to prevent accidental slips and falls.
8. Keep the area around the pool free of toys, furniture, and other items that could be tripped over.
9. Clearly mark the depth of the pool in various areas so swimmers are aware of where it is safe to dive or jump.
10. Prohibit diving in shallow areas to prevent head injuries.
11. Use buoys and floats to designate swimming zones and to keep swimmers within safe areas.
12. Always have rescue equipment such as life rings, reaching poles, and a first aid kit near the pool.
13. Encourage swimmers to shower before entering the pool to reduce the introduction of contaminants.
14. Discourage swimming if someone is experiencing diarrhoea or other illnesses that can contaminate the water.
15. Keep a list of emergency contact numbers readily available in the pool area.
16. Use a pool cover when the pool is not in use to prevent accidental falls.

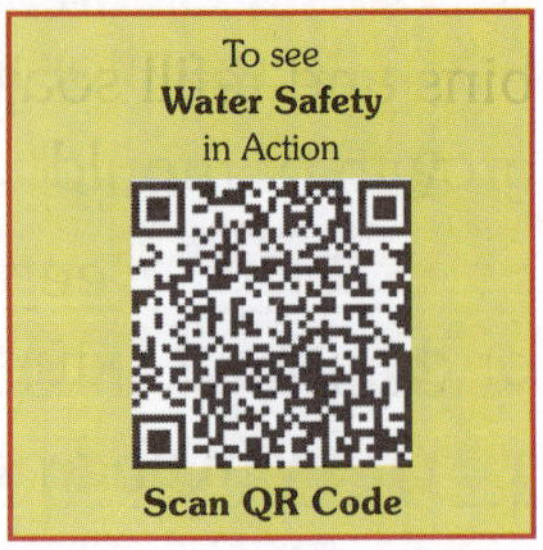

Fig. 4.6 Swimming Pool

Fig. 4.7 Swimmer

Schedule for Playing Area

Daily: Sweep and mop the floors with an appropriate cleaning solution to remove dust, dirt, and spills. Address any spills or stains immediately to prevent slipping hazards.

Weekly: Deep clean the floors if needed, especially in high-traffic areas.

Daily: Wipe down all equipment, including machines, free weights, and cardio machines, with disinfectant wipes or sprays after each use. Ensure that all surfaces are cleaned, including handles, seats, and screens.

Weekly: Inspect all equipment for any damage or wear. Tighten any loose parts and repair or replace damaged items to ensure safety.

Daily: Clean and disinfect mats after each use to remove sweat and bacteria.

Weekly: Inspect mats for wear and tear. Replace mats that are excessively worn or damaged.

Daily: Clean and disinfect all surfaces, including lockers, benches, and floors. Empty trash bins and refill soap dispensers. Ensure proper ventilation to reduce moisture and prevent the growth of mould.

Weekly: Deep clean lockers and check for any maintenance issues such as broken locks or damaged fixtures.

Daily: Clean and disinfect toilets, sinks, and floors. Refill soap dispensers and paper products. Address any leaks or maintenance issues promptly.

Weekly: Inspect for any signs of wear or damage.

Daily: Clean and disinfect shower areas to prevent moulds and mildew. Ensure that all showerheads are functioning properly.

Weekly: Replace shower curtains or liners if needed and inspect for any damage.

Daily: Clean and disinfect water fountains to prevent the spread of germs. Ensure that they are functioning properly.

Weekly: Inspect for any issues and repair or replace faulty parts as needed.

Daily: Ensure that wipe dispensers are full and functional. Clean the areas around all dispensers to maintain hygiene.

Monthly: Check the contents of first aid kits to ensure that they are complete and that supplies are not expired. Restock items as needed.

Fig. 4.8 Gym

After completing this session, you should be able to:

- Demonstrate knowledge about players' health
- Describe the hygiene and health in play area

ACTIVITY

Materials Required:

Props and equipment mentioned in the above session.

1. Conduct a safety & hygiene survey in your school playground.
2. Undertake the maintenance of ball before and after the play.
3. Rearrange the props after the class.
4. Write a paragraph about importance of play area of inspection

Subjective Questions

1. List the steps to maintain hygiene at the playground.
2. What should be the hygiene tips for the person who supplies food and drinks during play?
3. What are the inspection and maintenance points of sports facilities and kits?

Win Prizes

ATTENTION READERS

Win Prizes

We request for your frank assessment regarding various aspects of the book as given below:

A TEXTBOOK OF PHYSICAL ACTIVITY TRAINER

Subject Code 845| Skill Education
(As per Latest NEP Guidelines)

Class XII

By: Dr. Rakesh Bharti, Dr. Mali Ram Yadav

Please Fill up the Sheet in Neat and Clean Writing

(i) What topics of your syllabus, important for your examination point of view, are not covered in this book?

....

....

....

....

(ii) What are the chapters wherein the treatment of the subject matter is not systematic or organised or updated?

....

....

....

....

(iii) Have you come across misprints/mistakes/factual inaccuracies in the book? Please specify the chapters and the page numbers.

....

....

....

....

(iv) What other books on the same subject have you found/heard better than the present book? Please specify in terms of price and quality.

....

....

....

....

(v) Further suggestions and comments for the improvement of this book.

....

....

....

....

(PS: If need be please attach a separate sheet to write your views)

OTHER DETAILS

(i) Who recommended you this book? (Please tick (✓) in the box near the option relevant to you.

Teacher ☐ Friends ☐ Bookseller ☐

....

....

....

....

(ii) Name of the recommending teacher, his designation and address:

....

....

....

....

(iii) Name and address of the bookseller you purchased the book from :

....

....

....

....

(iv) Name and address of your institution (Please mention the University or Board as the case may be)

....

....

....

....

(v) Your name and complete postal address:

....

....

....

....

(vi) Course you are enrolled in:

....

....

....

....

The best assessment will be awarded each month: The award will be in the form of our publications as decided by the Editorial Board.

Please mail the filled up coupon at your earliest to:

S.K. KATARIA & SONS®
4885/109, Prakash Mahal, Dr. Subhash Bhargav Lane,
Opposite Delhi Medical Association, Daryaganj, New Delhi–110002 (INDIA)
Phone: +91-11-43551243, Mobile: +91-9871775858, 7678425209
e-mail: katariabook@gmail.com, katariabooks@yahoo.com
Website: www.skkatariaandsons.com